CW00589698

ISBN 978-0-266-75019-2
PIBN 10884186

FB &c Ltd, Dalton House, 60 Windsor Avenue, London, SW19 2RR.
Company number 08720141. Registered in England and Wales.

For support please visit www.forgottenbooks.com

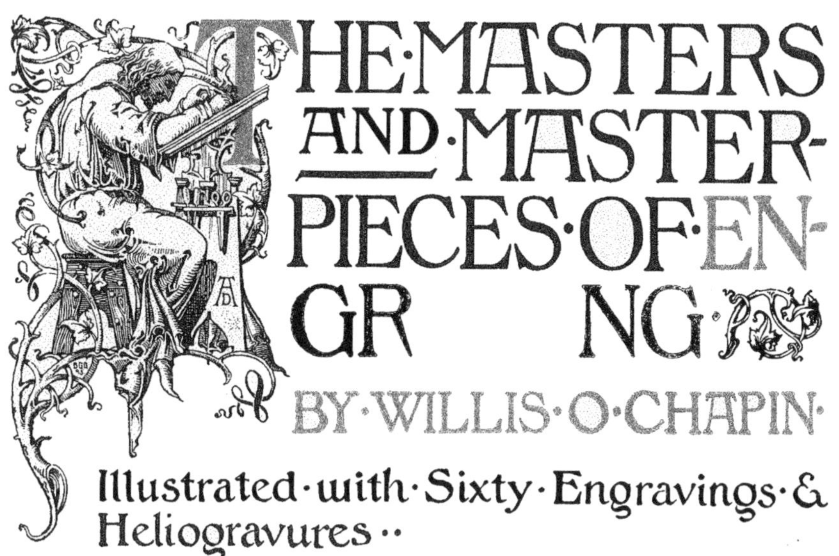

THE MASTERS AND MASTER-PIECES OF ENGRAVING

BY WILLIS O. CHAPIN

Illustrated with Sixty Engravings & Heliogravures ..

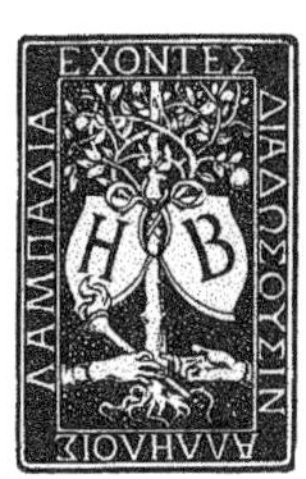

NEW YORK · HARPER & BROTHERS
PUBLISHERS · · · · · M·DCCC·XCIV

PREFACE

ENGRAVING, like painting, has an extensive literature of its own. The present volume is designed for the general reader as a condensed survey of the art from its beginnings to our own time. To give some account of the engravers themselves, and of the history and theory of their art; to trace the progress and development of engraving in the works of its representative masters, has been the writer's purpose. The illustrations are intended to show, as far as possible, the different styles and processes. The heliogravure reproductions are from originals in the British Museum.

To the various sources of his information the writer makes frank acknowledgment. Many of the more important are mentioned in the text. He is also indebted to Mr. Louis Fagan, late of the British Museum, Mr. Frederick Keppel, and Mr. W. J. Linton for valuable suggestions and criticisms. He trusts that his work may, to some extent, accomplish its purpose in leading to a more familiar knowledge in an important department of art education.

BUFFALO, N. Y., 1893.

CONTENTS

CHAPTER IV

DUTCH AND FLEMISH ENGRAVERS

CHAPTER V

ENGRAVING IN FRANCE

CHAPTER VI

ENGRAVING IN ENGLAND

CHAPTER VII

REVIVAL OF WOOD-ENGRAVING

CHAPTER VIII

VARIOUS MODERN ENGRAVERS

ENGRAVINGS AND HELIOGRAVURES

ILLUSTRATIONS

THE MASTERS
AND MASTERPIECES OF ENGRAVING

CHAPTER I

INTRODUCTORY

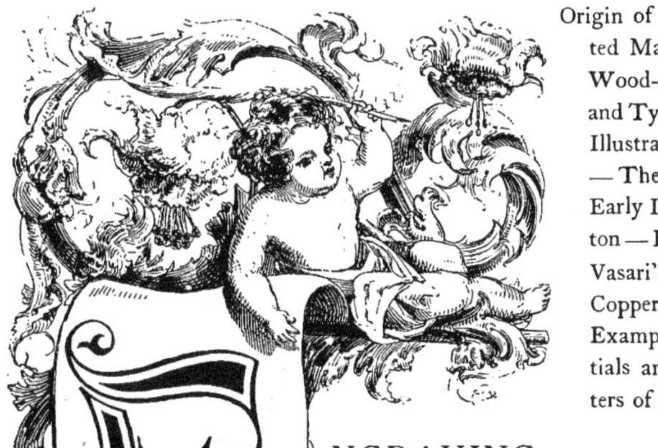

Origin of Engraving—The Early Dotted Manner—Earliest Examples of Wood-engraving—The Block-books and Typography; Gutenberg—Early Illustrated Books—Books of Hours—The *Hypnerotomachia Poliphili*—Early Illustration in England; Caxton—Engraving on Metal Plates—Vasari's Account of the Origin of Copper-plate Engraving; Earliest Examples—Engravers' Marks; Initials and Monograms—The Masters of Engraving

ENGRAVING, as one of the fine arts, is of comparatively recent origin. Its advent was coincident with the revival of classical learning and the general resuscitation of art; its career of usefulness has been contemporary with that of its sister art, printing. As an industry, as a means of recording events and displaying ornamental work, engraving was practised in remote antiquity; but as an art of carving designs upon the surface of wood or metal to be multiplied by impressions upon paper, its history cannot be definitely traced further back than the early years of the fifteenth century.

There can be little doubt that relief engraving was the method first employed, suggested by the familiar practice of stamping initial letters, signatures, and designs; and as printing from the surface, or projections, of the block or plate, instead of from the incised lines, required considerably less skill and labor. It was but the practical application of a process already well known. Whether the earliest form of relief engraving was upon wood, the black lines of the design being relieved against the white paper, or the "early dotted manner," called the *manière criblée*, upon metal plates, the design being brought out by an arrangement of dots and spaces which appear white in the impression, cannot now be determined.

Although the latter process was much employed in the early part of the fifteenth century in Germany and the Netherlands, the earliest known dotted print bearing a date is the 'St. Bernardino of Siena,' in the National Library at Paris. This print, found at Mainz in the year 1800, bears the date 1454, considerably later than the earliest dated wood-cut or copper-plate engraving. The same collection also contains two other dotted prints, which, although not dated, have been assigned to the year 1406, but, as many claim, upon insufficient evidence.

It has often been asserted that the early makers of playing-cards were the first to make practical application of wood-engraving in Europe; but these *briefmalers*, or card-colorers, are to be distinguished from the *formschneiders* (figure-cutters), who were wood-engravers in the proper sense. The former practised a rude form of wood-engraving as an industry, while the works of the latter are the beginnings of an art. In the early years of the fifteenth century rude wood-cuts of Bible subjects and of saints and martyrs of the Church were scattered through Upper Germany, the Low Countries, and Flemish provinces. To many of these were added legends of the saints, short prayers, pious ejaculations, and various other inscriptions of a religious character, cut upon the same blocks in rude black-

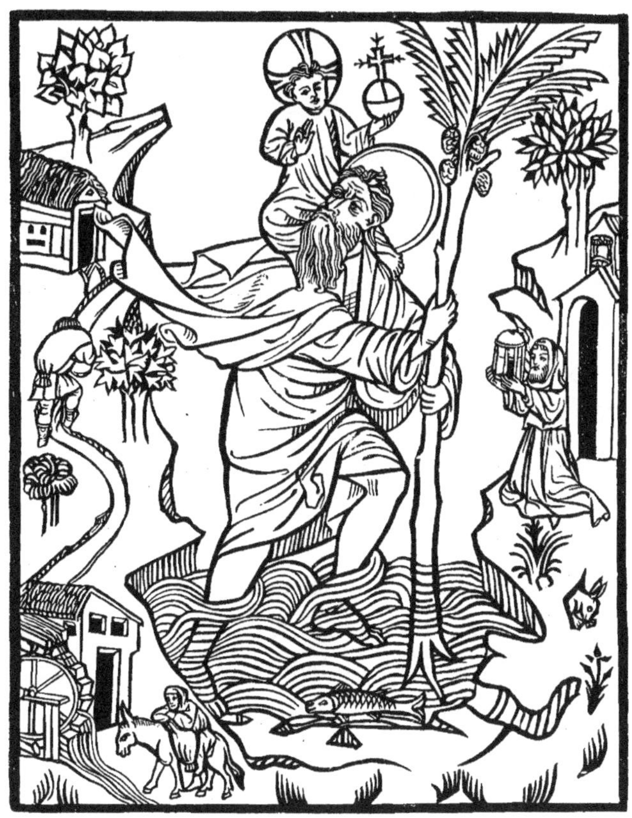

ST. CHRISTOPHER (1423)

letter. There can be little doubt that many of these cuts were produced in the convents and circulated in the interests of the Church.

The earliest dated wood-cut of accepted authenticity is the famous 'St. Christopher of 1423,' discovered in 1769 by Heinecken, in the library of the Carthusian convent of Buxheim, near Memmingen, in Suabia. This time-honored and much-discussed relic was brought to England, and was for a long time in the famous library of Earl Spencer, at Althorp; quite recently it has found a permanent resting-place in the new library established by a noble generosity at Manchester. It measures eleven and a quarter inches high, and eight and one-eighth inches wide. According to the mediæval legend, St. Christopher is represented carrying the infant Christ across a stream, supporting himself by a palm-tree. On the right bank a hermit kneels before his cell, holding a lantern to guide the saint, who, however, is looking in the opposite direction; on the left is a mill, which, although directly in the foreground, is of insignificant proportions compared to the saint; in the "distance" a peasant carries a sack towards a cottage on the top of a cliff. This cut is merely an outline, rudely colored by hand or with a stencil, and contains an inscription to the effect that each day the image of St. Christopher is looked upon the beholder will meet no violent death, alluding to a superstition common at this period in all Catholic countries. In 1844 a wood-cut representing the Virgin surrounded by saints was discovered at Malines, bearing a date alleged to be 1418. This cut, now in the Royal Library at Brussels, represents the Virgin and Child in a palisaded garden with SS. Catharine, Barbara, Dorothea, and Margaret; angels holding wreaths hover over the group. It is considerably superior in design, drawing, and execution to the 'St. Christopher,' but the genuineness of the date has not been established. There is also in the Imperial Gallery at Vienna a 'St. Sebastian,' dated 1437. The Scotch verdict—not proven—has been applied to various other examples, from time to time brought forward, with alleged early dates. There may be and doubtless are still earlier cuts without dates, but we know definitely that wood-engraving was practised as early as 1423; how far back of this time the art extends is a matter of conjecture. But while the *incunabula* are of great historical value, as showing the beginnings of the art, they are of very little artistic importance.

All of these early wood-cuts were rudely executed by unskilled workmen, who ought rather to be called wood-cutters than engravers. Until the middle of the fifteenth century wood-engraving was not recognized as a separate craft, and until the time of Dürer it had scarcely reached the dignity and importance of an art.

It must be remembered that these early cuts preceded typography and the roller press, and that the impressions were obtained by placing dampened paper upon the inked blocks and rubbing (*au frotton*) with a cloth or roller. To bind together a number of these sheets was the first step in "Block-book" making. These Block-books, as they are called, did not become common until the second half of the fifteenth century. According to Dutuit (*Manuel d'Estampes*), the *Exercitium super Pater Noster* is "one of the first productions of engraving on wood." The same authority also states of the first edition, without text, that "one cannot be much mistaken in placing it as far back as 1420." Other important examples, as regards the history of wood-engraving, are the *Apocalypse*, or History of the Life and Revelations of St. John the Evangelist; the *Biblia Pauperum*, or Book of the Poor Preachers; the *Historia Virginis*, as typified in the Song of Solomon (*Cantico Canticorum*), one of the finest of the Block-books in design and arrangement; the *Ars Moriendi*, often reprinted in various languages; and the *Ars Memorandi*. To these is often added the famous *Speculum Humanæ Salvationis*, or Mirror of

Human Salvation, a work pervaded throughout with the symbolism and mysticism of mediæval religious sentiment. The text in the first edition of this work was printed from movable type, although some later copies are partly xylographic. This book has been the subject of much controversy, and all sorts of conflicting theories have been advanced concerning its origin. It was assigned by some to Laurent Coster, of Haarlem, to support the claims made in his behalf as the inventor of typography; but it is now generally conceded that the first edition of this work did not appear before 1460, by which time printing from movable type was well known.

These Block-books were often gilded and rudely daubed with colors in imitation of the illuminated manuscripts. By the middle of the century they had become common both in Germany (especially along the Rhine) and the Netherlands. The quaint, picturesque cuts show the influence of the school of Van Eyck, and to the wood-cutters of the Netherlands are ascribed many of the best examples.

After the Block-books had become common, there are indications of attempts, both in Germany and the Netherlands, to invent a quicker and less costly mode of multiplying the numerous manuscripts and treatises, *Speculums* and *Donatus*, to supply the constantly increasing demand, by employing smaller blocks containing single words and even letters. The large blocks were available for only a single work, and were both fragile and costly, aside from the impossibility of correcting mistakes or varying inscriptions, while smaller blocks could be used indefinitely, and, if broken, could be quickly replaced. The evolution of typography from the engraved wood block thus began. The familiar legend that Laurent Coster, churchwarden of Haarlem, while cutting letters from beech-bark wherewith to amuse his grandchildren, discovered quite by accident the use of movable type, need not be repeated. Like Papillon's sensational account of the Cunii and the origin of wood-engraving, it has been relegated to the realms of fiction. Printing has recorded the origin of other arts, but not its own. Typography is not to be regarded as a deliberate invention, or the result of an accidental discovery; it was the outcome of numerous attempts and partial successes, until at last the problem was successfully solved—shall we say by Johann Gutenberg, of Mainz?

The early history of wood-engraving is so closely connected with that of the printed book that it is difficult to speak of the former without some allusion to the latter. The earliest dated specimens of typography are the famous copies of the *Letters of Indulgence*, issued by Pope Nicholas V., and printed at Mainz in 1454; while the earliest complete book, printed wholly from movable metal type, is the so-called *Gutenberg Bible*, possibly commenced by Gutenberg, but issued by Fust and Schoeffer about 1455–56.

The early printers, like the early wood-engravers, were especially numerous and active in the cities along the Rhine, and at Nuremberg, Augsburg, Strasburg, Ulm, and even as far south as Geneva. Among the most important of their publications, as regards illustration, were *Breydenbach's Travels*, printed at Mainz in 1486; the *Schatzbehalter* and *Nuremberg Chronicles*, printed at Nuremberg in 1491 and 1493 respectively; and Sebastian Brandt's *Ship of Fools*, printed at Basle in 1497. Of these the *Nuremberg Chronicles* stands at the head for the great number of its illustrations. The cuts in this famous folio, exceeding 2000 in number, are sufficiently rude and inaccurate; the same cut often answers for portraits of a number of persons, and others represent each a number of different cities or buildings, besides "stock-heads" for kings, bishops, saints, etc. Many of the designs for this work and for the *Schatzbehalter* were made by the famous Franconian master, Michael Wolgemut, the early instructor of Albrecht Dürer, but certainly do not give us a very exalted idea of his abilities. The many other quaintly illustrated books of this early period concern rather the archæologist and lover of old books and early typography than the student of the general history of engraving. The real importance of wood-engraving dates from the time of Albrecht Dürer.

Before the close of the century printing had found its way into France, and the printers of Paris and Lyons began to issue numerous works; the former devoted themselves chiefly to learned works in Latin and French, while the latter turned their attention to popular literature. Wood-engraving was practised in France soon after the middle of the fifteenth century, but until the *Livres d'Heures*, French engraving could boast of very little of importance.

The Books of Hours, so popular in France in the fifteenth and sixteenth centuries, were at first in manuscript, often engrossed and embellished with miniatures in the most sumptuous manner, and resplendent with gold and the bright tints and colors so popular in the Middle Ages. At a later period many of them were printed from type, and the borders beautifully ornamented with exquisite miniature designs and vignettes. In some instances the outline only was printed, to be filled in by the colorist; but frequently the entire design was printed in colors from engraved blocks or plates, although the unique and beautiful illuminated copies were naturally more highly prized. These books were not always confined to religious subjects; they sometimes contained profane legends, and secular and classical subjects, and often a medley of miniature figures and designs, surrounded with foliage and ornamental framework. They were prized for the decorative skill and typographical beauties which they displayed, rather than for the literary quality of their contents. This form of art culminated in the books published at Paris during the last quarter of the fifteenth and the first quarter of the sixteenth centuries by Simon Vostre, Philip Pigouchet, Antoine Vérard, Thielman Kerver, and the famous Geoffroy Tory. The *Danse Macabre* of Guyot Marchant, with its spirited and characteristic designs, also belongs to this period, having been first published at Paris in 1485.

The early printers, travelling from place to place, stopping at monasteries and towns, wherever they could find employment, crossed the Alps, attracted by the priceless manuscripts of Italy. They found that a knowledge of wood-engraving had preceded them. From the outset the process seems to have been employed in illustrating books, especially at Venice and Rome, the chief seats of early printing in Italy. Among the multitude of these early illustrated books were editions of Dante and Ovid, but by far the most important and popular of all, in point of illustrations, was the *Hypnerotomachia Poliphili*, a mystical and romantic work of the most curious construction. Its author was the Venetian monk Francesco Colonna, and it was first published at Venice, by Aldus, in 1499. Many editions and copies of this famous work have appeared, and its graceful designs and illustrations have been ascribed to various great masters.

Printing was introduced into England by William Caxton, who is said to have acquired a knowledge of the art while travelling as a merchant in the Low Countries. Upon his return to London, in 1475 or 1476, he set up a printing establishment in Westminster. The first book printed in the English language with wood-cut illustrations was Caxton's *Game and Playe of the Chesse*, second edition published about 1476. This was followed by the *Myrrour of the World*, 1481; *Golden Legend*,

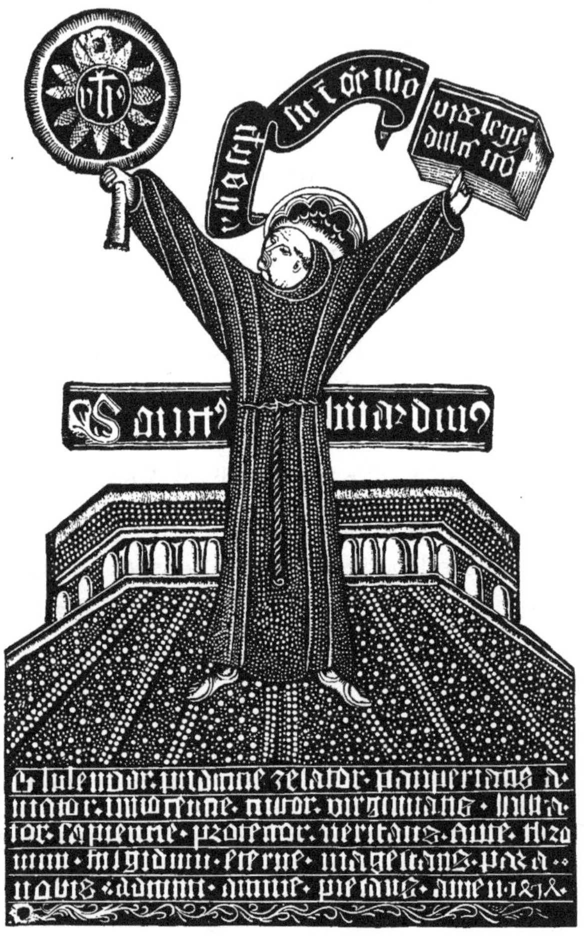

ST. BERNARDINO OF SIENA (1454)

Early Dotted Manner

1483, and other works rudely illustrated in the same manner. Although wood-engraving was probably practised in England soon after the introduction of printing, many of the wood-cuts in the books published by Caxton and his successor, Wynkyn de Worde, were undoubtedly of foreign origin. English engraving for a century later was of little importance, although books by English authors were illustrated abroad, as the *Utopia* of Sir Thomas More, for which Holbein designed illustrations at Basle, before his visit to England in the reign of Henry VIII.

The numerous illustrated works issued by Aldus Manutius, of Venice; the Trechsels, of Lyons; Christopher Plantin, of Antwerp; Geoffroy Tory, of Paris, and other famous printers, whether illustrated with wood-cuts or from engraved metal plates, did much to elevate and encourage the art of engraving. In various costly and elegant editions of these early books the printer omitted the initial letters of the chapters, leaving blank spaces to be illuminated and embellished by the rubricators, who often displayed rare taste and skill in their beautiful designs. The exquisitely engraved vignettes which head the chapters in modern books are without doubt an outgrowth of this practice.

With the advent of typography the age of manuscripts began to pass away, although for a time the new art encountered the hostility of the monks and transcribers. It is said that there were many persons, especially in Italy, who disdained to own a printed book which any person could possess. But this feeling could not long resist the influence of so manifestly important and useful an art. The Block-books in use among the common people also gradually disappeared before the invasion of typography. Although the rude specimens of book-making of our fifteenth century ancestors are preserved in our libraries and collections among the rare and curious, and are looked upon with a feeling akin to pity, as showing the poverty of mediæval civilization, they possess a deeper interest and significance, for they lifted the veil of ignorance and superstition which enveloped the Dark and Middle Ages, and turned upon them the light of philosophy and science; they inaugurated the age of enlightenment and progress, forming an epoch in civilization and culture as well as in art—a realization of the dream of Archimedes.

As wood-engraving and typography were foreshadowed by the well-known practice of stamping designs, so the early goldsmiths, whose art, transmitted from the Egyptians, Phœnicians, Greeks, and other nations of antiquity, had come down with the remains of Roman civilization, needed only the knowledge of printing upon paper, or its early substitutes, from the incised lines of their designs to inaugurate the modern art of engraving. That many of these early goldsmiths possessed rare artistic powers and great mechanical skill is abundantly shown by their many beautiful designs engraved upon crosses, candelabra, and various articles of the Church service, vessels of the banquet, toilet articles, arms, armor, coffers, and seals, and by enamelling and setting of precious stones, and all manner of similar work. They possessed all the means for printing impressions upon paper or its substitutes; but until the fifteenth century there is no evidence that a single impression was ever so taken, or a single plate engraved for such purpose.

The art of taking impressions upon paper from these incised designs was for a long time believed to have been of Italian origin, upon the authority of Giorgio Vasari, an Italian painter, architect, and author of the sixteenth century. Vasari's abilities as painter and architect are overshadowed by his fame as author, in which character he will be frequently mentioned in the following pages. His famous history of the Italian artists from Cimabue to his own time, *Le Vite de' più eccellenti Pittori, Scultori, e Architetti*, dedicated to Cosmo de' Medici, was first published at Florence in 1550, and afterwards partly rewritten and republished in 1568 with additions and portraits. Many subsequent editions have also appeared with important notes and corrections. These biographies, of which there is an excellent English translation, are written in a charming style, and contain many curious and amusing anecdotes, legends, and

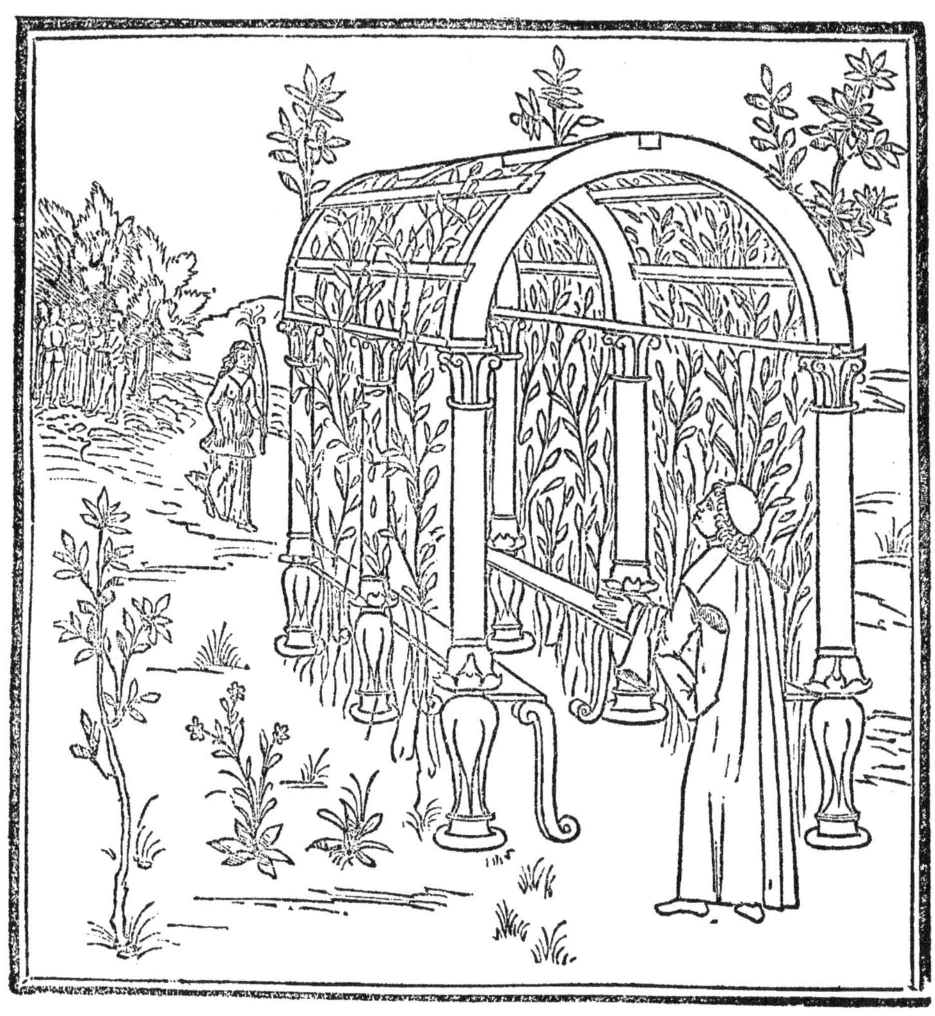

WOOD-CUT FROM THE "HYPNEROTOMACHIA POLIPHILI" (1499)

traditions, and preserve much valuable and interesting information concerning many Italian artists of the fourteenth, fifteenth, and sixteenth centuries. The author is said to have received much assistance from literary scribes, and although his statements may generally be relied upon, he seems to have been somewhat simple and over-credulous, and in some instances his errors and confusion are unpardonable.

In his chapter on "Marcantonio of Bologna," Vasari gives the following account of the origin of engraving: "The commencement of the practice of copper-plate engraving was made by Maso di Finiguerra about the year of our Salvation 1460. Of every work which this artist engraved on silver, preparatory to its completion in *niello* (*i.e.*, filling the lines with a black composition to bring out the design), he took the impression in clay, then poured melted sulphur over it, whereby the impression was repeated, and appeared blackened with smoke, displaying in oil the subject which appeared on the plate of silver. He then did the same on dampened paper and with the same color, going over the whole very gently with a round roller, the result being that these pictures not only appeared as if printed, but have the effect of those designed with the pen." Vasari then proceeds to narrate that Finiguerra was followed by the Florentine goldsmith Baccio Baldini, and by Andrea Mantegna, and others, who carried the art of engraving to great perfection.

Vasari's narrative long remained unquestioned, and was still further credited upon the discovery in 1797 by the abbé Zani, in the Paris Library, among the prints formerly belonging to Mariette, of an impression from a *niello* plate, a so-called "Pax," and ascribed by him to Finiguerra, and its origin to about the year 1452. This plate, made for the Church of San Giovanni at Florence, is still preserved in the Uffizi Gallery. The design, containing about forty figures, represents the 'Crowning of the Virgin,' and is of great beauty. There is a plaster cast of this Pax in the British Museum. But Finiguerra is no longer credited with this performance; it has been ascribed to various masters, but recent researches have shown that it must still be regarded as of unknown origin.

Vasari's account of the origin of engraving in Italy, although no longer credited, is not irreconcilable with a previous knowledge of the art in Germany, of which country he had very vague ideas. There is at Berlin a set of seven prints of the Passion, one of which, a 'Flagellation,' bears the date 1446. There is also a print by a German master whose mark is a 𝔓, known as 'La Vierge immaculée,' and dated 1451, although some doubt exists as to the genuineness of this date. The British Museum also possesses a series of twenty-seven prints of the Passion, apparently belonging to the Cologne school, one of which, representing the Last Supper, bears an inscription in which it is claimed the date 1457 is to be made out. Passavant also mentions a round print of German origin, a 'Décollation de Sainte Catherine,' with the date 1458. The discovery of these early prints, and the elaborate and skilful technic of the German Master of 1466 and his contemporary Martin Schongauer, go far to show that the origin of copper-plate engraving, as of wood-engraving and printing, belongs to Germany.

Thus the early history of engraving, as of most arts, is veiled in obscurity. Until the sixteenth century but few names appear. Many of the fifteenth century engravers identified their works only by their initials or monograms, or by some design, device, or rebus. In many instances their names, and even the time in which they worked, are unknown. In Italy, for example, we have the "Master of the Die," the "Mousetrap," the "Compass," the "Bird," etc., and in Germany the "Master of the Crab," the "Anchor," the Master of 1446, and that famous unknown artist, the Master of the initials 𝔈. 𝔖., or the Master of 1466. But the age of uncertainty soon passed away; before the close of the century engraving had become an important branch of art, and schools for its cultivation had sprung up in various cities of Germany and Italy. Soon after the beginning of the sixteenth century names and dates were commonly inscribed upon the plates, and shortly afterwards the names of the publishers were added.

From the outset, engraving has been the handmaiden of painting. Dürer, Rembrandt, Van Dyck, and Claude, eminent as painters, are also among the masters of engraving. Raphael and Rubens founded schools of engraving to disseminate a knowledge of their works, while of the many modern artists who have practised the art in some of its forms may be mentioned such familiar names as Wilkie, Turner, Millet, Daubigny, Fortuny, Meissonier, and Jacque.

In the following pages will be mentioned those great masters of engraving whose works mark epochs in the history of their art: the *peintres-graveurs*, original artists, who engraved their own designs with the graver or by means of aqua-fortis, and of whom Dürer and Rembrandt are almost ideal exponents; and that important and numerous body of engravers, of whom Marc Antonio Raimondi is the great prototype, who have engraved the designs of other artists, and to whom we are indebted for artistic and faithful translations of the masterpieces of painting into another language of art, whose mode of expression, by reduplication of impressions, has made them common blessings.

CHAPTER II

ENGRAVING IN ITALY

From Goldsmith to Engraver — The German and Italian Schools Contrasted — Botticelli and Baldini — Mantegna — Campagnola; *opus mallei* — Marc Antonio Raimondi; Typical Engravings after Raphael; Portrait of Aretino — Reproductive Engraving — School of Marc Antonio — Parmigiano; Etching — A New School of Engraving; Cort and the Caracci — Agostino Caracci's Portrait of Titian — Followers of the Caracci — Engraving under Urban VIII. — Della-Bella — Ribera and Goya — Castiglione, Canaletto, and various other Etchers — Piranesi — Italian Wood-engravers — Engraving in the Chiaroscuro Manner — Early Chiaroscuros by German Engravers — Ugo da Carpi — Antonio da Trento and Vicentino — Christopher Jegher — Andrea Andreani — Bartolommeo Coriolano — Dęcline of Engraving in Italy

IT is definitely known that impressions on paper from incised metal plates were taken in Italy soon after the middle of the fifteenth century, and it is quite likely that the practice can be carried back to a somewhat earlier period. These little prints, however, of which several hundred of undoubted authenticity have come down to us, representing a great variety of subjects, are not *engravings* in the proper sense, but impressions worked off by the goldsmiths, either to prove their ornamental designs before applying the *niello*, as already described, or as curiosities, or memorials of their work. They are, therefore, as a rule, unique, and it is seldom that more than a single impression of the same subject is found. The Italians seem to have made but little practical use of their knowlege of engraving until the last quarter of the century, although across the mountains in Germany engraving plates expressly for printing purposes had already become an important branch of art, and the skilful technic of the Master of 1466 and Martin Schongauer shows that their art was no longer in its infancy.

Although the transition from *niello* work to modern engraving cannot be definitely traced, it was undoubtedly at Florence that engraving in Italy broke from its bondage to the goldsmith. Under the powerful patronage of the Medici, Florence had long been the home of the arts. Her painters, sculptors, architects, and goldsmiths were honored and rewarded as in no other city, and the time has been extolled by Vasari as "an age of gold for men of talent."

The period of transition from ancient to modern art, which began in Italy in the latter half of the fifteenth century and ended with the sack of Rome, also witnessed the birth, growth, and maturity of Italian engraving. During the Renaissance the masterpieces of ancient sculpture, Italy's great inheritance, were beginning to reappear, to shed their lustre upon a later art, and to awaken a new interest in the nude figure and in the subjects of classical mythology. The Italian engravers, like the Italian painters, soon rose to the highest eminence in their delineation of the human face and form, and the best examples of their works are still unrivalled for purity and correctness of outline, graceful contours, and masterly simplicity of drapery and surroundings. Their slender, graceful figures are in striking contrast to the homely models of their German contemporaries. In Germany, engraving seems from the outset to have been practised by original artists, while the Italian engravers devoted themselves chiefly to multiplying the drawings of contemporary painters. But their lack of originality was compensated by severe discipline in drawing, and their prints, as a whole, are as characteristic of the Italian love for grace of action and beauty

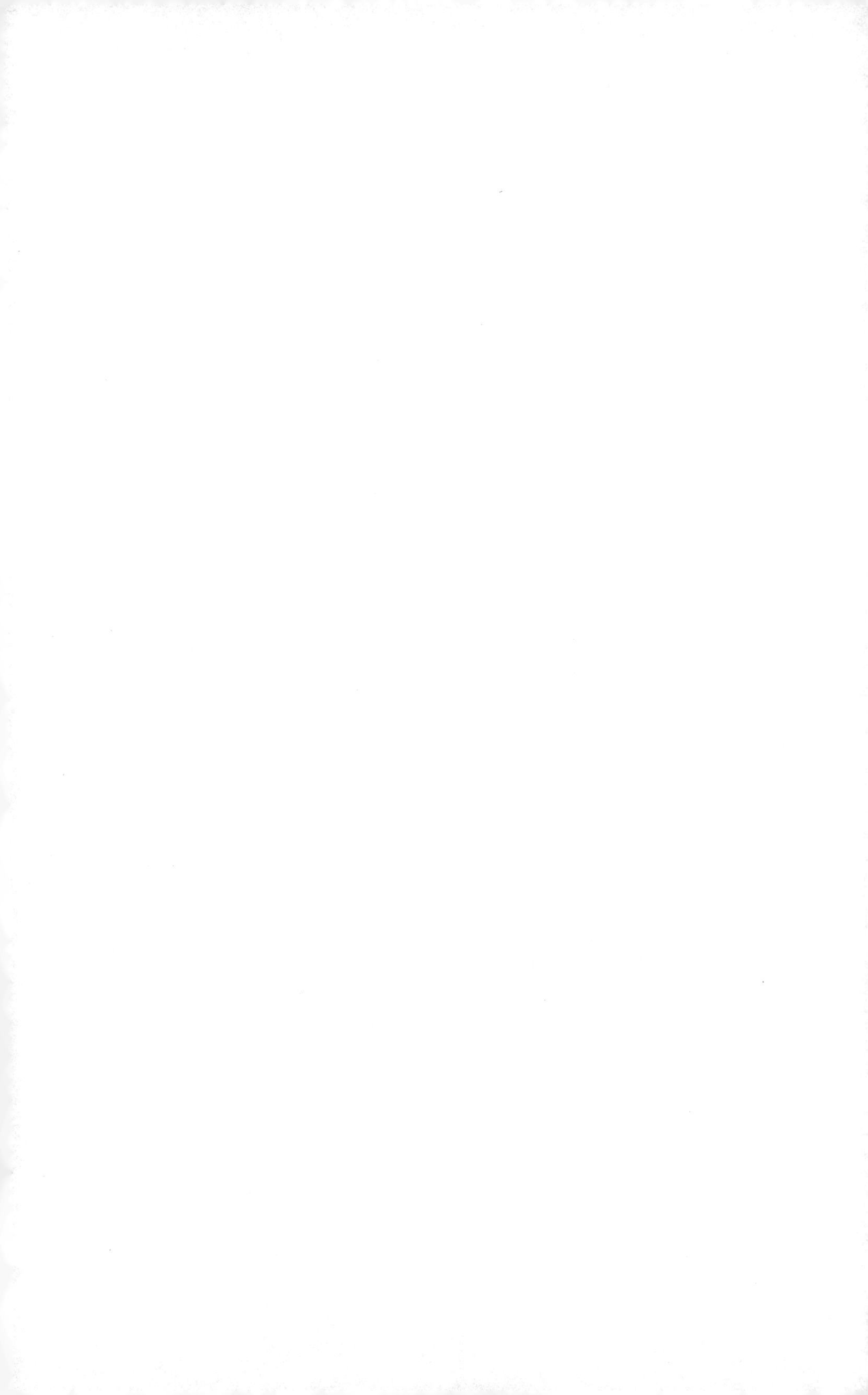

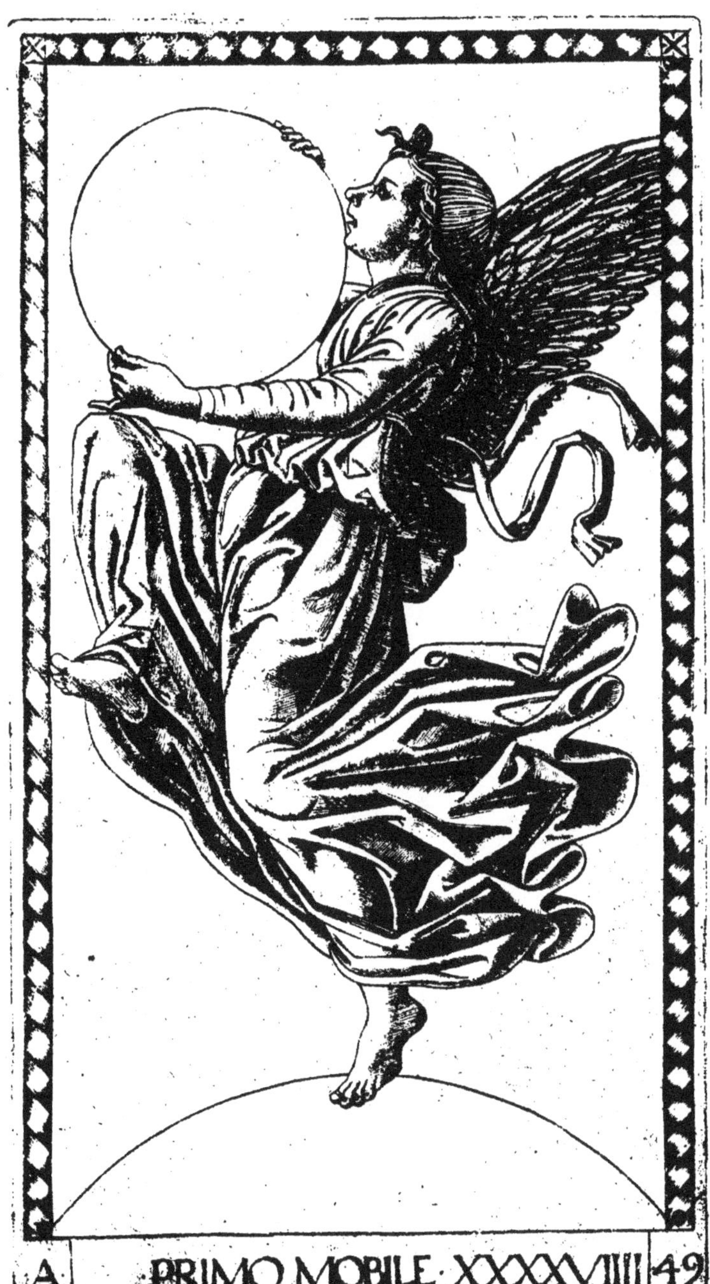
A
PRIMO MOBILE · XXXXVIIII
49

of form and expression, as the works of their German contemporaries are typical of the Northern feeling for romance and realism.

But the schools of Italy and Germany were destined to exert upon each other a reciprocal influence. The technic of Dürer was a revelation to the Italian engravers, and from the point of contact of these schools dates the gradual development of the resources of the art. In return, the Italian influence pervaded Germany until the art of that country lost many of its national characteristics.

The early engravers entertained exceedingly narrow views as to the province of their art. With a system based upon abstraction, they represented only certain qualities of an object; limitations imposed, to a certain extent, by technical inexperience. In a modern engraving we find textures, local color, and a system of light and shade. In the works of the early schools we find none of these qualities to any considerable extent. The Italian engravings of the fifteenth century, for example, are little more than outlines shaded in the most conventional manner, generally by parallel lines drawn diagonally.

The beginning of engraving in Italy may be traced to Florence, and to the last quarter of the fifteenth century. The first engravers whose names appear were the eminent Florentine artists Sandro Botticelli and his pupil, the goldsmith and engraver Baccio Baldini. According to the narrative of Vasari, whose account of the origin of engraving is far from trustworthy, Baldini, who flourished about 1460–85, acquired his knowledge of the art directly from Finiguerra, its alleged inventor. Although very little is known of Baldini, all authorities agree that he engraved the designs of Botticelli, "being himself deficient in drawing," and that he sometimes worked in conjunction with his master, whom he excelled in mechanical skill, as the latter was superior in design; but there is great difficulty in distinguishing their respective prints. It is believed by many that Botticelli did little more than supply the subjects. They are credited with a variety of sibyls, prophets, saints, planets, religious and mythological subjects, playing-cards, book illustrations, and designs for jewellers' ornaments. Of the prints now ascribed to Baldini, the series engraved for *Il Monte Santo di Dio* of Antonio Bettini, printed at Florence in 1477, and the illustrations engraved from Botticelli's designs for the edition of Dante's *Inferno*, published at Florence in 1481, and attributed by Vasari to Botticelli, are among the earliest engravings of Italian origin. The former is believed to be the earliest book with copper-plate illustrations. But the most characteristic examples of their art are their Prophets and Sibyls, which were popular alike in Italy and Germany. Although the technical skill of these Florentine artists was greatly inferior to that of their German contemporaries, the best examples of their prints show a characteristic love for beauty, subtilty of expression, graceful design, and classical purity of drawing.

The eminent goldsmith-engravers Pollajuolo and Robetta were also among the pioneers in their art, and have left us interesting examples of their skill; but towards the close of the century the school of Florence declined in importance, and was soon surpassed in Northern Italy, where schools of engraving had arisen at Mantua, Bologna, Venice, Modena, Milan, Parma, and other cities. Among the last, but the greatest of the early schools, came that of Rome, inspired by Raphael, which reached its highest point in the works of his pupil Marc Antonio Raimondi, the most eminent of all Italian engravers.

Of the numerous other engravers belonging to this transition period, the most important were Mocetto, Brescia, Giovanni del Porto, called the "Master of the Bird," and Andrea Mantegna. In point of technic, Mantegna was by far the greatest of the Italian engravers who preceded Marc Antonio. He was the first to develop the resources of his art, and the earliest whose works attracted any considerable attention outside of his own country. In his own time, Mantegna's fame as an engraver was scarcely less than his renown as a painter. He was one of the master-spirits of his time—bold, original, and successful; the founder of a school of engraving, and a pioneer through whose influence and example the engraver's art began to flourish in many of the cities of Northern Italy.

Mantegna was born near Padua in 1431 of humble parentage, and, according to Vasari, was a shepherd-boy. Some of his early drawings attracted the attention of the painter Francesco Squarcione, an enthusiastic collector and admirer of antique models, who instructed him in the principles of art and inspired in him an ardent love for the antique. Mantegna soon rose into eminence as a painter of altar-pieces and frescos, and about 1463, having married the daughter of the Venetian painter Jacopo Bellini, and thereby estranged himself from his master, he entered the service of the Gonzaga family at Mantua; thence he went to Rome, towards the close of the century, upon the invitation of Pope Innocent VIII., to decorate the Belvedere Chapel in the Vatican. This chapel no longer exists, having been ruthlessly demolished by Pius VI. in his enlargement of the gallery. After a residence of two years in Rome he returned to Mantua, where he died in 1506, at the age of seventy-five years. Mantegna was held in high esteem at the Mantuan Court, and from the humble occupation of shepherd he rose to become a man of great consequence, receiving the honor of knighthood, and numbering among his many illustrious patrons and admirers Lorenzo the Magnificent, who, like himself, was an ardent admirer of the antique. Ariosto mentions him with Leonardo, Bellini, and others in canto xxxiii. of the "Orlando Furioso."

As an engraver, Mantegna's style is imposing and often spirited and forcible, although naturally somewhat primitive and deficient in variety. His peculiar shadings, made by oblique lines drawn in a perfectly formal manner from right to left, without crossing, add to this monotony, and show a mechanical skill in handling the graver greatly inferior to that of his German contemporary, Martin Schongauer, whose shadings, generally in curved lines, are much more effective. But Mantegna's technical inexperience certainly did not restrict his choice of subjects, or prevent him from giving to them their true character and sentiment. Some of his prints possess an antique air, as though copied from an ancient bas-relief. Good impressions have become scarce and valuable. As characteristic examples may be named the 'Virgin and Child,' 'Entombment,' 'Resurrection,' 'Combat of Sea-gods' (copied in pen-and-ink by Dürer, and one of the figures reproduced in his print 'Effect of Jealousy'), 'Bacchanals,' 'Hercules and Antæus,' 'The Flagellation,' and that rare and interesting series, the 'Triumphs of Cæsar,' from his own paintings for the theatre in the Castle of Mantua, where the comedies of Terence and Plautus were performed. The original paintings were afterwards taken to England, and becoming successively the property of Charles I. and Cromwell, are still preserved at Hampton Court. Although much injured, they are still the most celebrated of Mantegna's paintings, and it is said that when his prints of the same subjects first appeared they were considered the most important engravings that had been produced in Italy.

The engraved works of the accomplished scholar and artist Giulio Campagnola, of Padua, also merit attention, for he was one of the earliest engravers who employed the dotted manner known as *opus mallei*, a style of engraving which must not be confounded with the *manière criblée*, which left the design in relief, indicated by white dots. Much of this dotted work in Campagnola's prints is extremely delicate, and appears to have been done with a sharp point or punch upon a very soft metal. His prints are few and rare, and are mostly from designs by Bellini, Giorgione, and Mantegna. The large print of 'St. John the Baptist holding a Cup' affords a good example of this dotted work, the background being curiously composed of dots, while the figure of the saint is strongly outlined with the graver. Campagnola's reputation as a painter was great in his own time, but of his abilities in this direction we have no other proof than the judgment of his contemporaries, for none of his paintings are known to exist.

The works of the engravers already named sufficiently illustrate the state of engraving in Italy before the time of Marc Antonio; we now approach the period in which its real masters appear — Albrecht Dürer in Germany and Marc Antonio in Italy—who carried the art of engraving from the point to which it had been brought by their predecessors to a degree of perfection in some respects never excelled, if, indeed, quite equalled.

Marc Antonio Raimondi, the founder of the famous Roman school of engravers, was born at Bologna about the year 1488, or perhaps a few years earlier. At this time, according to Vasari, the goldsmith-painter Francesco Raibolini, better known as Francia, was living in Bologna "in much glory and peacefully enjoying the fruits of his labors," and among his multitude of pupils was Marc Antonio, who, "as being more ingenious than the rest was brought much forward." Francia, if not a great artist, was at least agreeable and beloved as a man, and among his accomplishments as "master of the four arts" was that of designer and engraver of ornamental work, in which art he instructed Marc Antonio, who at this period engraved a few plates of inferior merit and produced a number of *nielli.*

After leaving Francia, Marc Antonio "conceived the desire, which is felt by so many men, of seeing somewhat of the world and of the mode of proceeding in use among the artists of other lands," and accordingly journeyed through Upper Italy to Venice, where he was attracted by the works of Albrecht Dürer, then at the zenith of his fame, and a quantity of whose wood-cuts "certain Flemings" had brought to Venice and exposed for sale on the Piazza of St. Mark, and which seem to have acquired great and immediate popularity on account of their novelty and superior execution. About the year 1510 Marc Antonio was in Florence, and in the following year, attracted by the fame of Raphael, he went to Rome, where his career was destined to mark a memorable era in the history of his art. Here he remained until 1527, when he fled to Bologna to escape the sack of Rome, and disappears from history.

Marc Antonio's prints number more than 300, and are divided, according to the period in which they were executed, into four classes. To the first class belong his earliest works engraved at Bologna under Francia; the second includes his copies of Dürer's wood-cuts, and his other prints engraved before his arrival in Rome; the third, his masterpieces engraved at Rome under the influence of Raphael; and in the fourth class are placed those engraved after the death of Raphael.

Marc Antonio's earliest prints, engraved under the influence of Francia, are naturally archaic in composition and sentiment, and their technic shows rather the *niellist* than the engraver. Of these, 'Pyramus and Thisbe,' engraved by 1505, is a good example. At Venice he commenced his famous copies of Dürer's wood-cuts, an undertaking which contributed in great measure to that excellence in drawing and masterly handling of the graver which characterize his later works. These copies, or, more properly, translations, are engraved upon copper, and imitate the effects of the original wood-cuts; they are not fac-similes of the lines. During his career, Marc Antonio re-engraved in this manner nearly eighty of Dürer's wood-cuts. These copies are of various degrees of excellence, the most important being the series of the 'Life of the Virgin' and the 'Little Passion,' of which more particular mention will be made when we come to speak of Dürer. When Marc Antonio engraved these copies his own reputation had not yet been established, and it is said that he sought to profit unjustly by Dürer's fame, by reproducing his signature as well as his designs "with the most faithful similitude," so that "they were supposed to be by Albrecht Dürer himself, as whose works they were accordingly bought and sold." His copyism is certainly excusable, but his forgery of Dürer's signature, and his deceit in passing off his copies as the originals has not added to his moral reputation. Vasari states that Dürer "fell into a most violent rage, and leaving 'Flanders' (Nuremberg) he at once repaired to Venice," and obtained from the Signoria a decree prohibiting the Italian engraver from attaching his signature to future copies—a somewhat improbable story, as we shall presently see.

During the period of Marc Antonio's residence in Florence, sometimes called the transition period of his career, he engraved the beautiful print known as 'Les Grimpeurs' (The Climbers), three figures taken from Michael Angelo's famous cartoon of the battle of Pisa. As this print is dated 1510, it may have been finished after his arrival in Rome.

This brings us to the most important period of Marc Antonio's career, the time during which he was Raphael's engraver. Dürer and Rembrandt were original artists, and engraved their own designs; Marc Antonio engraved the designs of others, and became in this way one of the great masters of his art. As a draughtsman he has scarcely been excelled, although his drawing in the details of his subjects is not always to be commended. Within certain limits his technical skill was very great, uniting classical purity of outline and grace of form with great delicacy of technic and a singular subtilty and refinement of expression. While somewhat dry and monotonous, his style was well adapted to the works he engraved. It was sufficient to interpret the drawings and preparatory studies of Raphael, but wholly inadequate in richness and variety to interpret his paintings, or those of his contemporaries, as a modern engraver would represent them. His style was not pictorial, and was deficient in effects of chiaroscuro and local color, and his knowledge of expressing textures was very imperfect; but it must be remembered that he did not aspire to these qualities, and that in his own domain he was completely successful.

Marc Antonio possessed an exquisite sense of Raphael's genius and ideals; indeed, the spirit of the "divine painter" seems to have taken complete possession of him. There are still preserved a number of Raphael's drawings in which certain parts are merely indicated by a few bold strokes, while in the engravings the ideas are so completely realized that the lines appear those of Raphael; in other plates there are essential variations from the originals, evidently suggested by the great artist and carried out by his engraver. The outlines and contours, and the grace and expression of his figures are in a number of instances so perfect that some of his admirers affect to recognize the hand of Raphael in tracing the designs, or, at least, in correcting the outlines upon the copper, particularly in the fine prints of 'Adam and Eve' and 'The Judgment of Paris.' That some of his prints were engraved under the immediate supervision of Raphael is not unlikely. Other typical examples are the superb print of the Roman 'Lucretia,' which is said to have first attracted Raphael's attention to the engraver; the 'Massacre of the Innocents' (B. 20); 'Dance of Cupids;' 'St. Cecilia;' 'The Five Saints;' and the figure called 'Poetry.' By these and other prints of a similar character Marc Antonio's fame soon extended into Germany and Flanders, and mainly through his influence the German engravers who succeeded the school of Dürer became Italianized.

We now come to the last period of Marc Antonio's career. Whether influenced by Francia, Dürer, or Raphael, we see but little of his own personality and much of the mind that guided and inspired him. His best works were produced under the inspiration of Raphael, but after that master's death this reflected genius disappeared, and his subsequent works betray a haste and lack of refinement and interest, and a general relapse into mannerism and mediocrity.

At this period Marc Antonio engraved chiefly from the designs of Giulio Romano, Raphael's most celebrated pupil, who sometimes stooped to represent the dissolute manners of the time. He engraved after this master a series of twenty plates "of figures, the character of which was highly offensive; and, what was still worse, Pietro Aretino wrote a most indecent sonnet for each, insomuch that I do not know which was the more revolting, the spectacle presented to the eye by the designs of Giulio, or the affront offered to the ear by the words of the Aretine." These designs, however, seem to have been popular, and the prints were "discovered in places where they ought least of all to have been expected," a circumstance which so greatly enraged Pope Clement VII. that, to escape his wrath, Romano fled to Mantua and Aretino to Venice; the engraver, who remained behind, was thrown into prison, from which he was released only upon the repeated entreaties of Cardinal Ippolito de' Medici and the sculptor Baccio Bandinelli, Benvenuto Cellini's bitter rival, then in the pope's service at Rome; "and certain it is," proceeds Vasari, "that the endowments which God has conferred on men of ability ought not to be abused, as they too frequently are, to the offense of the whole world and to the promotion of ends which are disapproved by all men." To show his gratitude, Marc Antonio engraved after Bandinelli a fine print, 'The Martyrdom of St. Lawrence,' "wherein there is a large number of nude figures who are roasting San Lorenzo on a gridiron." This work was considered to be "a truly beautiful one," and so pleased Pope Clement that he took the engraver under his especial protection. Bandinelli, however, disapproved of certain liberties taken with his design, and complained to the pope that his work had not been faithfully rendered, but upon comparing the engraving with the drawing, Pope Clement declared that the engraver had not only committed no fault, but had even with great judgment corrected many in his original, and the envious Bandinelli "received exactly what he deserved as the recompense of his ingratitude and discourtesy." The original red-chalk drawing by Bandinelli is still preserved at Munich, and the alleged

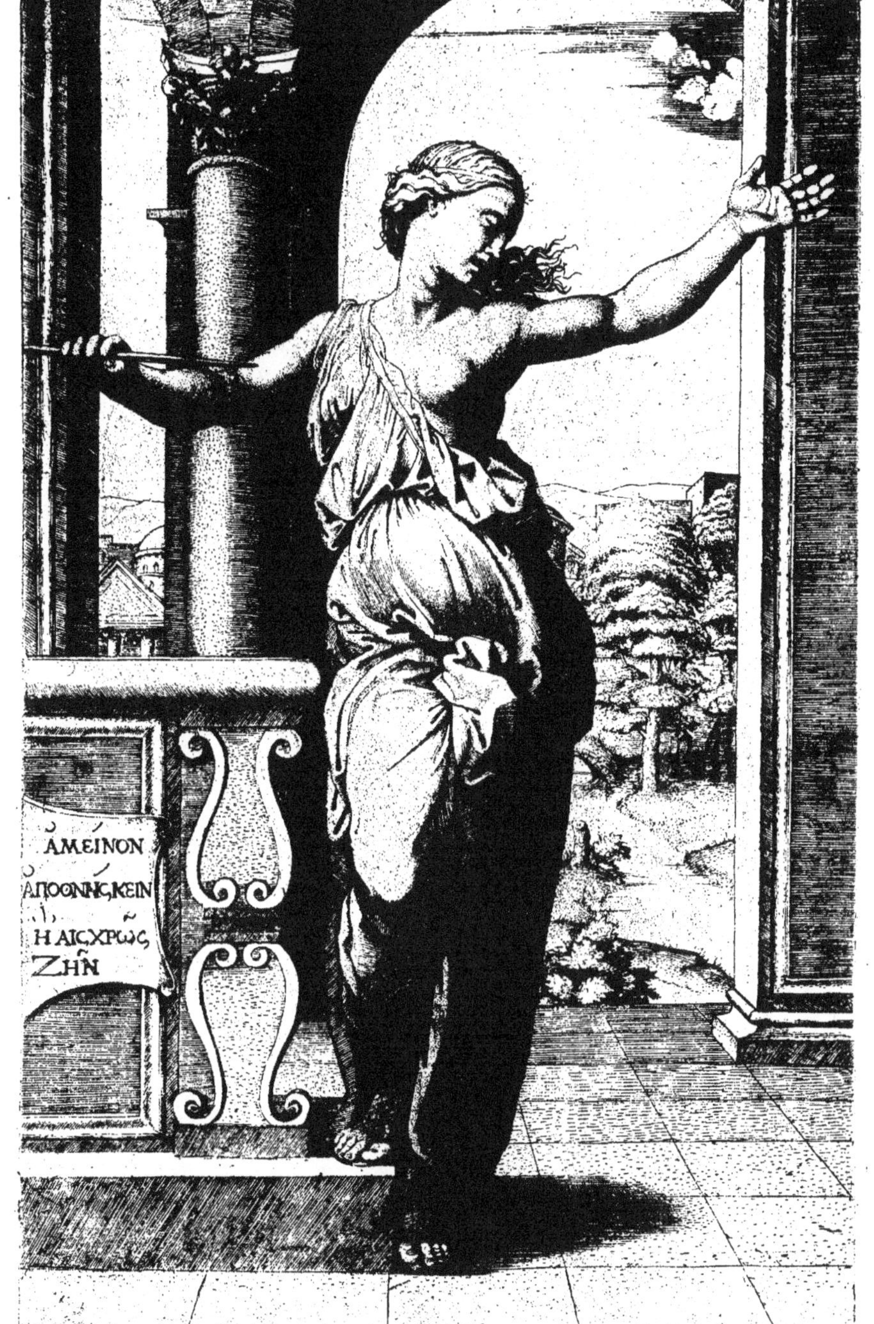
ΑΜΕΙΝΟΝ
ΑΠΟΘΝΗCΚΕΙΝ
Η ΑΙCΧΡΩC
ΖΗ͂Ν

indecent designs, which are still preserved, seem hardly to have warranted the severe measures taken by the pope.

Marc Antonio also engraved a number of fine portraits, of which that of the poet Pietro Aretino, after Titian, ranks among his choicest, rarest, and costliest works. His portraits of Pope Clement VII. and the Emperor Charles V. are also admired. He engraved portraits of the following popes, viz.: Leo XII., Adrian VI., Clement VII., Pius II., Paul II., Sixtus IV., Innocent VIII., Alexander VI., and Pius III. Fine early impressions of Marc Antonio's prints are now rare and exceedingly valuable, and when offered for sale excite almost as fierce competition as those of Rembrandt and Dürer.

Marc Antonio's works are chiefly valuable as preserving and multiplying the drawings and preparatory studies of Raphael. He stands at the head of all reproductive engravers, the consummate perfection of his art consisting in his complete realization of the spirit of his originals. His subjects are clothed in classic forms in which grace and beauty predominate. His work does not enter into competition with that of Dürer or Rembrandt in originality, nor with modern engravers in variety of resources.

The school of Marc Antonio numbered many engravers of eminence, but none whose works, in drawing and expression, approached the excellence of their master. Of his immediate pupils, Agostino de' Musi, called, from his birthplace, Veneziano, and Marco Dente, known as Marco da Ravenna, were the most successful. Agostino appears to have been for a time a pupil of Campagnola, and to have studied the works of Dürer at Venice, but he was afterwards a fellow-pupil with Marco Dente in the atelier of Marc Antonio at Rome. The sack of Rome, which compelled their master to seek refuge in Bologna, drove

Agostino to Florence, and cost Marco Dente his life. In technical skill the best works of these engravers are but little inferior to those of their master, although much below them in draughtsmanship. They engraved chiefly from the designs of Raphael, Giulio Romano, and Bandinelli, and their prints are numerous, but in fine impressions extremely scarce. They sometimes worked in conjunction with each other and with Marc Antonio, whose style they imitated in a deceptive manner. At Florence, Agostino endeavored to attach himself to Andrea del Sarto, but having engraved one of his pictures in an unsatisfactory manner, that painter would have no more of him.

Among the later disciples of the school of Marc Antonio were the unknown Roman engraver called, from his mark, the "Master of the Die," Giovanni Caraglio, and Enea Vico, of Parma, and Giulio Bonasone, of Bologna, who practised their art for a considerable period after the death of Raphael and Marc Antonio. Concerning the identity of the first of these engravers many surmises have been made, but, aside from his prints, very little about him is known. As a draughtsman he excelled Agostino de' Musi and Marco Dente, and a number of his prints have been incorrectly ascribed to Marc Antonio. We can form an idea of the period during which he flourished from the dates, 1532 and 1533, which appear on his prints, and from his portrait of Pope Julius III., whose pontificate did not commence until 1550. His best work is to be found in his thirty-two plates of the 'History of Psyche,' after Coxie, the "Flemish Raphael." Caraglio, who flourished as an engraver in the second quarter of the century, is described by Cumberland as "a great but modest engraver as well as a fine artist." He is said to have acquired his superior skill as a draughtsman and the fine expression of his heads in the studio of Marc Antonio, his reputed master. He also became famous as an engraver of gems and medals at the Court of Sigismund I. of Poland. Enea Vico, a very voluminous engraver, was popular alike at Rome and Florence, and engraved a number of fine subjects after Michael Angelo, of which 'Jupiter and Leda' is the best example. He also engraved from his own design a portrait of the Emperor Charles V., surrounded by emblematical figures, which he is said to have presented to the Emperor with ceremony. Like Caraglio, he was also an engraver of gems and medals, and his *Medals of the Empresses*, with biographies, published in 1557, contains some of his best work. Bonasone was also a voluminous engraver, and his career extended to the last quarter of the century. He endeavored to give to his works greater breadth and more pronounced effects of light and shade than those of Marc Antonio, but most of his prints are dry and uninteresting, and are defective alike in drawing and execution.

Among the last worthy successors of the school of Marc Antonio were the Mantuan engravers Giorgio Ghisi, and the family of Scultori, consisting of Giovanni, Adamo, and Diana, until recently considered members of the Ghisi family. Giorgio, the chief of these engravers, was also a very celebrated artist in damascene work. By these engravers we have many plates after Raphael, Giulio Romano, Michael Angelo, and other eminent masters, engraved in a manner similar to that of Marc Antonio, although in comparison most of their works are dry and monotonous. Diana was one of the earliest female engravers, but there were many others before the close of the century. Although we have mentioned but a few of the numerous followers of Marc Antonio, none of especial importance have been omitted; indeed, some of the later works of the engravers already named show evidence that the school was already on the wane.

While the works of Marc Antonio were still the models for the Italian engravers, another process of engraving was coming into favor, in which the lines were bitten into the plates by aqua-fortis, instead of being laboriously ploughed with the graver. Although etching was well known to the early goldsmiths and armorers, its first practical application as a process of engraving was for a long time attributed to a native of Lombardy, Francesco Mazzola, called *Il Parmigiano*, to the exclusion of the prior claim of the German engravers. Parmigiano seems, however, to have been one of the earliest of the Italian engravers who made extensive use of etching as a complete process. While many of his early works in this direction show an unfamiliarity with the management of the aqua-fortis, his later attempts are somewhat more successful, although nearly all of his plates are imperfectly bitten and rudely retouched with the graver, and show rather the freedom of the skilful draughtsman who occasionally took up the needle than the careful technic of the professional engraver. The graceful arrangement and spirit of his designs, the beauty and sweetness of the expression of his heads, and his attention to chiaroscuro compensate in a measure for the imperfections of his technic. Parmigiano was also a very celebrated designer of wood-cuts to be printed in the chiaroscuro manner.

Many curious stories have been told of Parmigiano's charm of person and conversation, and of his art, manners, and lute-playing. Born in 1504 at Parma, he was surrounded by the art of Correggio, whose beautiful style he followed in his earlier works, but at the age of twenty he was attracted to Rome by the fame of Raphael and Michael Angelo. Here he received flattering attention from Pope Clement VII., and rose rapidly into fame as the fortunes of Marc Antonio were declining. But the smiles of fortune were of short duration. Upon the sacking of Rome by the German and Spanish soldiery of the Constable de Bourbon, the career of Parmigiano, like that of many other Roman artists, was rudely interrupted. Like Marc Antonio he fled to Bologna, but soon returned to Parma, where he received a commission to paint an extensive series of frescos. At this time a change came over his character; he became weary of his task, and, having received money in advance of his contract, became so neglectful and indifferent to his work that he was imprisoned; being released upon his promise to amend, he decamped, instead, to Casal Maggiore, where, becoming "strange and melancholy," he died in 1540. His troubles have been attributed to a fatal infatuation for alchemy; "running after such whimsies as the congelation of mercury, in the hope of rendering himself richer than he had already been made by the gifts of Nature and Heaven;" but his biographer, Padre Affò, regards this account as one of Vasari's numerous gossiping stories with shaky foundation.

During the decade immediately following the death of Parmigiano there flourished an engraver concerning whose identity much confusion has existed, and of whom very little is known. The works now attributed to Andrea Meldolla have until recently been ascribed in part to the artist called Schiavone and partly to Parmigiano. The latter was quite evidently his model, for most of Meldolla's prints are after designs by Parmigiano, whose grace, expression, and feeling are preserved with fidelity. Many of his plates, like those of Parmigiano and other early etchers, were badly corroded with the aqua-fortis, and rudely retouched and scratched upon with the point, although a few of the later examples show marked advancement in technical skill. It is believed that many of his plates were of pewter, which accounts for the frequent alterations and the scarcity of clean, sharp impressions.

Soon after the middle of the sixteenth century the influence of Marc Antonio, which for a generation had attracted to Rome many engravers, not only from all parts of Italy, but from Germany, France, and the Netherlands, began to decline. The meridian point had been passed, and the art now began to retrograde and languish. The interest in engraving no longer centred in a single direction, nor in the qualities of a single school, and the engravers, free to follow their own inclinations, were striving to cultivate a more brilliant and pictorial style than that of Marc Antonio. The first great impulse in this new direction came from without. Cornelis Cort, a Dutch engraver who had acquired considerable reputation at home, went to Italy soon after the middle of the century and settled in Venice, where, for a time, he resided in the house of Titian. He afterwards established at Rome a school of engraving which was destined to mark something like an epoch in the history of his art. He advocated the cultivation of a broad, free style, and the use of larger plates, and his works are especially noted for their fine landscape backgrounds. While some of his early prints after the Flemish masters are interesting, his fame as an engraver rests mainly upon his interpretations of Titian, although the best engravings after that master belong to a later period, for Titian was much less fortunate in his engravers than either Raphael or Michael Angelo.

The movement inaugurated by Cort was given a far greater impetus by his accomplished pupil Agostino Caracci, whose works became models for imitation as those of Marc Antonio had been. The great masters had passed away, and no worthy successors had appeared, and the various schools of painting and engraving had degenerated into affectation and mediocrity; but towards the close of the century arose the famous Bolognese family of Caracci, who attempted to restore to art its former glory.

The Caracci family numbered three men of genius—Agostino, his brother Annibale, and uncle Lodovico. Differing greatly in disposition and character, the reputation of these artists rests upon different grounds. The Caracci were of humble origin: the father of Agostino and Annibale was a tailor, and Lodovico's father was a butcher; but through industry and merit they rose to a high place in the history of art. Not only was Agostino one of the most renowned artists of his country, but he was also scholar, poet, and philosopher, and his polished manners and elegant tastes won for him many friends among the learned and noble. Annibale was averse to studies, dull of comprehension, sarcastic, and envious of his brother's social success, and loved to remind him of their lowly origin, and the life of the brothers was one of continual discord and mortification; yet, as painters, their combined talents were essential to the highest success of either, and their art was never so effective as when it united the taste, learning, and invention of Agostino with Annibale's grace, vigor, and beauty of execution; but at last Annibale's jealousy separated them, and their subsequent works lack much of the genius which characterizes their joint productions.

Agostino Caracci was born at Bologna in 1557, and was intended by his father for the goldsmith's craft; but he soon entered upon his career as an artist, at first in Bologna, afterwards studying painting at Parma and engraving under Cornelis Cort, at Venice. He returned in 1589 to Bologna, where he remained until about the year 1600, when he accompanied his brother to Rome. As an engraver he was the most eminent of his time. His style resembles the bold, free technic of Cort, but shows greater skill and refinement, and is characterized by singular beauty of expression, although lacking in effects of chiaroscuro, an omission common in the works of the early Italian engravers.

The prints of Agostino Caracci are numerous and interesting; they comprise portraits, biblical and mythological subjects and landscapes, both from original designs and after various masters, chiefly Paolo Veronese, Tintoretto, Titian, and Correggio. Many of his engraved subjects are of large size, some composed of a number of sheets. As typical examples may be named 'The Crucifixion,' and 'St. Jerome regarding the Virgin in the Clouds,' after Tintoretto; 'St. Francis in Ecstasy,' after Francesco Vanni, in which a beautiful angel hovers over the sleeping saint; 'The Virgin, St. Catherine, and St. Anthony,' after Paolo Veronese; and 'Pan Conquered by Love;' *omnia vincit amor*. Of his portraits, that of Titian, a bold, picturesque work, bearing the date 1587, eleven years after that master's death, shares the honors of the school in portraiture with Marc Antonio's portrait of Aretino. Agostino Caracci was also famous as a designer and draughtsman, and frequently corrected bad drawing in his originals, a service seldom rewarded with gratitude.

There are a few plates by Annibale and Lodovico, partly etched and finished with the graver in a free and masterly manner, which display admirable taste and drawing, but the fame of these artists rests mainly upon other grounds than their skill as engravers. Annibale was eminent as a painter, and possessed great technical abilities, but his powers of design were limited, for he was alike ignorant of history and fable, and when engaged upon his famous frescos in the Farnese Palace he was obliged to have frequent recourse to Agostino and others for his designs.

Lodovico Caracci was considerably older than his nephews, and it was at his persuasion that they became painters. He was the founder of what is known as the "Eclectic" school, and was more renowned as a teacher than as a painter or engraver. With the assistance of his nephews he opened at Bologna the famous *Academia*, its object being, as the name of the school implies, to select the pre-eminent qualities in the works of the great masters, avoiding their defects, and to fuse the whole into an original system, modified by the artist's own personality. According to his precepts, the painter is expected to familiarize himself with the ideals and methods of the great masters until "every borrow'd grace becomes his own;" the design and expression of Raphael, the power of Michael Angelo, the coloring of Titian, the grace of Parmigiano, etc., according to the sonnet of Agostino. The Caracci numbered among their pupils Domenichino, Guido Reni, Albani, and other eminent artists, and their influence extended far into the seventeenth century.

Among the most distinguished followers of Cornelis Cort and Agostino Caracci were Francesco Villamena and Cherubino Alberti. Villamena is believed to have been Agostino's fellow-pupil under Cort at Venice, but his numerous works are inferior to those of his prototypes. The numerous works of Alberti show a genius at times approaching that of Agostino Caracci, and are far above the average of his time. He engraved some remarkable friezes from Caravaggio's paintings in the manner called "sgrafitto," expressed by hatchings in the plaster, a style much used at this period to ornament the exteriors of palaces and public buildings, and of which Caravaggio's famous friezes in the Vatican and palaces at Rome were among the most important examples. Upon the sack of Rome, Caravaggio retired to Naples, whence he went to Sicily, where he is said to have been robbed and murdered by his servant. Although his famous friezes have long since succumbed to the ravages of time and weather, or have been destroyed in rebuilding, many of the designs have been preserved in the prints of Alberti, Galestruzzi, Goltzius, and other engravers.

As the works of Marc Antonio are typical of the highest state of engraving in Italy in the first half of the sixteenth century, so the progress made in the art during the latter half of the century is shown in the works of Agostino Caracci. After the death of Agostino in 1602 a period of decadence followed, extending over two centuries, during which time there were but few Italian engravers whose works are important either for exceptional merit in point of art or as showing any improvement in the mechanical processes.

When Cardinal Barberini became pope in 1623 under the title of Urban VIII., Rome once more became an art centre, and the artists of France, Germany, and the Netherlands, as well as those of Italy, were once more attracted to the Imperial City. Among those who were received with especial favor were the French painters Nicholas Poussin and Claude Lorraine. It was during Urban's pontificate that Galileo was summoned to Rome to make his famous recantation. Notwithstanding the instability of his temporal power in Italy, the complications caused by the Thirty Years' War which was raging in Germany, the intense national jealousy which had sprung up between the French and the Italians, and the growing supremacy of literature over art, Urban still found time to encourage artistic talent of all kinds. During this period a school of engravers flourished in Rome whose works, collectively, are important, if not especially interesting. Their similarity and want of individuality, however, render particular mention unnecessary; they can generally be distinguished at a glance by the bees of the armorial bearings of the Barberini family which swarm about them.

We turn away from these monotonous works to the spirited etchings of the Florentine artist Stefano Della-Bella, who was a fellow-pupil of the French engraver Callot in the atelier of Canta-Gallina at Florence. In the earlier part of his career Della-Bella imitated Callot, from whom he acquired his happy manner of arranging his figures, and much of the grotesque humor and philosophical spirit displayed in his prints; but he afterwards adopted a manner of his own which shows his peculiar genius to greater advantage. The prints of each of these eccentric artists number more than 1400, comprising all manner of subjects; we could wish that they had produced less and worked with greater care. The amazing finesse and freedom with which Della-Bella handled the point has scarcely been surpassed. His brilliant, spirited, and picturesque works show remarkable fertility of invention, infinite taste and judgment in the arrangement of his subjects, and an almost endless variety in the grouping of his figures. For these qualities Callot and Della-Bella are esteemed far above a number of their contemporaries who possessed greater mechanical skill.

In the year 1640, five years after the death of Callot, Della-Bella visited Paris, where he was taken under the protection of Cardinal Richelieu. During his residence of about ten years in France he made for Richelieu drawings of the siege of Arras and La Rochelle, which he also engraved, and chief among his many views of Paris made during this period is his fine plate of the Pont Neuf, from his own drawing, which belongs to the year 1646. The picturesque bridges and buildings along the river in Paris have ever been favorite subjects with artists, and the representations of Zeeman, Callot, Silvestre, Perelle, Della-Bella, Méryon, Lalanne, Martial, and other artists, belonging to different periods, possess great historical and topographical value aside from their artistic interest. After leaving Paris, Della-Bella returned to Florence, where he died in 1664. He has left us a portrait of himself in a Persian costume.

In the early part of the seventeenth century the Spanish artist Josef de Ribera (1588–1656), called *Lo Spagnoletto*, went from Valencia to Italy, where he soon became infatuated with the rugged style of Caravaggio, whose works, with their harsh and violent contrasts of light and shadow, were at this time held in extraordinary estimation. After a career abounding in adventures and misfortunes, Ribera settled at Naples, where he became the leader of the school of realistic painters known as the "Naturalisti," who, under the Spanish rulers of Naples, enjoyed privileges not accorded to other artists. The influence of Raphael and Correggio, visible in his earlier works, rapidly disappeared after his arrival in Naples. He became an ascetic, and his subsequent works are stern and vigorous in execution, and present violent contrasts in chiaroscuro, and his conceptions are terrible and repulsive. He loved to portray tortures and flayings, and like his fiery countryman Goya, he seems to have revelled in scenes of suffering and death; he is said to have been much patronized by the Jesuits. The jealousy of his school drove from Naples Guido Reni and other followers of the graceful eclecticism of the Caracci, in whose expulsion

Ribera is said to have taken an active and rather disgraceful part. A number of his etchings are highly esteemed by connoisseurs. Among these are 'The Martyrdom of St. Bartholomew,' his masterpiece; 'St. Jerome, with an Angel Blowing a Trumpet;' 'Bacchus,' 'Silenus,' and 'Poetry.' As an etcher, Ribera's works possess delicacy and versatility of technic, purity and precision of drawing, and vigor and truth of expression. Goya's subjects are numerous and of unexampled brutality. His prints (mentioned for convenience in the present chapter) include a series of 'Bull-fights,' 'Caprices,' 'Disasters of War,' 'The Garotte,' and some portraits after Velasquez.

Guido Reni, Salvator Rosa, Maratti, and Tiepolo also used the point with great freedom, but, like many other painters, ancient and modern, they employed the process rather as a convenient method of multiplying their drawings than on account of its artistic possibilities, and their prints, while interesting, are not characteristic examples of the art.

Of the numerous other etchers of the Southern school a few only will be mentioned. The distinguished artist Castiglione (1616–70) etched a large number of plates, imitating in many of them the manner of Della-Bella and Rembrandt. The best of these represent caravans, processions, troops of animals, and pastoral subjects. Castiglione visited nearly every important city of Italy, most of which still possess examples of his paintings. Pietro Santi, or Bartoli, also called "Il Perugino," from his birthplace, Perugia, is best known by his multitude of plates, mostly etched, representing ancient monuments and remarkable buildings, Roman antiquities, bas-reliefs, and similar subjects. His success in this direction, however, was completely overshadowed in the following century by that of Piranesi. He also engraved a number of subjects after Raphael, Giulio Romano, the

Caracci, and others, and a series of forty-two plates from "Raphael's Bible."

Of the Venetian engravers of the seventeenth and eighteenth centuries but little will be said. In the latter half of the seventeenth century Valentin Lefébre, a Flemish artist, settled in Venice, and etched numerous plates after Titian, Paolo Veronese, and Tintoretto, which were published in a large folio volume in 1682; but these prints are little more than simple sketches, and preserve only the composition of the originals, without conveying any adequate idea of their effects. In the eighteenth century we have the well-known Venetian artist Canaletto (1697–1768), whose views of picturesque Venice are to be found in almost every important gallery of Europe. Canaletto also etched a series of thirty-one "Views in Venice" in a spirited and pictorial manner; of these the 'Tower of Malghere,' in the Lagunes, is a good example. There is also a series of forty etchings from Canaletto's pictures by his pupil Viscentino.

That eccentric and voluminous etcher of architectural subjects, Giambattista Piranesi, also belongs to this period. His characteristic works are still widely known on account of their great size and multitude, and their topographical and artistic value. Piranesi was born in Venice in 1720. After studying architecture in his native city he went to Rome, where he received instruction in theatrical painting and engraving; returning to Venice, he twice attempted to start as a practical architect, but the attractions of Rome, and of art, were too strong for him, and he went back to devote the greater portion of his life to etching the ruins, ancient architecture, and antiquities of Rome and its vicinity. His skill as a draughtsman of architectural subjects was great, and his knowledge as a practical architect enabled him to appreciate and interpret the important and distinguishing features in the buildings and structures which he represented. Into many of these views he also introduced groups of figures, and produced brilliant and striking effects by his skilful arrangement of light and shade. His plates are generally etched in a bold, free manner, supplemented by burin work.

Piranesi's plates are mostly of large size, and number more than 2000. Most of these were first published by his son Francesco, also an engraver of architectural subjects, who set up a printing establishment for this purpose in Rome. Some of the editions contain a text, printed in different languages in different volumes, and to some of the volumes is prefixed a portrait of the artist engraved by Polanzani in the form of a mutilated statue. Later editions have been published at Paris in the present century. Among the most important and interesting examples are exterior and interior views of the Colosseum, St. Paul's, St. Peter's, and the Pantheon; Santa Maria Maggiore; the Columns of Trajan and Antonine; the Arches of Constantine and Septimus Severus; the Farnese and Quirinal Palaces; the Baths of Diocletian; the Campo Vaccino; Roman Aqueducts; and many fine plates of ancient statues, sarcophagi, furniture, vases, candelabra, classical ornaments, and a vast multitude of similar objects. There are also a number of views of Roman buildings engraved by Piranesi's daughter Laura, who is believed to have gone with her brother to Paris soon after her father's death.

Piranesi possessed a fiery, impetuous disposition, and indefatigable zeal and industry. The picturesque freedom and vigor with which he handled the needle gained for him the sobriquet, "The Rembrandt of Architecture." He was a member of many societies, and was made a "Cavaliere" by Pope Clement XIII. He died at Rome in 1778.

Of the other eighteenth century engravers, there still remain to be noticed Francesco Bartolozzi, Luigi Schiavonetti, Giovanni Volpato, and Vincenzio Vangelisti, all celebrated in their time, although many mediocre artists of this period acquired a reputation which in the judgment of succeeding ages their abilities scarcely justified. Bartolozzi and his pupil Schiavonetti will be mentioned with the engravers of England, with whom they became identified by association and by long residence in that country, and Volpato and Vangelisti in connection with their more famous pupils, Raphael Morghen and Longhi.

Before concluding the present chapter, an account of engraving in the chiaroscuro manner should be given, as this process reached its highest excellence in Italy. Until the second quarter of the sixteenth century, the Italian wood-engravers in the ordinary manner followed for the most part the simple style of the cuts in the *Hypnerotomachia Poliphili*, although a much more elaborate style prevailed in the North. But towards the middle of the century cross hatching was employed, and the work became much more elaborate and delicate, displaying considerable skill in execution as well as excellence in design. The best works were produced at Venice, where, in addition to the smaller cuts, the process was also employed by Niccolò Boldrini, Francesco Denanto, and others, to reproduce in large dimensions, and with pronounced effects of light and shade, drawings and even paintings by eminent masters. Some of these cuts are of gigantic size, composed of a number of sheets joined together, following, no doubt, the example already set in Germany. Boldrini, the chief of these engravers, is believed to have studied under Titian at Venice, where he engraved after that master a number of large cuts in a remarkably bold and effective manner.

But the enthusiasm of the German wood-engravers was not shared by those of Italy except in chiaroscuro engraving. By this process effects of color were obtained by printing in a number of shades or colors from wood blocks successively superimposed upon the same sheet of paper, each block containing only a portion of the design. The arrangement and number of the blocks, the tints and colors employed, and various details of the process varied according to the skill and fancy of the engraver, and the effects to be produced. The early engravers in this process seldom employed more than two blocks in addition to the outline block, and in some instances printed the outlines from metal plates. Different impressions from the same blocks vary greatly in quality, according to the care and skill bestowed upon them by the printer. A more elaborate form of this process is now much employed, and printing in colors is practised with the greatest success, not only in Europe, but in our own country.

Our interest in chiaroscuro engraving arises mainly from its novelty and historical value. It was much employed in the sixteenth century to imitate the drawings, sketches, cartoons, and even paintings of eminent artists, particularly Raphael, Parmigiano, and Titian. But notwithstanding its inferiority to other processes, and its decline in artistic importance, the singular skill displayed by some of these early engravers, the novelty of the effects produced, the fact that many eminent artists made designs to be engraved in this manner, and the historical importance attached to these works by connoisseurs and collectors lend a certain degree of interest to this branch of engraving, which, like most of the other processes, is now believed to be of German origin.

The earliest existing chiaroscuro engravings are from designs by German artists, principally Lucas Cranach, Hans Baldung Grün, Hans Schäufelin, and Hans Burgkmair, and the origin of the process has been assigned to the last decade of the fifteenth century. Although there can be little doubt that it was first practised in Germany, chiaroscuro engraving owes its development to the artists of Italy, who were attracted to the process by its capabilities in the way of pictorial effects, and delicate shadings and gradations of color. Although many of their prints engraved in this manner are coarse and unattractive, there are also many beautiful pieces in which the most eminent designers and the most skilful engravers contributed to the result.

There are a number of German chiaroscuros bearing dates as early as 1506, 1509, and 1510, and still earlier examples have been claimed; but the first engraver who practised this process with any considerable success was Jost De Necker, a skilful Flemish wood-engraver who settled in Augsburg about the year 1510, and engraved chiefly from the designs of Burgkmair and Schäufelin. His portrait of Hans Baumgartner, Maximilian's counsellor, dated 1512, and printed in three tints, is one of the finest early chiaroscuros of German origin.

In Italy, where this process reached its maturity, Ugo da Carpi is believed to have been its earliest exponent. This artist, who was born about the middle of the fifteenth century, and died at Rome about the year 1520, gained by his works in this direction a more lasting reputation than from his paintings. The validity of his claims as the inventor of the process, presented to the Venetian Senate in 1516, were for a long time

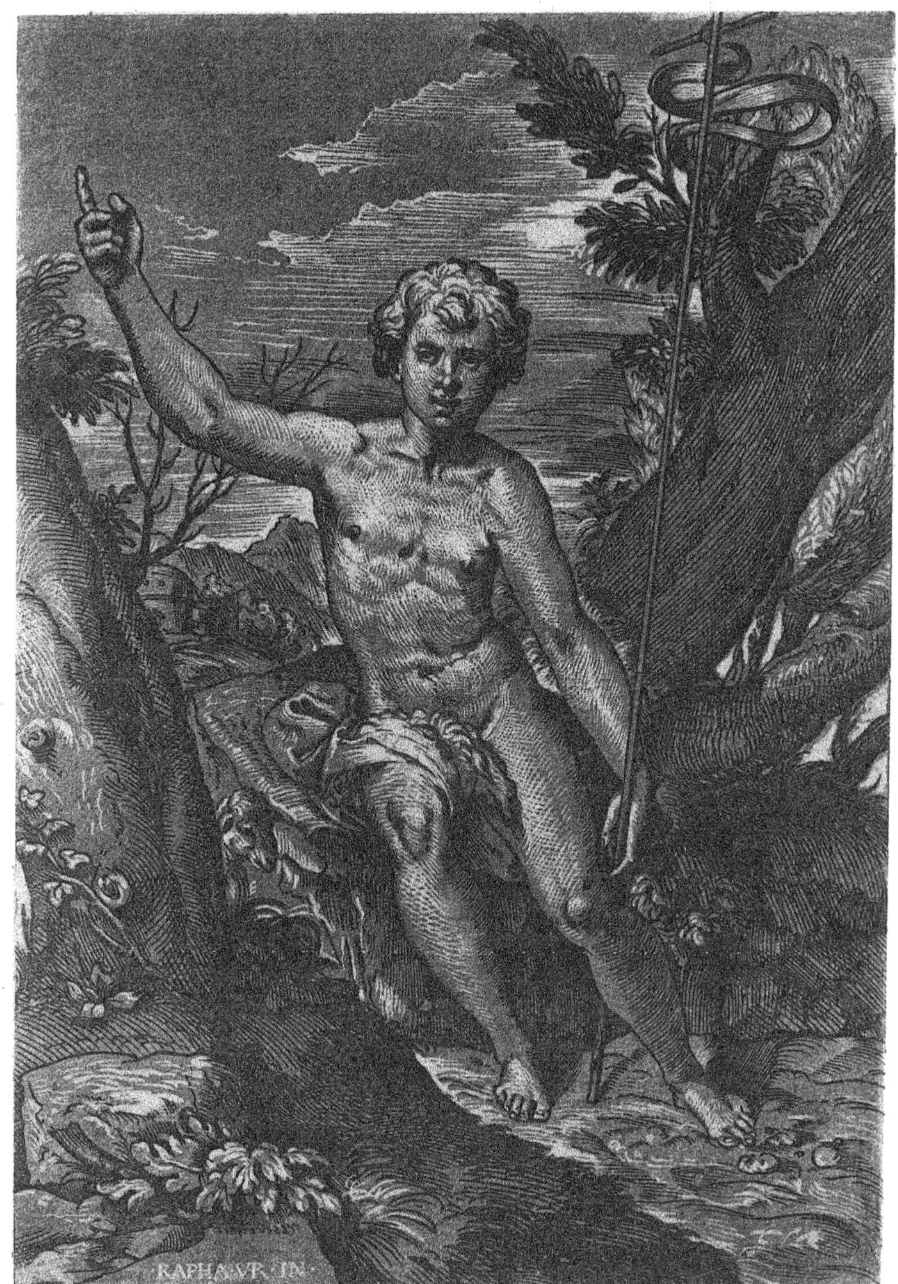
RAPHA·VR·IN·

recognized upon the authority of Vasari, but are no longer admitted. The earliest date which appears upon any of his prints is 1518, although he is known to have worked several years before that time. As typical examples of his prints may be mentioned his 'Sibyl,' after Raphael, and 'Diogenes,' after Parmigiano. Ugo's style was original and striking, and in many of his prints he obtained peculiar effects by a repetition, or "reiteration," of impressions in the same color or shade without using the outline block.

Ugo da Carpi was succeeded by Antonio da Trento and Vicentino, who worked until about the middle of the sixteenth century, and did much to improve and popularize the process. Antonio was a pupil of Parmigiano, and is also said to have received instruction from Ugo da Carpi. After engraving in the chiaroscuro manner some fine subjects after Parmigiano, whose easy, graceful style he preserved in a remarkable manner, he decamped with many valuable drawings, engravings, and wood-cuts belonging to his master; according to Vasari, "he must have taken himself fairly to the devil, seeing that no news was heard of him from that time forward." Among the artists who assisted in the decoration of Fontainebleau in the reign of Francis I. appears the name of Antoine Fantose, who is believed to have been the faithless Antonio. The best examples of his prints are 'The Martyrdom of St. Peter and St. Paul,' and the 'Tiburtine Sibyl,' both after Parmigiano.

Among the other engravers who worked in this manner were Christopher Jegher, who engraved a number of fine subjects at Antwerp, under Rubens, of which the 'Repose in Egypt' may be named, and Andrea Andreani, a very distinguished engraver in this process, who worked in Rome in the latter part of the sixteenth and during the early years of the seventeenth century, and carried the art to a still higher perfection. Andreani engraved many fine subjects after Parmigiano, to whose designs the early engravers in this manner showed a singular partiality, even employing some of his etched plates to obtain outlines and shadows. He also engraved a series of prints of Mantegna's 'Triumphs of Cæsar,' and two immense pieces, dated 1587, from Beccafumi's paintings in "sgrafitto" in the pavement of the Cathedral of Siena. In addition to his own work, Andreani procured blocks cut by other engravers which he retouched, and in a number of instances supplemented by additional blocks, and published the whole as his own, thus obtaining credit to which he was not justly entitled. This deception has thrown suspicion upon works which may have been wholly his own.

The last of the chiaroscuro engravers who will be named was Bartolommeo Coriolano, who worked in Bologna in the second quarter of the seventeenth century. This engraver was a pupil of Guido Reni, and his correct and spirited drawing, and the fine character and expression of his heads, show the influence of the Eclectic school of which he was a disciple. His best prints are after designs by Guido, although a few of his later prints after the artist called Guercino also possess considerable merit. A set of prints which he dedicated to Urban VIII. obtained for him the order of knighthood of Loretto. The most esteemed of his chiaroscuros are 'The Virgin with the Sleeping Infant,' 'The Virgin and Child with St. John, the Baptist,' and the 'Four Sibyls,' all after Guido. Although some of his works were printed from three blocks, he generally confined himself to two, the first containing the outlines and deeper shadows, and the second bringing out the tints and gradations. At this period chiaroscuro engraving was practised by many engravers in Italy, Germany, France, and the Netherlands; but it soon degenerated rapidly in importance until it was no longer practised as a fine art.

We have now traced in a general way the history of engraving in Italy from its first dawnings in Florence, the home of Italian art; we have seen its development under Mantegna and his contemporaries, and its perfection under the magic touch of Marc Antonio. Under Cort and the Caracci we have witnessed its progress in the direction of broader and more pictorial effects, and have noted its subsequent decline. The principal Italian painter-etchers have been mentioned, and a brief outline of the early history of chiaroscuro engraving has been given. The revival of engraving in Italy, and the achievements of Raphael Morghen and the Milanese school of engravers, will be narrated in a subsequent chapter.

CHAPTER III

THE EARLY ENGRAVERS OF GERMANY

The National Character of German Art — The Master of 1466 — Martin Schongauer and his imitators — Albrecht Dürer — The Apocalypse, Great Passion, Life of the Virgin, and Little Passion — Designs for the Emperor Maximilian; the Triumphal Arch and Triumphal Car — Dürer's Principal Copper-plate Engravings — Works upon Art — Maximilian I., the Great Patron of Wood-engraving — The Triumphs of Maximilian; The Wise King; Theuerdanck, and other series — Hans Burgkmair, Hans Baldung Grün, and others — Nuremberg and Augsburg; Dürer and Holbein — Dance of Death and Bible Figures — Early Wood-engravers; Andreae and Lützelberger — The Little Masters; Small Subjects and Ornamental Designs — Albrecht Altdorfer — The Behams: Hans Sebald and Barthel — George Pencz — Heinrich Aldegrever — Italian Art in Germany — Decline of Engraving in Germany

ALTHOUGH Germany had no Vasari, "the commencement of the practice of copper-plate engraving" is now ascribed to her artists rather than to those of Italy. The story of Finiguerra's alleged discovery, so minute and plausible, has been reluctantly abandoned before the indisputable proofs afforded by earlier examples of German origin. At a time when Baldini and Mantegna were struggling with the mechanical difficulties of their art, the engravers of Germany had already become expert in the technical processes. The mediæval spirit of the North, religious, mystical, and romantic, was faithfully reflected in contemporary engraving. While the artists of Italy had constantly before them the examples of early art, the Gothic artists of the North drew their inspiration from the stores of tradition and romance, national legend and myth; they chose their models from the homely scenes around them, from the only types with which they were familiar. If instead of graceful outlines and simple surroundings we often find attenuated figures in awkward attitudes and a superabundance of stiff and complicated draperies, we also find an intensity of expression and sentiment, and an abundance of ideas characteristic of the time and country. At a later period, the intense national character of German art, to us its greatest charm, began to disappear before the all-pervading influence from the South.

The earliest of the German engravers to claim our attention is the master of the Gothic initials 𝔈. 𝔖., generally called the "Master of 1466" from a date which appears on his prints. He is believed to have been both goldsmith and engraver, and to have worked in the cities along the Rhine and at the court of Burgundy; but we know very little about him—not even his name, although many surmises have been made. He is surrounded with a mystery which has defied investigation. The works of this accomplished artist exhibit all the Gothic peculiarities, with scarcely a trace of the humanistic influence which was to revolutionize German art. He possessed a finer, subtler genius than any of his predecessors, and inaugurated a new era in the practice of his art, occupying a position in its history not unlike that of the Van Eycks in painting. His style is as vigorous and spirited as it is quaint and archaic, and his works are full of sentiment and expression; his technic is remarkable for delicacy and precision. His numerous prints represent scenes from the Gospels, canonical and apocryphal, particularly the Gospel of Mary, besides innumerable saints, and even playing-cards and a few improprieties. Bartsch mentions 136 prints by this master, and others have since been discovered, some quite recently, among them a considerable number of playing-cards, of which the series, now numbering forty-two, has been reproduced in fac-simile by the Chalcographical Society. There can be little doubt that their author was an artist of great prominence in his own time, and that he had many pupils and imitators.

Of far greater importance, however, are the works of Martin Schongauer, who was born in the Alsatian town of Colmar before the middle of the century, and was the first great master of the school. By early training a goldsmith, he left his father's shop, it is said, to enter the studio of the Flemish painter Rogier Van der Weyden, Van Eyck's famous pupil. He returned about 1465 to Colmar, where he passed most of the remainder of his life; and here he died in 1488, having won during his short career the admiration of his contemporaries, both by his works and personal qualities. He was also called Martin Schön, and Hübsch Martin, and in France "Le beau Martin." Of Schongauer's personal history we know very little. In the general neglect of the Gothic artists many of his best paintings and the authentic records concerning him disappeared—a serious loss, for Schongauer was the most eminent and original of the German artists who preceded Albrecht Dürer.

Under Schongauer the art of engraving continued its march of progress. His inventive powers would be considered remarkable in any age, and in drawing and technic he far surpassed the other predecessors of Dürer, whose fame has so completely overshadowed most of the earlier artists of Germany. He engraved his own designs, of which more than 100 are known, mostly of religious subjects. Chief among these is the large print of 'Christ bearing the Cross,' a work highly esteemed and often copied in his own time, which shows his creative powers and technical skill to great advantage. The figure of Christ in this print was adapted by Raphael, with slight modification, in his 'Spasimo di Sicilia.' Schongauer's other important prints include the 'Death of the Virgin,' a fine example; 'Coronation of the Virgin,' 'Conversion of St. Paul,' 'Angelic Salutation,' 'Temptation of St. Anthony,' 'The Annunciation,' 'Flight into Egypt,' and 'St. Anthony carried into the air by Demons;' "with forms of the most fanciful and varied character that can be imagined." The last of these designs was copied in colors by Michael Angelo, then at the beginning of his career. There are also two sets of little prints known as 'The Wise and Foolish Virgins,' suggested, no doubt, by the statuettes of the Virgins of the parable which adorned the porches at the "brides' door" in many of the mediæval churches of Germany, and of which the churches of St. Sebaldus and St. Lawrence at Nuremberg still afford fine examples. Of Schongauer's ornamental designs, the crook, or head of a bishop's pastoral staff, and a censer are the best examples.

Schongauer had many imitators, and many of his prints were copied by other engravers, and their copies sometimes passed off as the originals. The copies made by the Meckenens, Franz von Bocholt, and the artist known as Wenceslaus of Olmutz are the most important. Israel von Meckenen and his son of the same name, voluminous engravers, worked in conjunction, engraving both original works and many copies of celebrated prints by other engravers, among the latter fine copies of Schongauer's 'Christ bearing the Cross,' and 'Death of the Virgin.' They also engraved a series of the 'Life of the Virgin,' of considerable merit, and have left us their own portraits. In addition to their numerous religious subjects and ornamental designs, they engraved many prints of subjects from ordinary life, which scenes they were almost the first of the German engravers to represent. Their works possess far less interest and merit than those of Schongauer, and are remarkable for their quantity and variety rather than for their quality. Wenzel of Olmutz is best known by his copy of Schongauer's 'Death of the Virgin.' The much contested prints signed with a W have also been attributed to him, but more recently the old opinion seems to have revived that they were engraved by Michael Wolgemut, of Nuremberg.

The works of the engravers already mentioned sufficiently illustrate the successive stages of engraving in Germany before the time of Albrecht Dürer, and we will therefore pass by the numerous contemporaries of the Master of 1466 and Schongauer, and come at once to that great master who stands forth as the representative artist of Germany.

Albrecht Dürer was born in Nuremberg, May 21, 1471, and was the third of a family of eighteen children of a Hungarian goldsmith of the same name. The elder Dürer, who had settled in Nuremberg in 1455, was a man of irreproachable character, skilled in his craft, in which he intended his son Albrecht to become his successor. But the latter soon wearied of the mechanical work of his father's calling, and determined to become a painter. At the age of fifteen he was apprenticed to the Franconian master, Michael Wolgemut, an eminent painter and designer of wood-cuts, and now credited with a number of copper-plate engravings. During this period he made rapid progress, and upon the expiration of his apprenticeship in 1490 he set out upon his wanderings, according to custom, visiting various cities of Germany, and possibly going into Italy. He returned to Nuremberg about four years later, "And when I reached home," he writes, "Hans Frey treated with my father

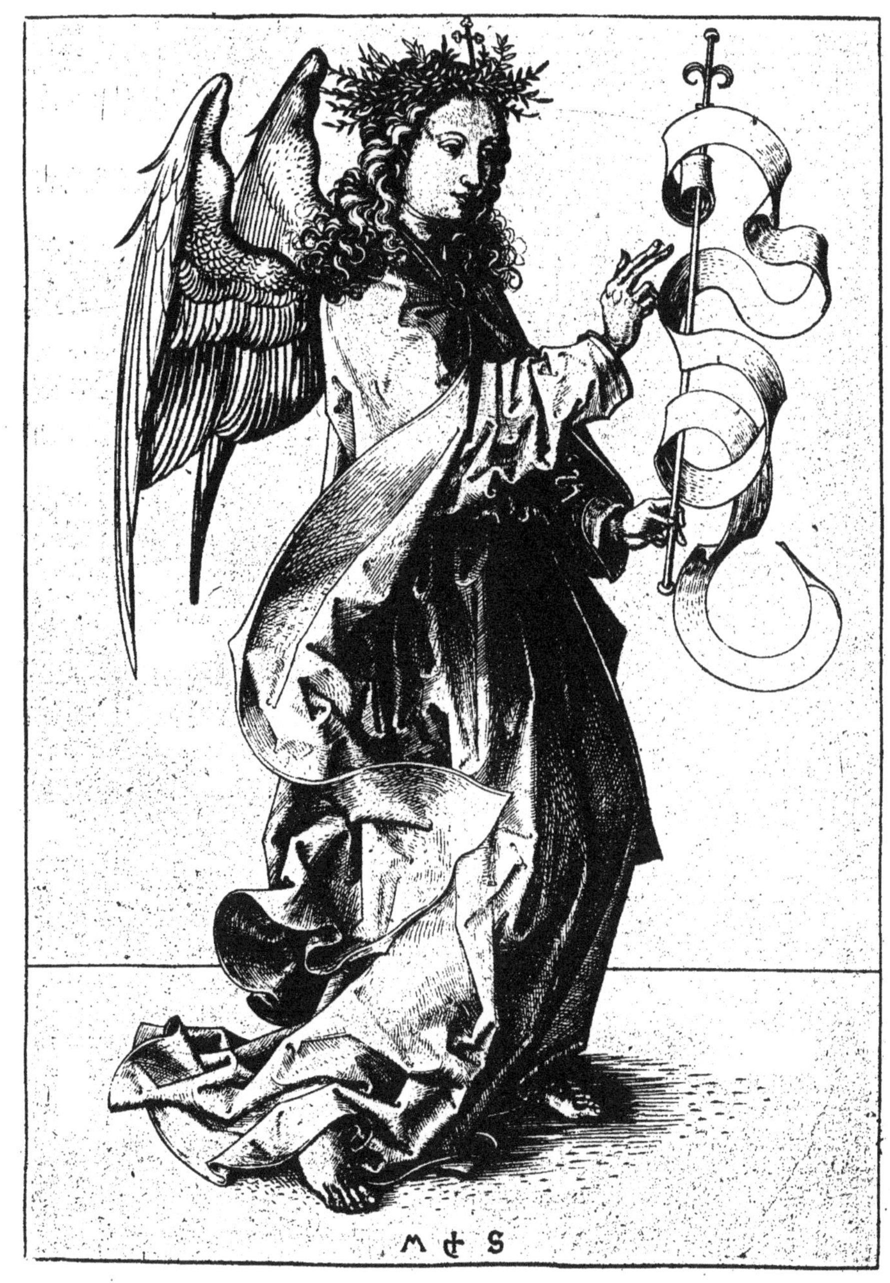

and gave me his daughter Agnes, and he gave me 200 gulden with her, and the marriage was celebrated on the Monday before St. Margaret's Day in the year 1494." The familiar and disputed story of their domestic infelicity need not be repeated. Dürer took his young wife to his father's house, where they continued to reside until 1509, when they removed to the large house near the Thiergarten Gate, which is still shown to visitors as one of the interesting places of the city.

To this period belong some of the best of Dürer's engraved works, and also the designs for the *Apocalypse*, a series of fifteen large cuts, boldly engraved, and first published at Nuremberg in 1498. These cuts mark an epoch in the history of wood engraving. In grandeur of conception and excellence of execution they far surpassed anything of the kind which had previously appeared, and inaugurated the age of successful wood engraving. Other similar works soon followed. Some of the cuts of the *Great Passion* were probably designed as early as the beginning of the sixteenth century, and to the years 1504 and 1505 are assigned most of the twenty cuts of the *Life of the Virgin*.

In the autumn of 1505 Dürer journeyed to Venice. According to Vasari the object of this visit was to protect himself against the forgeries of Marc Antonio. Without entering into the details of this famous controversy, it is sufficient to state that during the period of his residence in Italy Dürer may have complained of his treatment at the hands of the Italian engraver, but it is scarcely to be believed that this was the motive of his journey, especially as it is known that he had received a commission from the German merchants of the Fondaco dei Tedeschi for an altar-piece to adorn their church of San Bartolommeo. This picture, 'The Feast of the Rosary,' or 'Rose

Garlands,' is now in the monastery of Strahow, near Prague. Dürer was received by the venerable Giovanni Bellini, the teacher of Titian and Giorgione, with all the distinction due to so eminent an artist, but incurred the jealousy of most of the painters. Although he remained in Italy for a considerable period, we find but little trace of the Italian influence in his subsequent works; if anything, he was more than ever impressed with the excellence of his own style of art.

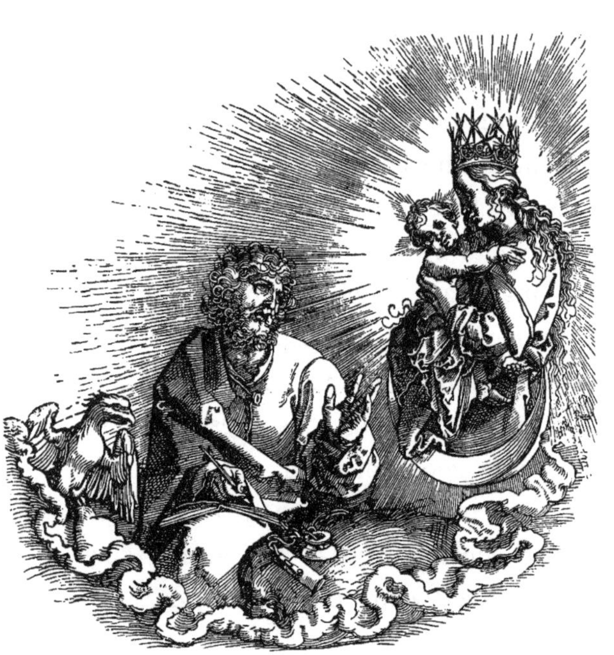

VIGNETTE TO THE "APOCALYPSE"
By Albrecht Durer

Early in 1507 Dürer was back again in Nuremberg working industriously. He completed the two series of wood-cuts, the *Great Passion* and *Life of the Virgin*, which he had begun before his Venetian visit. The first of these series was composed of eleven large cuts and a vignette, and the latter of nineteen large cuts and a vignette of the Virgin seated on a crescent holding the infant Christ. The latter series contains some of Dürer's best work. It commences with the High Priest's rejection of Joachim's Sacrifice, and depicts the home life of the Holy Family, including the Birth, Presentation, and Marriage of the Virgin; the Visitation, Nativity, Adoration, Circumcision, Presentation, the Flight and Rest in Egypt, Jesus disputing in the Temple, Parting from His Mother, Death of the Virgin, and the Assumption. To the series already named was added another of thirty-seven small cuts known as the *Smaller Passion* or *Little Passion*. All of these series were published in book form about 1511.

At this period Dürer commenced his famous designs for the Emperor Maximilian. Two of these works deserve particular mention: *The Triumphal Arch* and *The Triumphal Car*. The former was composed of no less than ninety-two blocks joined together, making a stupendous picture about ten and one-half feet high and nine feet wide, one of the grandest and most imposing works ever engraved upon wood. This famous work was commenced probably in 1512, soon after Maximilian's visit to Nuremberg, and bears the date 1515, doubtless the year in which the drawings were completed, for the actual engraving of the blocks was not finished for a number of years later. *The Triumphal Arch* contains three gates, or entrances, of which the largest, the central, the Gate of Honor and Power, is surmounted by a figure of Fortuna holding the Imperial Crown; the Emperor's genealogical tree adorns the wall. The side gates, surmounted by towers, are those of Praise and Nobility. Other blocks represent scenes in the Emperor's life, and the escutcheons of various countries and provinces subject to his rule. *The Triumphal Car*, composed of eight pieces, forms a subject over seven feet in length; the largest cut, the Car, measures about eighteen inches in height.

In Dürer, Maximilian found an artist able and willing to aid him in his schemes for self-glorification. Besides the Arch and Car, Dürer contributed to the so-called *Triumph of Max-*

imilian a number of designs, although the greater portion of this work was designed by Hans Burgkmair of Augsburg. He also made a great variety of other designs and drawings for the

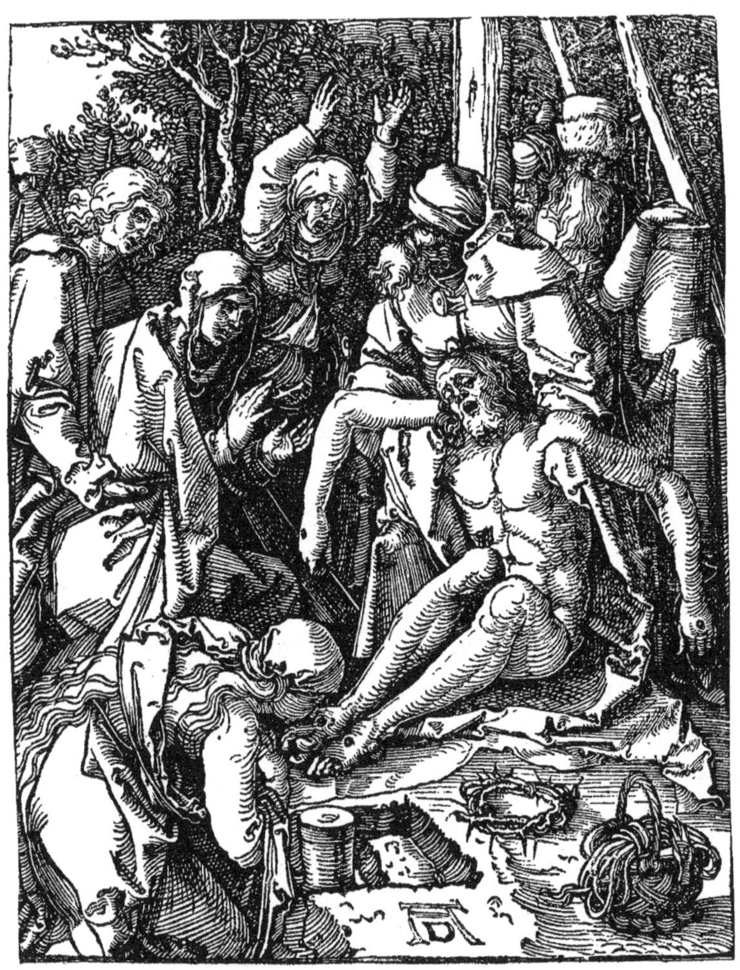

WOOD-CUT FROM DÜRER'S "SMALLER PASSION"

Emperor, among them the remarkable decorations in the famous "Prayer-book of Maximilian," and while at Augsburg, during the Diet of 1518, he drew a charcoal portrait of the Emperor which is still preserved in the Albertina. Maximilian's generosity exceeded his supply of gold, and Dürer received little for his services beyond the advantages of the imperial patronage and a small pension.

We now come to the famous journey into the Netherlands, of which Dürer has left an ample and entertaining account in his journal. Accompanied by his wife and her maid Susanne, he left Nuremberg in July, 1520, while the plague was raging, and in due course of time arrived safely at Antwerp, whence he made excursions to various points of interest. The chief object of this visit was to meet the newly-elected Emperor Charles V., and obtain from him a ratification of the grants of Maximilian, the latter having died in the previous year. After considerable delay and difficulty a confirmation of his pension was signed at Cologne.

Dürer's journal of this expedition is highly curious, recording many important facts and incidents which throw light upon the condition of civilization and art, with the most trifling details of his expenditures. At Antwerp he met Quentin Massys and other Flemish artists, and made the acquaintance of Erasmus. He was entertained with distinction by various guilds and societies, and his reputation as an artist, together with his attractive manners and generous disposition, won for him numerous friends and patrons in this sixteenth-century London, and, indeed, wherever he went. The Archduchess Margaret, Regent of the Netherlands, was also exceedingly gracious to him, although he complains that for all he had given her and done for her she had not made him the least recompense.

Although Dürer made many drawings and portraits during his visit to the Netherlands, and had taken with him a supply of his engravings and wood-cuts, he states that in all his dealings he received less than he gave, and borrowed money with which to return home. He describes a banquet given in his honor by the painters in their Guildhall, and states that at its close he was escorted home with torches. He gives a glowing description of the grand procession in honor of the Virgin, which he witnessed at Antwerp on the Sunday after the Assumption, in which all the guilds of tradespeople participated, and tells us that his wife had her pocket cut off in St. Mary's Church on St. Mary's Day with two gulden in it. At Brussels he saw some wonderful curiosities, "brought to the King from the new gold country (Mexico), including a sun entirely of gold, a whole fathom broad, and a moon all of silver, quite as large," besides all sorts of curious arms, armor, costumes, and other strange objects, and expresses his astonishment and delight at the ingenuity displayed by men in foreign lands. After his return from Cologne he went out to Zeeland to see an enormous whale which had stranded at high tide, and records his narrow escape from shipwreck. While still at Antwerp he heard of the seizure of Luther, and, supposing him dead, thus apostrophizes: "And is Luther dead? Who henceforward will so clearly expound to us the Gospel? Aid me, all pious Christians, to bewail this man of heavenly mind, and to pray that God may send us another as divinely enlightened. Where, O Erasmus of Rotterdam, wilt thou stop? Behold now how the tyranny of might and the power of darkness prevail! Hear, thou champion of Christ! Ride forward, defend the truth, and deserve the martyr's crown." But Erasmus was not flattered by the prospects of martyrdom, and calmly stated that "his gifts did not lie that way."

Towards the close of 1520 Dürer returned home to Nuremberg, having contracted in the Netherlands a malady from

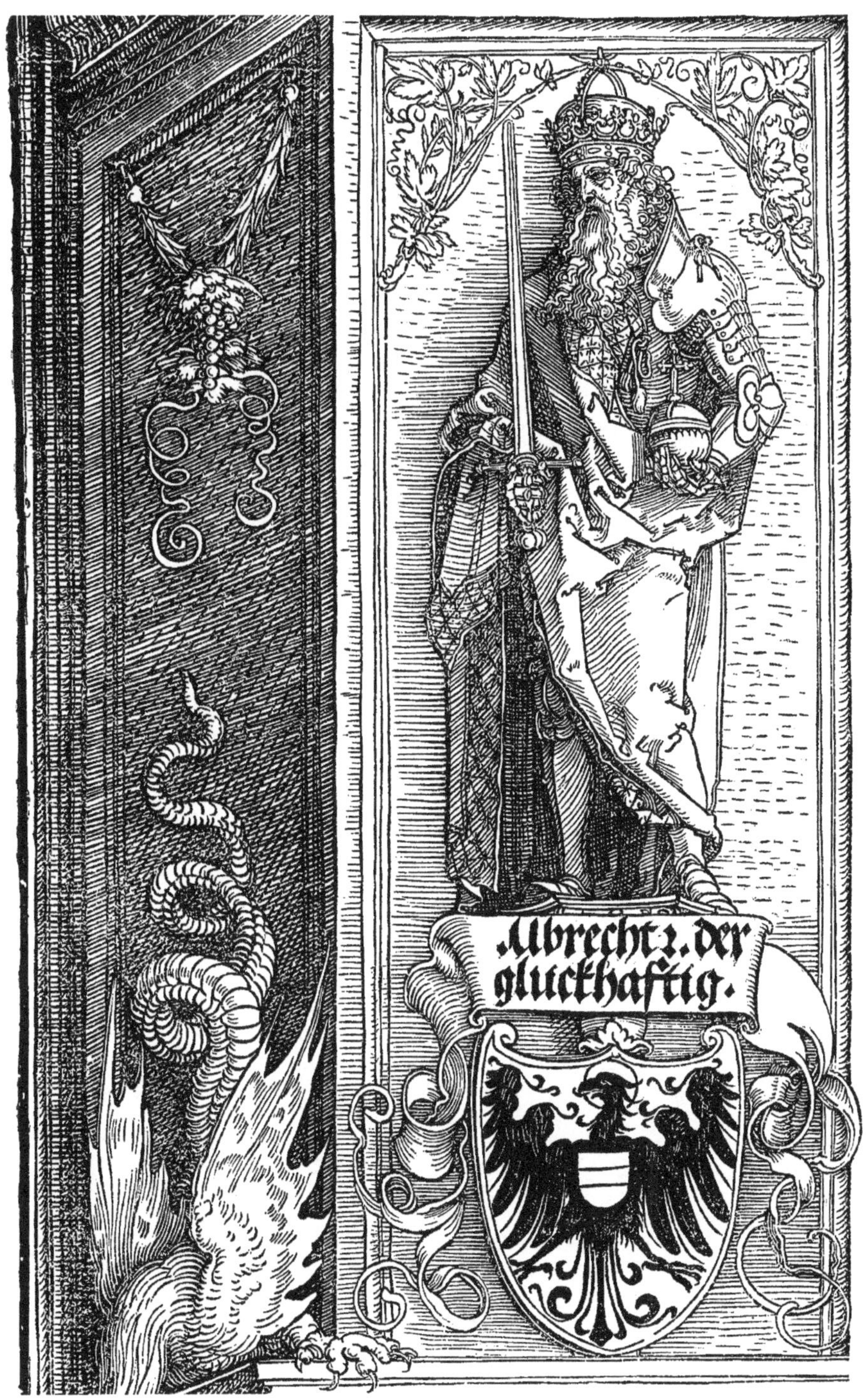

DETAIL FROM "THE TRIUMPHAL ARCH OF MAXIMILIAN."

which he never recovered. But notwithstanding his enfeebled constitution, he continued to work until his death, which occurred suddenly, April 6, 1528, in Passion-week, eight years after the death of Raphael. The inscription on his tombstone was written by Pirkheimer, who soon followed to the grave his early playmate and constant companion. The death of so eminent an artist and so good a man was lamented throughout Germany.

The literary remains of Dürer, recently collected and published, show him as a dutiful son, but not an affectionate husband; a hard-working artist, and a deep student of the theory and principles of art; with strong opinions of his own; striving for truth, yet, with the restless Gothic spirit, led away by all kinds of fantastic conceits; close in a bargain and by no means lavish with his pfennigs, yet fond of the enjoyments of life and of the admiration of his fellow-men; attractive in person and manners; somewhat vain of his accomplishments, and appreciating his own importance; drinking and gaming in moderation; an influential burgher of Nuremberg, devoted to his country and loyal to his emperor; devout in his religion, but inclined to rebel against the abuses of the Church; practical, systematic, and exact in everything he undertook; fond of sight-seeing, and possessing an insatiable curiosity and thirst for knowledge of all kinds—in short, a representative of every side of the life of his age, a faithful historian of the Germany of the Renaissance and Reformation; a master whose art embodies the ideals of his time and country, and whose works for this reason must always be of intense interest.

Although Dürer had received lucrative offers from Venice and Antwerp, according to his own statement he preferred to live in Nuremberg in a moderate manner than to be rich and great elsewhere, although he had received from his own townsmen in return for his art "a truly mean and ridiculous sum," most of his patronage having come from princes and foreigners. However, we find that he enjoyed at Nuremberg, beyond any other German artist, social and intellectual advantages. Wilibald Pirkheimer, scholar and man of science, and its foremost citizen, was his intimate friend and companion. He was also on terms of intimacy with Lazarus Spengler and other distinguished citizens. The Emperor Maximilian was his friend and patron, and he numbered among his admirers Luther, Melancthon, Erasmus, and many of the great artists and scholars of his time.

In the versatility of his talents, Dürer was almost as remarkable as his great contemporary Leonardo, with whom he is often compared and contrasted. It has been said of them, as of Cæsar and Alexander, that only the differences between them were greater than their many resemblances. Not only was Dürer painter, engraver, and designer, but author, philosopher, and inventor; interested in geometry, natural history, architecture, fortification, music, and almost every other branch of art and science. By preference he was an engraver; educated as a goldsmith, his love for minute finish and perfection of detail never left him. With him art meant the expression of almost every fact and thought connected with the object or person represented. He studied Nature in detail. It has been aptly said that he drew plants as though illustrating a work on botany, and expressed the forms and cleavage of rocks in a manner that would delight a geologist; that he drew bones and muscles like an anatomist, and furniture as though designing for a cabinet-maker. Although fond of introducing landscape backgrounds into his scenes, he had no idea of the breadth and beauty of landscape as now represented. Every tree, cottage, or fence, however distant, is clearly shown. His interiors are detailed drawings of every object within sight. To suppress details and matters of secondary importance, in order to emphasize some important fact or truth, seems never to have occurred to him. Unity, concentration and general effect he seldom thought of, but filled his best plates with a superabundance of details—the more the better. Even his largest print, 'St. Eustachius,' is crowded with individual objects. Mere beauty of form or line was of little importance compared with accuracy and expression, and in all his works there is scarcely a single beautiful female face or figure. His costumes are often glaring anachronisms, but this was a fault common to the northern artists. His system of chiaroscuro and knowledge of local color were very imperfect, and his rendering of perspective was almost equally defective, although he speculated much upon this subject. He revelled in a deep and subtle philosophy, and was fond of theorizing, and his works are pervaded with the deep religious feeling and philosophical speculations of his time. He represented the manners, customs, and ideals of his age and country, with their religious and romantic features, and for these qualities we are chiefly interested in his art. Vasari states that "he would have equalled the greatest masters of Italy if he had been born in Tuscany, and if the study of the antique had helped him to impart to his figures as much beauty and elegance as they have truth and delicacy." In that event, however, Gothic art would have lost its greatest representative.

Dürer's services to the art of wood-engraving were of inestimable value. He found the process devoted to inferior designs and practised by unskilled workmen. He extended its boundaries, and raised it from a crude mechanical craft to the dignity of an art, lavishing upon his designs the riches of his poetic imagination and inventive genius, making it by example, as well as precept, one of the most popular arts of the Renaissance.

While Dürer and other early masters furnished the designs, and in many instances drew them upon the blocks, the actual cutting of the blocks was left to the *formschneiders*, whose task it was to cut away the superfluous wood, leaving the lines of the design standing in relief. Wood-engraving was valued as a means of multiplying in fac-simile the designs of eminent masters; but it remained for later artists to develop its possibilities in the direction of delicacy and refinement, and of representing tones, textures, and various other qualities common in the best modern work. It is said that many of the best of Dürer's designs, among them many of the blocks of *The Triumphal Arch*, were engraved by Hieronymus Andreae of Nuremberg, one of the most skilful wood-engravers of the time.

As a copper-plate engraver Dürer's skill in handling the graver, in vigor and absolute certainty, has scarcely been surpassed. Although his prints are engraved in the manner peculiar to the time, his style is none the less interesting if now quaint and archaic. His three allegorical prints, 'St. Jerome in his Chamber,' 'Melancholia,' and 'The Knight, Death, and the Devil,' the first two engraved in 1514 and the last in the preceding year, represent the culmination of his creative powers and technical skill. These prints are engraved in a peculiarly expressive manner, and are literally crammed full of meaning. They possess a quality of mystery, weirdness and introspection, combined with a deep, subtle philosophy and a humanistic feeling, characteristic of the early period of the Reformation, a prelude strain echoed by Goethe. St. Jerome, robed as a cardinal, is writing at a table in the centre of his cell, engrossed in holy work; symbolic, it is said, of the growing feeling for humanity typified in the works of Erasmus. Before him is a crucifix, near the window is a skull, and beside him lies the lion, so deferential to this saint. The winged woman in the print inscribed 'Melencolia—I.,' a print engraved with intense energy, is a picture of gloomy meditation. She is surrounded by the implements of art, science, and magic, and the scene is weirdly lit up by a comet and rainbow. It has been suggested that this print was the first of a projected series of engravings to illustrate the ancient theory of the Four Temperaments, in which Dürer believed. The last of these prints mentioned by Dürer as 'The Horseman,' but now generally called 'The Knight, Death, and the Devil,' represents a knight, clad in complete armor, riding through a wild, rocky landscape, accompanied by Death, who holds up his hour-glass, while the Devil follows behind. The Knight, with a triumphant air, pursues his way fearlessly, regardless of his grim companions, for Death is no longer the conqueror.

The prints just described are perhaps the best known of all Dürer's works, and have been made the subject of endless discussion as to their full meaning. Other famous examples are 'Adam and Eve' (1504), exceedingly fine and often copied, and a fine impression of which was purchased for the Berlin Museum at a recent sale for £410, said to be the highest price ever realized for a print by Dürer; 'St. Eustacius,' or 'St. Hubert,' said to represent the Emperor Maximilian, and esteemed so highly by the Emperor Rudolf that he ordered the plate gilded; 'The Prodigal Son,' 'Coat of Arms with a Skull' (1503), 'The Nativity' (1504), 'Nemesis,' or the 'Great Fortune,' 'St. Jerome in the Desert,' 'St. Anthony,' 'Effect of Jealousy,' also called the 'Great Satyr;' 'Triton carrying away Anymone,' 'The Great White Horse,' 'The Virgin with a Monkey,' 'The Virgin by the Wall,' and the series of beautiful plates known as the 'Small Passion,' on copper, to distinguish it from the 'Little Passion,' engraved on wood. There are also many others scarcely less important. Among Dürer's engraved portraits, for which he was justly famous, are those of Erasmus, the Emperor Maximilian, Melancthon, and Pirkheimer. Dürer executed a few etchings and dry-points, but aside from these his plates were engraved wholly with the burin. Nearly all of his works bear his initials or monogram, and of many of his engravings and wood-cuts there are deceptive copies and inferior modern impressions.

Dürer was the author of a number of treatises relating to art, among them works on mensuration and fortification, and a *Treatise on Human Proportion*, written after his return from the Netherlands. The last-named work, published posthumously, is illustrated with nude figures, male and female, with scales of proportions, rules, calculations, "words of distinction," arbitrary divisions, subdivisions, etc., in endless profusion. The "average man" of the composite photographers is foreshadowed in his theory that the variations of individuals from the "typical man" will, in an infinite number of instances, counteract and nullify each other, thus giving the type of man as he actually is. Dürer also contemplated a large encyclopedic work, of which those named were really parts, which was to embody the results of his study and observation, and to cover the whole domain of art, and to be called "Food for Young Painters."

The last works of Dürer were his fine paintings of the "Four Evangelists," now at Munich, where his own portrait of himself is also preserved, which shows him with long flowing hair, and with a countenance intellectual and melancholy. His engraved works, now so universally popular, for a long time met with little favor in France and England, but at the present day, with the single exception of Rembrandt, no artist's engraved works are so eagerly sought for by both amateur and collector. In his own domain, with no great predecessors, contemporaries, or followers to share his renown, Dürer's art, like his grave, powerful, and picturesque personality, stands forth unique. His friend Melancthon has testified that his art was the least of his merits.

Contemporary with Dürer was an artist of great ability of whom very little is definitely known. He seems little more than a shadow, appearing and vanishing at intervals, yet exerting an influence upon German art distinctly felt. He is known as Jacopo de Barbarj, or the "Master of the Caduceus," from his mark, although in Germany he was called "Walsh" (a foreigner).

Jacopo was probably born at Venice about the middle of the fifteenth century, and appears to have been a wanderer, for at different times we catch glimpses of him in Italy, Germany, and the Netherlands. He undoubtedly lived for a time in Nuremberg, towards the close of the century, and seems to have been a great favorite with the artists there, and to have been brought into close relations with Dürer, whose style he influenced more, perhaps, than any other artist except Wolgemut; but he was back again in Venice before the year 1500, for he made a large bird's-eye view of that city which was finely engraved on wood and published in that year. Even this work shows Jacopo's connection with Nuremberg, for its publication was undertaken by Anton Kolb, a Nuremberg merchant of the Fondaco dei Tedeschi, or guild of the German merchants at Venice. But Jacopo soon left Venice, for Dürer informs us that he was not there in 1506; he is believed to have accompanied Count Philip of Burgundy to the Netherlands in that year, stopping at Nuremberg on the way, probably his last visit to the city with which he is chiefly identified. Dürer also states that while travelling in the Netherlands he saw a sketch-book by Jacopo in the possession of the Archduchess Margaret, for whom he had been *valet de chambre* and court-painter; but, although Dürer greatly admired and coveted this book, he did not succeed in obtaining it, as it had already been promised elsewhere. Jacopo died before the year 1516, for he is mentioned in an inventory of Madame Marguerite's effects, made at Malines in that year, as "the late Master Jacopo."

By this master we have nearly thirty prints, most of which represent subjects of classical mythology, although there are about ten prints of religious subjects. His style is very pure, and his graceful drawing shows the Italian influence, although his technic is often wholly German in style, acquired, doubtless, during his residence in Nuremberg. The print of 'Apollo and Diana,' representing the sun and moon, is a good example of his quaint style. His art forms a connecting link between the schools of Italy and Germany.

During the first half of the sixteenth century wood-engraving was at the height of its popularity in Germany, a popularity due in great part to its employment in the interests of the Reformation, which promised social and religious liberty, and to the encouragement and support given to the art by its great patron the Emperor Maximilian. The wealth and variety of German book illustration of this period can scarcely be appreciated. Following the example of Dürer, many eminent artists made designs for wood-cuts, among them Hans Burgkmair, Hans Schäufelin, Hans Baldung Grün, Hans Springinklee, Lucas Cranach, Albrecht Altdorfer, Hans Sebald Beham, and Hans Holbein. Under the instruction of such masters, a class of wood-engravers soon arose whose skill was equal to the most delicate and elaborate fac-simile work. Many remarkable series of wood-cuts were issued during this period at Nuremberg, Augsburg, Wittemberg, Frankfort, Basel, and other cities, of which a few deserve more than passing notice, for they show the development and perfection of early wood-engraving, and reflect the sentiment and ideals of the period of which they were the outgrowth.

Many works of this character were designed in honor of the Emperor Maximilian, who delighted in these pictorial records of his life and achievements. The most important and extensive, the *Triumph of the Emperor Maximilian*, consists, even in its incomplete condition, of 135 cuts, making a panorama more than 175 feet in length. In magnitude and grandeur this famous work may be classed with *The Triumphal Arch*, designed for the Emperor by Dürer. The original designs, 218 in number, and painted upon vellum, are still preserved in the Imperial Library at Vienna. While a few of the designs for *Maximilian's Triumph* are credited to Dürer, the greater portion are generally ascribed to Hans Burgkmair of Augsburg, whose mark appears upon many of the wood-cuts of the series. These cuts are executed with great spirit and picturesque effect, but are far from being exact reproductions of the original designs, varying in many important particulars. It is apparent that all of the designs were not drawn upon the blocks by one person, and the variation in the style and quality of the cutting shows that a considerable number of engravers were employed upon the work, their names in a number of instances appearing upon the back of the blocks engraved by them.

This great work, designed "for the praise and everlasting memory of the noble pleasures and glorious victories of the most serene and illustrious prince and lord Maximilian," shows, with all the pomp and splendor of a holiday parade, the countries and princes subject to the Emperor, with their heraldry; the cavalry and infantry regiments in his service; the guilds representing the various industries carried on in his domains; his knights, with their blazoned arms and glittering armor, and their richly caparisoned horses crowned with laurel; trophies of victories; prisoners in chains; and his musicians, jesters, hunters, etc., in almost infinite variety—all doing homage to the powerful and magnanimous but vain Maximilian, symbolizing his victories and displaying his power and resources. After Maximilian's death the further progress of this work appears to have been abandoned, and the engraved blocks, long supposed to have been destroyed, after many vicissitudes found their way, more than two centuries later, to Vienna, where a large folio edition, the first as a complete series, was printed from them in 1796.

Burgkmair also designed many illustrations for *The Wise King*, an autobiographical work designed by Maximilian in his own honor, containing 237 pieces, picturing events in the life of the Emperor, and the gradual development of his education in almost every art, science, craft, and sport, including kingcraft and the black-art, which latter he afterwards declared to be vain and ungodly; but it is not definitely known how many of these designs are Burgkmair's, as he received assistance from Hans Schäufelin and other artists. Other designs include the 'Genealogy of the Emperor;' the series of saints, male and female,

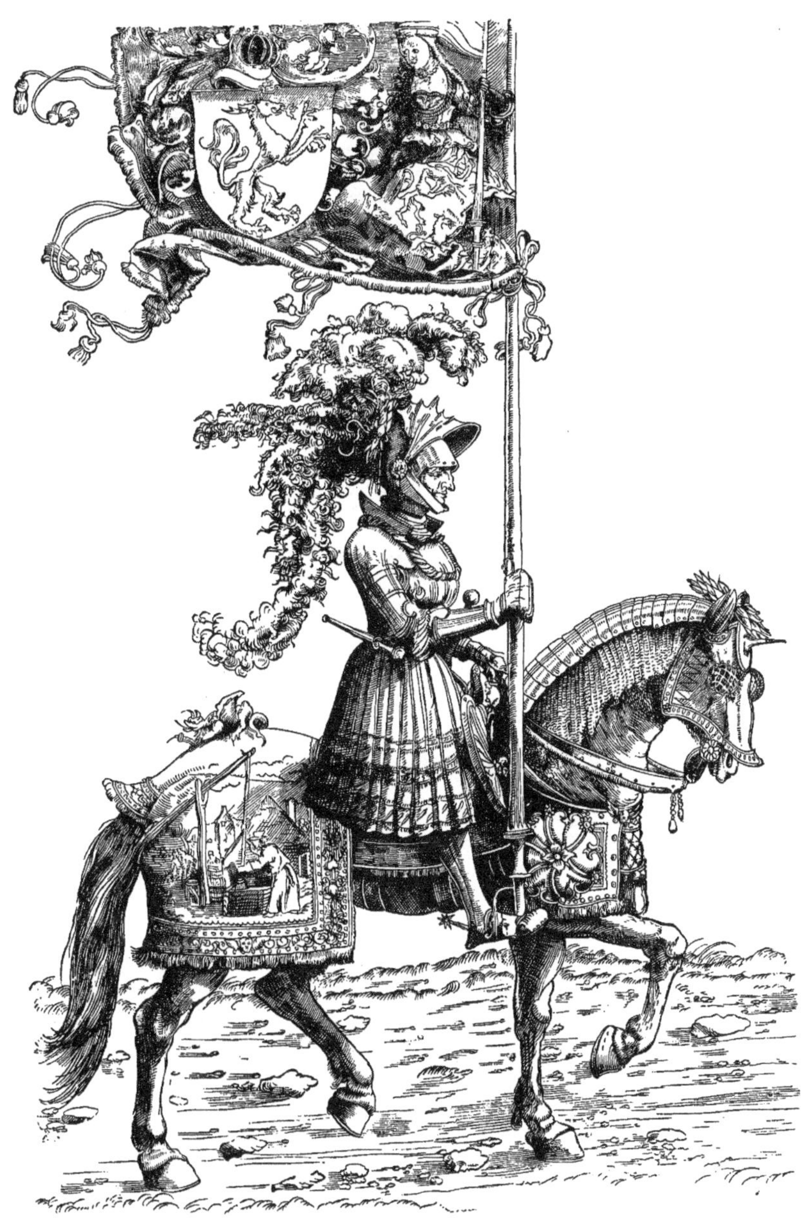

WOOD-CUT (REDUCED) FROM THE "TRIUMPH OF MAXIMILIAN"

Designed by Hans Burgkmair

related to the imperial family; an excellent portrait of Maximilian on horseback, and the same cut in chiaroscuro; and the famous chiaroscuro portrait of Hans Baumgartner. Burgkmair's designs for wood-cuts, both in sets and single, were almost endless in number, and illustrate the picturesque life and feudal spirit of the Germany of Maximilian, as the works of Dürer show its religious, mystical, and romantic features. Next to Dürer, Kaiser Max, "the last of the nomadic emperors," was the typical representative of his age and country.

Another interesting and edifying series are the 118 cuts of the *Theuerdanck*, an allegorical poem written, it is said, by Melchior Pfinzing, "singing Kaiser Maximilian's praise," and showing how its romantic hero, in the character of Sir Theuerdanck, through Virtue and Understanding, overcame his enemies, Envy, restless Curiosity (Fürwittig), and Daring, in no end of perilous adventures. The designs for these cuts are believed to have been made by Dürer's accomplished pupil Hans Schäufelin, and were engraved, it is said, by Jost De Necker, a Flemish wood-engraver who had settled at Augsburg. This work, upon which artists and printers are said to have been engaged for a period of five years, was designed, not for the booksellers, but for the Emperor and his friends, and therefore intended to be of surpassing excellence; but it is inferior both in interest and merit to the *Triumph*.

The works of Dürer's pupil and imitator, Hans Baldung, called Grün, probably from the color of his costume, and mentioned in Dürer's journal as "Grünhans," also present some interesting examples of early wood-engraving, although his designs are often fantastic and exaggerated. But of the vast quantity of similar works, both in sets and single, belonging to this period, only a few important and representative examples can be mentioned, such as the cuts in the *Hortulus Animæ*, designed by Hans Springinklee, another disciple of Dürer, and printed by Koburger in 1516; the twenty-six cuts of the *Passionale Christi*, designed by Lucas Cranach, and published at Wittemberg in 1521; the 'Repose in Egypt,' by the same master, representing the Virgin and Child surrounded by a troop of angels dancing; and the Bible cuts and *Apocalypse* of Hans Sebald Beham, which will be mentioned hereafter. But without devoting further attention to the school of Dürer, we will pass on to a very different style of art—that of Holbein.

It is worthy of remark that Germany's two great artists, Dürer and Holbein, were born respectively in the two free imperial cities of old Germany: Nuremberg and Augsburg. The ancient city of Nuremberg was the cradle of German art. Its history is lost in the mists of tradition. Early in the thirteenth century it became a free city, and rose rapidly in importance, until in the fifteenth century it became the centre of the trade of Europe. Its merchants were found in every mart, and in Venice they were organized into a powerful guild. The merchandise from Venice and the East passed through it to the Hanse towns, and riches flowed into it from every side. Its liberal government, its wealth, and the independent spirit of its citizens also made it a centre of art and learning. Its artists, scholars, and printers were renowned throughout Europe. Its glory culminated towards the close of the century, when its two great churches, St. Sebaldus and St. Lawrence, were completed, from which the respective sides of the city take their names. Here was born Albrecht Dürer, the greatest of German artists, and here his master, Michael Wolgemut, pursued his career. Adam Krafft and Peter Vischer enriched its churches and public buildings with sculptures, and the cobbler-poet Hans Sachs sang its praises in verse. Here many of the German artists received their early instruction, and from here made pilgrimages into Italy, and brought back a knowledge of that soft Southern art so strongly contrasting with the severity of their own Gothic style.

> "Here, when art was still religion, with a simple, reverent heart,
> Lived and labored Albrecht Dürer, the Evangelist of Art.
>
> "*'Emigravit'* is the inscription on the tombstone where he lies;
> Dead he is not, but departed—for the artist never dies.
>
> "Not thy Councils, not thy Kaisers, win for thee the world's regard;
> But thy painter, Albrecht Dürer, and Hans Sachs, thy cobbler-bard."

In our own time the walls and fortifications which withstood the battles and sieges of the Dark and Middle Ages are giving way to the still more destructive inroads of commercial prosperity. But although, like Venice, its ancient glory has forever departed, "the quaint old town of art and song" still remains, almost as mediæval in appearance as in the days of Dürer; and the famous house at the Thiergarten Thor, in which the great artist lived, and where he produced many of his best works, is still preserved in almost the same condition as when Dürer painted and Agnes nagged and scolded, or did not nag and scold, according to the true version of the story.

Augsburg, where Holbein was born about the year 1497, was, like Nuremberg, a centre of culture and refinement, as well as a place of great commercial and artistic activity. It is also famous in history as the scene of the publication of the great Confession, embodying the creed of the Protestants. Among Augsburg's many great artists none became so renowned as Hans Holbein, the son and pupil of a famous portrait-painter of the same name. Holbein was an artist of pre-eminent genius, whose career is remarkable in many ways. Although a greater painter than Dürer, his personality is much less striking, nor did he represent the many-sided Germany of his time. Putting aside the religious enthusiasm, vague dreaming, mysticism, and romantic spirit by which mediæval art was almost wholly influenced and controlled, he became the apostle of humanity, and his advent may be said to mark the beginning of modern art. His fame rests mainly upon his wonderful portraits and designs for wood-cuts, and upon the famous Madonnas at Darmstadt and Dresden.

At an early age Holbein became a skilful draughtsman, and although undoubtedly much influenced by Burgkmair, Maximilian's great artist, his powers did not mature until after his removal to Basel in 1515. At this time Basel was the home of Erasmus, and a liberal and progressive city in the encouragement of learning and the arts. It was also the stronghold of the Reformers, and the cradle of many of the new doctrines. Holbein soon became deeply interested in the philosophical school of Erasmus, and became an ardent reformer as well as a diligent artist. He found employment in designing title-pages, wood-cuts, and book illustrations for the printers, painting frescos, and other miscellaneous work, which soon led to something more remunerative. To the period of his residence in Basel belong some of his most important works, among them the designs for the famous wood-cuts of the *Dance of Death* and *Figures of the Bible;* the fifty pen-and-ink drawings illustrating the *Praise of Folly*, by Erasmus, which show his genius for satire and caricature; the portraits of Erasmus and Melancthon, and the famous Meyer Madonna at Darmstadt. That Holbein was a man of importance in Basel is shown by his intimacy with Erasmus, the burgomaster Meyer, the printer Froben, the lawyer Amerbach, and other distinguished citizens.

Holbein's intimacy with Erasmus seems to have changed the whole current of his life. The great writer and philosopher, the Voltaire of his century, was held in high esteem in England, and was in constant communication with Henry VIII. and his Minister, Sir Thomas More. Holbein undoubtedly relied upon his influence when he undertook the journey to England to better his fortunes. Basel was no longer an attractive place for artists. The political and religious disturbances had become so great that art found little encouragement. With letters to Sir Thomas More and others, we can imagine that he set out upon his journey with renewed hopes. He probably travelled on foot most of the way to Antwerp, for he was too poor to go on horseback, putting up at the famous inns along the road, after the manner of the rich. When he left Basel, in the autumn of 1526, the plague was raging, and the town was also prostrated by the fanatical reaction against the Reformation, for the people attributed their misfortunes to the anger of God. At Antwerp he met Quentin Massys and other Flemish artists, but was not received with the distinction accorded to Dürer. He arrived in England in the eighteenth year of the reign of Henry VIII., and was received by Sir Thomas More, whose *Utopia* he had illustrated at Basel. For a time he lived in the house of his patron, whose home life Erasmus had compared to a second Republic of Plato. Here he painted the large picture, 'The Family of Sir Thomas More,' which has since disappeared, although the original drawing is still preserved in the Basel Museum. At this period he drew with colored chalks or crayons the famous series of portraits still preserved at Windsor Castle; these were exhibited to the public at the recent

Tudor Exhibition. Most of these portraits were engraved by Bartolozzi, and published in the closing decade of the last century.

Holbein's residence in London was of short duration. Owing to the political disturbances and sickness which prevailed, he returned to Basel in 1528 to find that town in a worse condition than when he left it two years before. During the two years he remained the religious agitation was fiercest. The iconoclastic storm had burst in its full fury, ending in open war between the cantons. The town also suffered from floods and scarcity of provisions; and in the terrible winter of 1529-30, the wolves, driven by hunger, came down into the town in great numbers. This was certainly no place for art to flourish, nor for an artist to provide for the wants of his family; and about the year 1531 Holbein was again in London painting industriously. At first he was employed by the German merchants of the Steelyard, for whom he painted some of his finest portraits; but he was soon again in high favor with the King, and received the appointment of court painter.

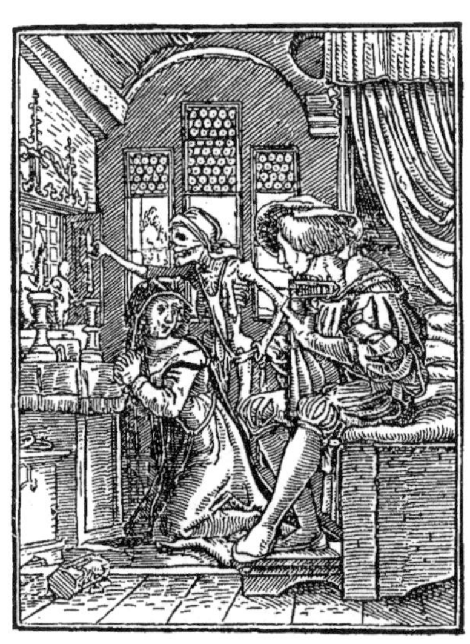

THE NUN
From Holbein's "Dance of Death"

Although we seldom hear Henry VIII. mentioned as an art patron, his patronage of Holbein created an epoch in British art. During the period of his residence in England few persons of eminence escaped his pencil or brush, and many portraits belonging to this period have been attributed to him for which he was in no way responsible.

In 1538, while Holbein was at the height of his fame, he once more visited his family at Basel—this time not in poverty, but as the representative of the King of England. Although he received liberal offers, he refused to remain, and returned to England. His last known work was a portrait of himself, painted in 1543, in which year he succumbed to the pestilence which swept over London.

As a painter, Holbein is represented in most of the great European collections, notably the Basel Museum, and every detail of his career which the most minute investigation could discover has been carefully recorded. But it is of his services to the art of wood-engraving that we are here chiefly concerned. Of his multitude of designs for wood-cuts, the two famous series, the *Dance of Death* and *Figures of the Bible*, are the most important. These designs were made and engraved at Basel, where some impressions were taken, judging from imperfect sets with German titles; but the first complete edition of these works, so far as is known, was published at Lyons by the Trechsels in 1538, while Holbein was a resident of the English court.

The "Dance of Death" was a subject often represented by the early artists. Its peculiar fascination to the mediæval mind was well understood by the monks and priests, who had long trafficked with the terrors of the ignorant, and had taught that the retribution after this life could be lessened by severe penances, weary pilgrimages, midnight vigils, bloody flagellations, and, above all, by offerings of money. It is no wonder that spectres started up and graves yawned and the gaunt skeleton of Death paraded through the world, confronting and terrifying the people wherever they went—painted in the market-places, on the gates of cemeteries, on the doors and walls of monasteries and cloisters, illuminated in their Horæ, and multiplied by wood-cuts. But the apparition which had so long terrified the people became by familiarity a source of satire and humor rather than of religious enthusiasm; and the Gothic artists, with a barbarous genius, put eyes of mockery into the hollow sockets, a malignant grin upon the ghastly features, and made the fleshless members gesticulate and mimic with all the postures and gestures of a caricaturist. They represented Death leading all to the grave, young and old, rich and poor, the great and the noble, as well as the oppressed and disdained. Although these representations were anything but cheerful, here, at least, all classes met on terms of equality, for Death was no respecter of persons.

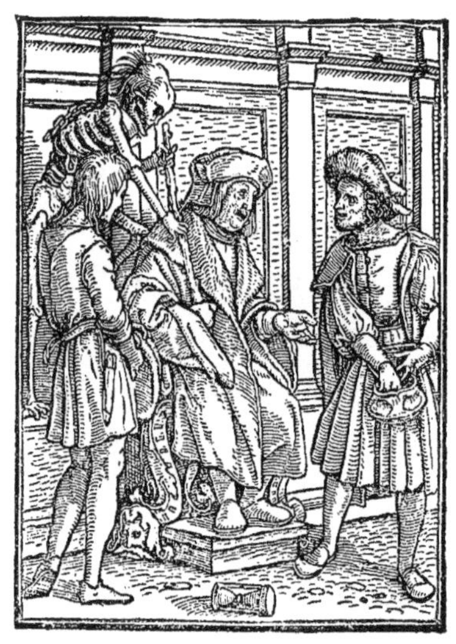

THE JUDGE
From Holbein's "Dance of Death"

The *Danse Macabre* of Guyot Marchant, published at Lyons in 1485, with its curious wood-cuts and Gothic characters, was one of the earliest, if not the first, of these series of wood-cuts which afterwards became so common in France and Germany. The Italian artists, however, with their traditions of antique art, had little sympathy with objects of distortion and deformity. They represented Death by an inverted or extinguished torch, a faded rose upon a sarcophagus, the butterfly escaping in glory from the chrysalis, or Atropos cutting the thread of life. Like the ancient sculptures, they recalled the life and deeds of the departed, carefully veiling the revolting contents of the charnel-house.

How different are these German representations as typified by Holbein's series! The skeleton of Death interrupts the joys and pleasures of life, and humbles every rank and condition of mankind, appearing in all its hideousness when least expected or desired. The kneeling nun turns from the altar to the youth who plays on the lute, while Death is putting out the taper which shall leave her in eternal darkness; the weary peddler turns questioningly to the delaying hand upon his arm; the miser counts his gold, the judge takes his bribe; but Death is present with his sneer, for they cannot escape him. Death plays the wedding-march for the bridal pair; the weary ploughman is accompanied by the skeleton, who runs along the furrow and beats his tired horses; Death pours the King's wine, and, dressed as a woman, walks with the Queen; the duchess is rudely awakened by the skeleton, whose companion, the "grim musician," plays on the violin; while the mother is cooking her meal, Death steals her child; Death stands behind the hypocritical preacher; the knight's armor is defenceless against Death's lance, and so on — almost every vice and passion, occupation and pursuit, typified in the persons represented. Not even the Pope, cardinals, or monks escape; Death's mockery, Death's triumph, is over all. "Death seems to live, and the living to be truly dead." Holbein's series achieved an extraordinary popularity, and many editions were printed from the original blocks, not to mention the numerous copies. Trechsel's title to the Lyons edition was *Les Simulachres et Historiées Faces de la Mort*, etc.

The Bible cuts, while possessing as a whole less merit and interest than the *Dance of Death*, were extremely popular; numerous editions appeared with text in different languages. There is also a series of initial letters known as the "Alphabet of Death," which shows Holbein's sympathy for the poor and oppressed, and keenly satirizes the rich and powerful and the dignitaries of the Church. In many of these cuts two skeletons are introduced, symbolizing the death of both body and soul. It is not unlikely that the feeling shown in these and similar cuts was aroused by the Peasants' War of 1514, and the misery which followed it. Other designs are attacks upon the papal party, ridiculing the sale of indulgences, and assailing its avarice, superstition, ignorance, bigotry, cruelty, and other abuses, and besides these there are many charming scenes of ordinary life which show that Holbein sympathized with the people, and contributed to their pleasures and education, as well as served them by advancing the interests of the Reformation, with which he was in keen sympathy.

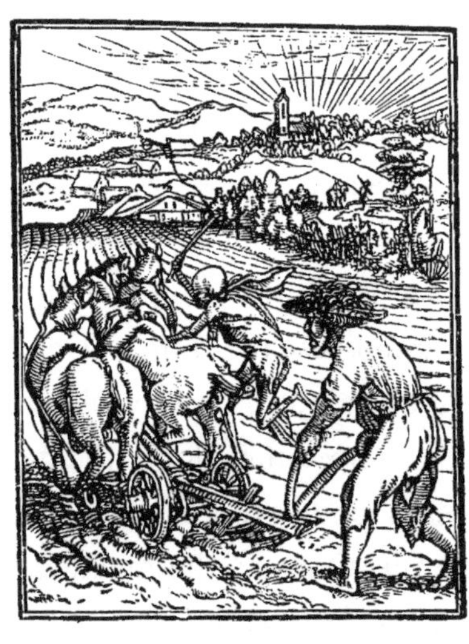

THE PLOUGHMAN
From Holbein's "Dance of Death"

If little has been said of the actual cutters or engravers of the wood blocks, a numerous body of workmen, it is because their work was almost purely mechanical, their skill consisting in their fidelity in following the lines of their designs, with very little originality of their own. The superiority of art over mechanical skill, however great, was understood by the artists who furnished the designs and obtained the credit of the performances; the names of but few of the actual engravers have reached us. There were two of these early engravers, however, whose works show the culmination of their art: Jerome Andreae, of Nuremberg, trained by Dürer to engrave his designs in the most skilful manner, and Hans Lützelberger, who engraved the designs of Holbein. These engravers certainly accomplished perfectly all that their masters required of them. Lützelberger was a native of Augsburg, but, like Holbein, removed to Basel, where he engraved the *Bible Figures* and the forty-one cuts in the Lyons edition of the *Dance of Death*, about 1522–26. The cuts in the latter series are in some respects the finest examples of early wood-engraving, presenting a refinement and delicacy of technic not to be found in the wood-cuts of the school of Dürer. The lines possess an artistic value which Holbein's drawings could scarcely have surpassed. Lützelberger also engraved, after Holbein, a fine portrait of Erasmus, and is credited with some of the blocks of the *Triumphs of Maximilian*. He is also said to have worked at Nuremberg under Dürer, but of this there is no direct evidence.

Only a few engravers between Lützelberger and Bewick will be mentioned. Following Lützelberger came Jost Amman, an able and prolific designer and engraver, who worked until near the close of the century, and whose designs have been freely borrowed by succeeding artists. There is a well-known series illustrating various trades and professions. In the following century Christopher Jegher engraved at Antwerp many fine subjects after Rubens, of which mention has already been made. In the first half of the eighteenth century we have Jean Papillon, a French wood-engraver of considerable ability, but best known as the author of an alleged history of wood-engraving, *Traité de la Gravure en Bois*, containing many absurd errors. But the history of wood-engraving from Lützelberger to Bewick is a history of its rapid degeneration. The art which

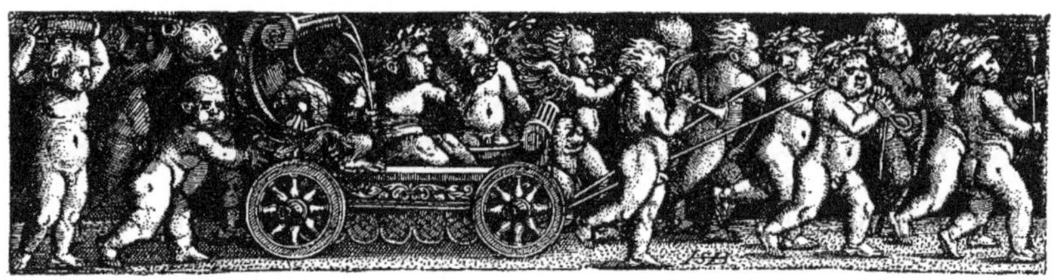

HEAD-PIECE, BY HANS SEBALD BEHAM

shone with such splendor in the days of Dürer and Holbein, and of the famous printers of Nuremberg and Lyons, had declined until but little of its former glory remained.

Of all the arts of the German Renaissance, wood-engraving has most faithfully reflected the popular sentiment and ideals. But as practised in the sixteenth century wood-engraving was a severe and conventional art. Until the time of Bewick the wood-cuts were, with very few exceptions, executed with the knife instead of the graver, and upon the plank, instead of a section cut across the grain of the wood. Modern wood-engraving is based upon different principles; as now practised, it is a very different art from that of Holbein's time. Between the old and the new methods stand the works of Thomas Bewick, whose services to the art will be mentioned in a subsequent chapter.

Previous to the sixteenth century, painting, except in connection with the Church, was but little practised. The greater portion of the early paintings were intended for altar-pieces and church decorations, with occasional portraits and heraldic devices for the nobility. The Renaissance, which commenced in Italy soon after the middle of the fifteenth century, crept northward slowly, the primitive schools of the North existing long after those of the South had been superseded. In Italy, the constant discovery of ancient sculptures and the beautiful remains of early art awakened a new interest in the subjects of classical mythology and the nude figure, an influence felt but little in Germany, whose artists now for the first time represented the aspects of ordinary life, scenes constantly passing before them, "manners-depicting representations." In Germany this change took place at first principally in engraving. The Church was still the greatest patron of painting, and nearly all of the subjects were still of a religious character. With engraving, a democratic art, the situation was different. From the outset it had met with immense popular favor, and its products, easily multiplied, were spread far and wide; that art was naturally more subject to passing influences.

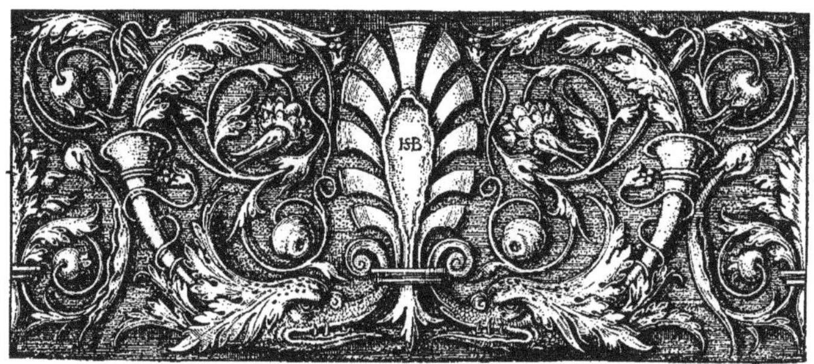

HEAD-PIECE, BY HANS SEBALD BEHAM

The period immediately following the time of Albrecht Dürer was made memorable in art by the "Little Masters of Germany," a coterie of accomplished artists whose works reflect the spirit of their age. The most important of these artists were Albrecht Altdorfer, Hans Sebald Beham, Barthel Beham, George Pencz, and Heinrich Aldegrever. The Behams and Pencz were natives of Nuremberg; Altdorfer lived at Ratisbon; and Aldegrever at Soest, in Westphalia. Although Dürer was their reputed master, there is no positive proof that any of them were ever his pupils, although his influence is plainly visible in their works. Until the recent researches of Dr. Adolf Rosenberg, our information concerning the lives of these artists, and more particularly the Behams, was of a very general character, although their works have long been well known to collectors. We are also greatly indebted to the late William B. Scott, whose interesting account of the Little Masters is based upon that of Herr Rosenberg.

Like most of the early engravers of Germany, the Little Masters were also painters, and their numerous ornamental designs show their connection with the craft which furnished so many of the early artists of Italy and Germany. As engravers, their works are of the most varied character, representing allegorical figures of virtues and vices; the days of the week with their planets; scenes of drinking and merry-making; village scenes; fairs, processions, costumes, courting scenes; landscapes; Bible histories; religious, classical, and mythological subjects; and an almost endless number of ornamental designs, executed with the greatest patience and exactness. The name "Little Masters" has been applied to these artists on account of the miniature size of most of their plates, some measuring less than an inch square. But although small in size, many of these little prints are grand in conception and almost faultless in execution, and their endless variety and quaint pointed character, together with the unique place which they hold in art, give to them a peculiar piquancy and interest. Judging from

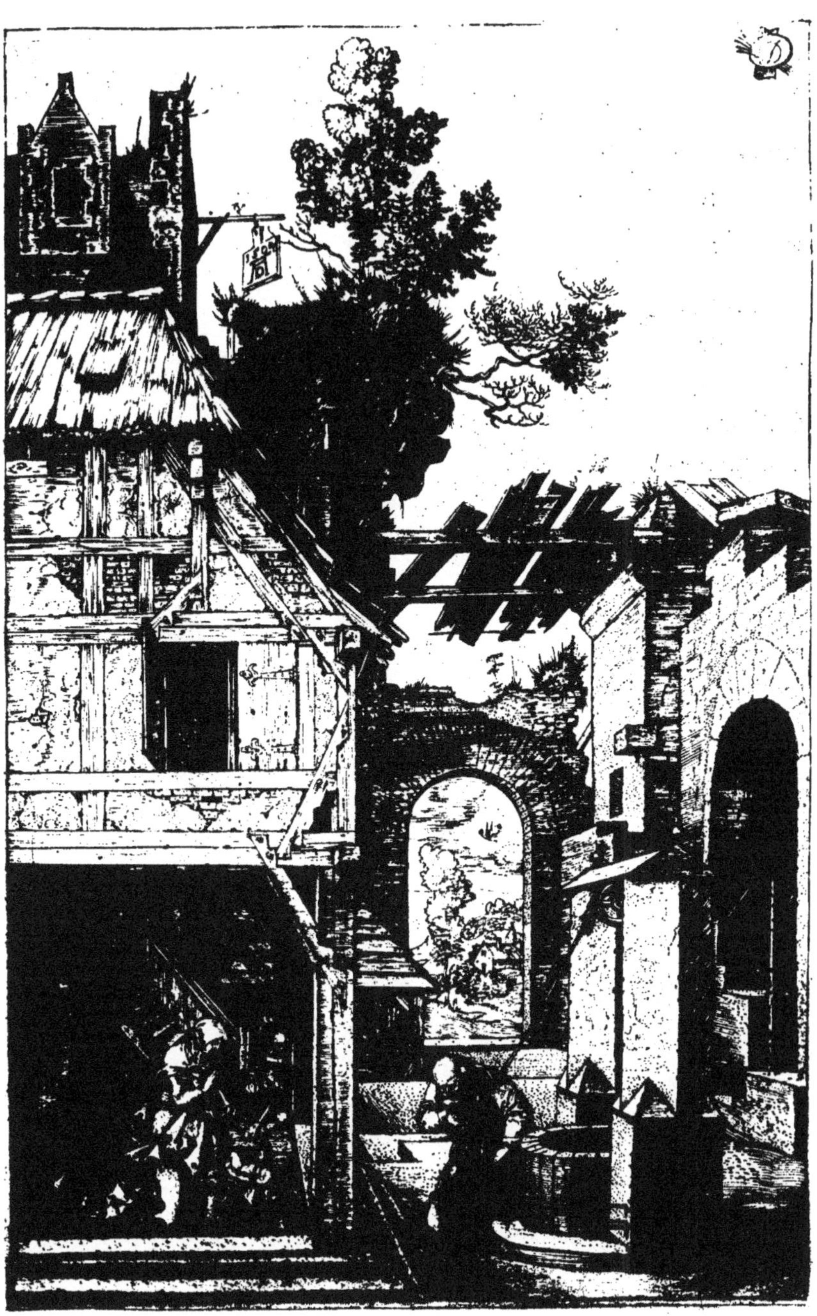

his example, even Dürer must have considered copper-plate engraving better adapted for small than for large plates; but that he favored large wood-cuts is sufficiently shown by his designs for the Emperor Maximilian.

First in point of time, but not in importance, comes Albrecht Altdorfer, who was born before the year 1480, and passed the greater portion of his life in Ratisbon (Regensberg), with which town his name is associated in many ways. Altdorfer was an artist of varied resources. In his own time he was most celebrated as an architect, although now known through his en-

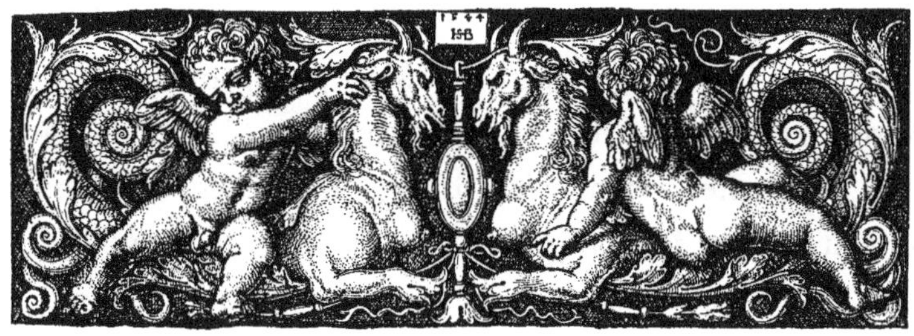

HEAD-PIECE, BY HANS SEBALD BEHAM

graved works and designs for wood-cuts. He was on intimate terms with Dürer, and is believed by some to have lived as apprentice with that master soon after the latter's marriage.

If not a native of Ratisbon, Altdorfer removed to that place before 1505, for in that year he received the freedom of the city. He was evidently a man of importance, for he held at different times a variety of honorable offices under the city government, among them city architect, member of the Rath, magistrate, and burgomaster. He was also bursar of the Augustinian monastery. He seems to have acquired riches as well as popularity, and his house, one of the most imposing in the city, is still shown to visitors with as much ceremony as that of Dürer at Nuremberg.

As a member of the town council, Altdorfer voted in favor of the expulsion of the Jews from Ratisbon in 1519. Until the latter part of his life he remained true to the mediæval faith, becoming even then only a mild advocate of the Reformation, and to the last a worshipper of the Madonna. He was, therefore, probably sincere in his opinions as to the propriety of expelling the Jews, whose exactions of usury had become extremely burdensome. Many persons, however, seized the opportunity to cancel the principal as well as the interest of their obligations in this questionable manner. The synagogue was completely demolished, and a church dedicated to Our Lady, now the Protestant parish church of Ratisbon, rose out of its ruins. It is related that "Our Beautiful Mary," approving this action, worked miracles upon the spot, so that the blind saw, the lame walked, and other remarkable things happened, and the place became a shrine for pilgrimages. Before its demolition, Altdorfer etched two curious views of this synagogue, one representing the interior of the vestibule, and the other that of the synagogue itself.

To this period belongs his famous 'Madonna of Ratisbon,' a rare and picturesque chiaroscuro from the figure then in the city cathedral. This print was eagerly purchased by the pilgrims, possibly, it has been suggested, as one of the miracles. Passavant also mentions a large exterior view of the new church, Altdorfer's largest wood-cut, measuring 23 × 18½ inches. These cuts, and the fact that gravestones from the synagogue were taken to serve as pavements in his house, and that he painted a number of pictures and a banner for the new church, show that the expulsion of the Jews was a source of profit to him as well as to others. As an artist, Altdorfer remained throughout his career true to the traditions of German art, and we look almost in vain for traces of the Italian influence so visible in the works of his contemporaries. His *genre* subjects, while quaint and fantastic, possess a peculiar charm which disappears when, with his ignorance of antique art, he attempts to render classical and mythological subjects; nor can his drawing of the human figure be highly praised.

Altdorfer has been called "the father of landscape-painting," having been, it is said, the first artist who made his landscapes of greater importance than his figures. He etched a number of landscape subjects, mostly of mountain scenery, in which the fir-tree is prominent. These are pictorial in effect, and express the breadth and beauty of real landscape; they are not studies of individual objects like Dürer's. He seems to have indulged his love for pine and fir trees upon every possible occasion, and many of his scenes are set in curious forests with backgrounds

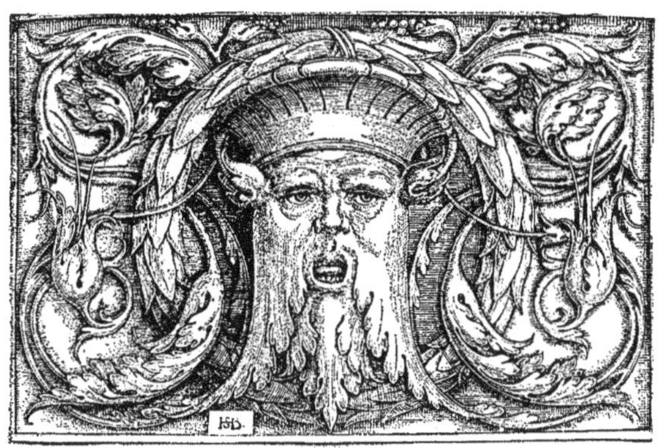

ORNAMENT, BY HANS SEBALD BEHAM

of ruins and mountains; even the Crucifixion is represented as taking place among fir-trees, and St. George vanquishes the Dragon in a beech wood; but such anachronisms were of frequent occurrence in early art.

Altdorfer's works comprise a large number of copper-plate engravings and etchings representing saints, biblical, mythological and secular subjects, ornamental objects and landscapes, mostly executed between the years 1506 and 1514, before his other duties led him to abandon engraving. Many of his religious subjects were taken from the apocryphal gospels, particularly the Gospel of Mary, a text which held great authority in the Middle Ages, and furnished many subjects to the early artists. We have also about sixty-five wood-cuts, mostly of religious subjects, among them forty miniature cuts representing the 'Fall and Redemption of Man;' this set has been reproduced in fac-simile by the Holbein Society. A quantity of his drawings is still preserved in the Berlin Museum and other collections. As a painter, his 'Battle of Arbela,' at Munich, is his principal work. Altdorfer died in 1538, and when the Church of the Augustines, in which he was interred, was taken down in 1840, a fragment of his tombstone bearing his name was discovered. Although inferior to the Behams, Pencz, and Aldegrever in most respects, yet the quaint, naïve character and individuality of Altdorfer's little prints render them almost as interesting as those of the other Little Masters.

The Behams, Hans Sebald, and Barthel were the most important of the Little Masters. The name Beham, or Behaim, was well known in Nuremberg as that of a patrician family. There was also Hans Behaim, the celebrated Nuremberg architect, Martin Behaim, famous in history for his discoveries in South America; and Sebald Beheim, a brass-founder, who cast many of the curious siege guns in use in the early part of the sixteenth century; and besides these were a number of others of the same name, all more or less prominent in Nuremberg at the time; but of the early history of our artists we know almost nothing, and no connection with any of these families has been traced; indeed, until recently, they were even believed to have been cousins instead of brothers. That they were famous in their time is evident; their works must have had an

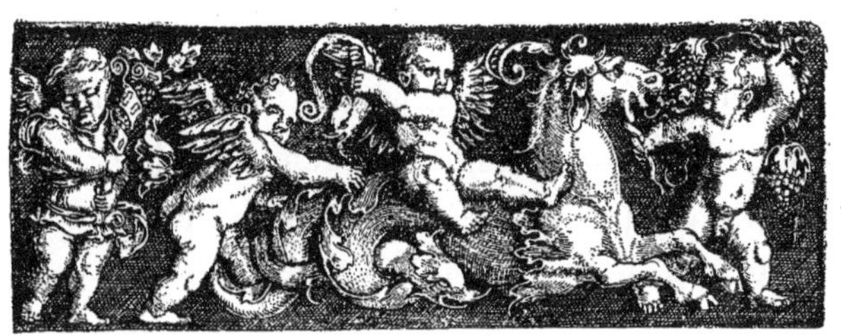

ORNAMENTAL DESIGN BY BARTHEL BEHAM

From reversed copy by Jacob Binck

enormous circulation, for their plates were printed from until the latest impressions are little more than spectres.

Born in Nuremberg in 1500 and 1502, respectively, the Behams were banished from that city for their heretical and socialistic opinions. Nuremberg had not escaped its share of the religious and socialistic agitations of the time. The extreme doctrines of Karlstadt and Münzer had obtained an influence over the people which alarmed the authorities. In 1524 the excitement culminated, and the Rath determined to check the growing evil by confiscating and burning communistic writings, and expelling the most violent and outspoken of the agitators. The Behams, particularly Sebald, were extreme in their doctrines. They believed that property and labor should be equally shared, and that the authorities should not be obeyed; and they disbelieved in most of the religious doctrines of the time. Stubborn, satirical, and daring, they openly paraded their objectionable opinions, and were described as "ostentatious, even insolent, young men, holding themselves high," and as dangerous citizens were accordingly expelled. In reading the account of their trial we cannot but admire their independent spirit, and pity their misfortune in not belonging to our own century.

After the decree of banishment, Sebald still continued to illustrate books for the Nuremberg printers, although he resided thereafter chiefly at Frankfort, where he died in 1550. Notwithstanding his banishment, he seems to have returned to Nuremberg, where, it is said, the old dislike revived, and he was again compelled to leave the city; but many evil reports seem to have been circulated of Sebald, of which some have proved unwarranted.

According to Neudorfer, Barthel entered the service of Duke William of Bavaria, who defrayed his expenses while travelling in Italy, where he studied the graceful models of antique art, and is said to have worked under Marc Antonio, whom he approached in drawing and skilful technic. During this, the flowering period of the Italian Renaissance, Raphael and Michael Angelo were painting their famous frescos in the Vatican, and that Barthel was familiar with these and similar works is shown by his friezes in the same style. He seems to have returned at intervals to Germany, where his works were widely popular; but our information concerning his life is very meager.

While the works of Hans Sebald Beham were exceedingly popular in his own time (more so, indeed, than those of any other of the Little Masters), his superiority rests chiefly upon technical grounds; his mechanical skill in handling the graver, both in vigor and delicacy, often equalling that of Dürer. In the higher qualities of art he was excelled by Aldegrever, and in grace and beauty of outline and expression his works are far inferior to those of his brother Barthel and George Pencz.

He had little acquaintance with Italian art; but although he never visited the South, he must have been familiar with the works of Marc Antonio, as he certainly was with those of Pencz and of his brother Barthel; but the æsthetic quality of Italian art had very little charm for him. He seems to have delighted in the vulgar naturalism common to so many of the German artists of his time, and to have been absolutely indifferent to grace and beauty in the human figure, as well as utterly incapable of entering into the spirit of antique art. Yet in the quaint, unconventional character of his works, and in their great variety and piquancy, there is a fascination not to be found in the works of others. Fertile in invention, strong in composition, and wonderfully neat and delicate in technic, his little prints are unique in art.

In his representations of classical subjects, Sebald seems to have chosen his models from the most vulgar peasant types around him. Some of his figures are almost comic in their ugliness. His nymphs are unpleasantly substantial, and his

HEAD-PIECE, ENGRAVED BY JACOB BINCK

gods and godesses are decidedly Teutonic in character, with little attempt at idealization. In his series of miniature plates representing the Labors of Hercules, the best examples of his mythological engravings, bearing dates from 1542 to 1548, the hero is represented as absurdly short and muscular, and with little of the physical grandeur commonly bestowed upon him. The Seven Liberal Arts are symbolized by maidens more substantial than æsthetic, and without the sculpturesque Italian character. The twelve months of the year are represented by boisterous peasants, capering along, vainly striving to catch up with Time. The Italian artists represented this subject by slender, graceful nymphs carrying pots of fire, flowers, fruit, or grain. There is also a series of very small prints representing the days of the week with their planets, and another of a wedding procession, a popular and often-repeated subject, representing sentimental peasants marching in couples to the flageolet and bag-pipe, while last comes the bride with her husband and father. There is another set, of larger dimensions, of wedding guests. Of his single prints may be named 'Adam and Eve in Paradise,' with the serpent presenting the apple; 'Leda and the Swan;' a plate inscribed 'Melencolia,' in emulation of Dürer; 'Judgment of Paris;' 'Coat of Arms, with the Cock;' a man trying to pull up a tree, inscribed '*Impossibile;*' Death walking with a maiden, to whom he exhibits his hourglass; sentimental couples around a table in a garden; and besides these are subjects of drinking and merrymaking, ornamental designs, head and tail pieces for books, and many copies from Barthel's prints, which last must have been exceedingly popular. All of the examples named were engraved at Frankfort, and bear dates ranging from 1531 to 1549.

Sebald stands pre-eminent among the Little Masters as a designer of wood-cuts and book illustrations. His series of eighty-one Bible cuts, made soon after his arrival in Frankfort, equalled or surpassed in popularity the similar series of Holbein. These designs were often re-engraved, and appear as illustrations in Coverdale's Bible. But far more interesting is the series of twenty-six cuts of the *Apocalypse*, masterly in drawing, and engraved in a manner worthy of Lützelberger. Besides these are many other cuts of Bible histories, and an immense series representing the costumes of the different orders of monks, who in his time almost literally swarmed in Italy and Germany. Judging from these and similar works, Sebald's religious opinions may have become more orthodox after his banishment. Sebald, like Dürer, also favored wood-cuts of large dimensions, and designed a number of subjects which were printed on several sheets united together. There is a large cut of the military fête held at Munich in honor of the Emperor Charles V., and there are two large friezes, each composed of four sheets, representing soldiers marching. But the most attractive of Sebald's wood-cuts is the large 'Fountain of Youth,' a beautiful design in Renaissance style, taken from the popular story brought home by Spanish mariners from the Caribbean Sea, of the rejuvenating stream for which Ponce de Léon sought so many years in vain.

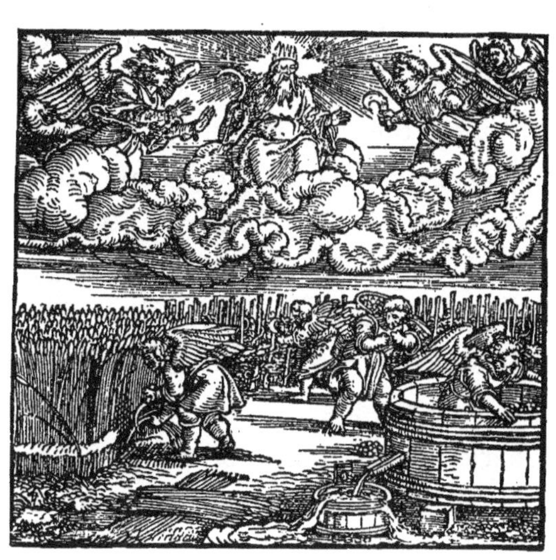

WOOD-CUT FROM THE "APOCALYPSE"
Designed by Hans Sebald Beham

We are told that Dürer had commenced a treatise upon the 'Proportions of the Horse,' but that his designs had disappeared, and that Sebald and Andreae, the suspected parties, had announced a similar publication, which was interdicted by the Rath until after the publication of Dürer's book. But Sebald's little book, published in 1528, is too unimportant, both as to text and illustrations, to have been the work of Dürer.

The death of Barthel Beham at the early age of thirty-eight cut short a career full of promise. We cannot but feel a certain tenderness for this accomplished artist, who achieved such popularity in his own time, but of whose personal history we know so little. Of his ninety-two prints, covering a wide range of subjects, at least fifteen were copied after his death by Sebald to supply the demand for impressions, and it is mainly by these copies that the scarce originals are known. Barthel's masterpieces are his three prints in the form of friezes, representing naked men fighting, called by Bartsch 'Combats d'Hommes nuds.' In purity and perfection of drawing and technic these prints are among the masterpieces of early engraving. Barthel also engraved a few portraits, of which that of the Emperor Charles V. is a masterpiece.

The works of George Pencz approached most nearly to the Italian models, while retaining the skilful and painstaking workmanship of the North. Born at Nuremberg before the beginning of the century, his career covered the most brilliant period of the Renaissance. That he was a person of importance in Nuremberg is evident, for although banished with the Behams, whose opinions he shared, he was not only allowed to return, but was even employed in restoring paintings, making drawings, and performing other similar work for the city for which he was well paid.

According to Passavant, our artist "left his home to frequent the school of Marc Antonio;" just at what period this occurred we are not informed. He was undoubtedly in Rome in 1539, for in that year he engraved, after Giulio Romano, the large 'Taking of Carthage,' signed and dated, but this was evidently not his first visit to Italy. Pencz is now credited with a number of fine engravings long ascribed to Italian masters. The most important of these, 'The Massacre of the Innocents,' the plate with the little fir-tree (*chicot*, B. 18), was until recently considered an authentic work of Marc Antonio, whose undoubted masterpiece of the same subject (B. 20) it closely resembles. The large plate of 'The Prisoners,' hitherto ascribed to Giorgio Ghisi, is also claimed to have been engraved by Pencz; his beautiful prints of 'Thomiris,' 'Medea,' 'Paris,' and 'Procris,' certainly show his ability to cope with the Italian engravers upon their own ground.

Pencz also engraved a number of miniature illustrations of Old and New Testament subjects, some of the former purely naturalistic in conception, and with very little religious sentiment, but, strange to say, he did not leave a single engraving of the Madonna. Of his New Testament subjects the 'Conversion of St. Paul,' and 'Christ Sleeping in the Storm,' are grand compositions. Other important plates are 'Sophonisba Drinking the Poison,' 'Triton Carrying off Anymone,' 'Six Triumphs of Petrarch,' and 'Virgil and the Scornful Lady.' The last of these subjects was also represented by Lucas of Leyden, Altdorfer, and other artists, and appears to have been a popular subject. Virgil was known in mediæval times às a magician. According to the story, he became enamoured of a Roman lady who, in jest, lowered a basket to receive him, but left it suspended in mid-air for the crowd to laugh at; whereupon Virgil rose to the occasion, and by his magic put out all the fires and lights in the city, and refused to remove the effects of his magic until the lady appeared naked upon a pedestal. One print represents Virgil in the basket, and the other the lady upon the pedestal supplying fire to relight the city. Chief among his engraved portraits is that of the Elector Frederick the Magnanimous, surrounded by the heraldry of the states subject to his rule. A few paintings by Pencz are known, mostly portraits. He died in 1550, the Rath at Nuremberg presenting his widow with 60 gulden to aid in educating his son, showing that our artist was not a success financially.

In his wonderful powers of invention, Heinrich Aldegrever (1502–58) was a worthy successor of Albrecht Dürer, whose style he followed, but with an originality and dramatic force quite his own. Although he lived in the ancient and conservative town of Soest, in Westphalia, and never visited either Nuremberg or Italy, he seems to have apprehended the artistic tendencies of the time; but while his drawing shows the Italian influence, he remained true to the sentiment and ideals of the North. With a technic remarkable for precision and delicacy, and an original and striking manner of realizing his subjects in a series of scenes or tableaux full of dramatic effect, his art is equally characteristic with that of Altdorfer, the Behams, and Pencz, while in the sum of his powers he was perhaps a greater artist than any of them.

The peculiar characteristics of Aldegrever's art are seen to the best advantage in his series of prints illustrating Bible stories, among them 'Susannah and the Elders,' 'Adam and Eve Driven from Paradise,' 'The History of Lot,' 'Joseph and His Brethren,' 'The Parable of the Good Samaritan,' and 'Dives and Lazarus.' The last of these series, dated 1554, consisting of five prints, contains some of his best work, picturing in a vivid manner the progress of the rich glutton, banqueting in luxury with his friends, to his death and subsequent punishment in the burning mountain, tormented by thirst and by the apparition of Lazarus, now happy and beautiful, sitting in glory with Father Abraham. Among Aldegrever's other subjects are three series of wedding processions, the 'Labors of Hercules,' 'The Seven Vices,' and the 'Monk and Nun,' two

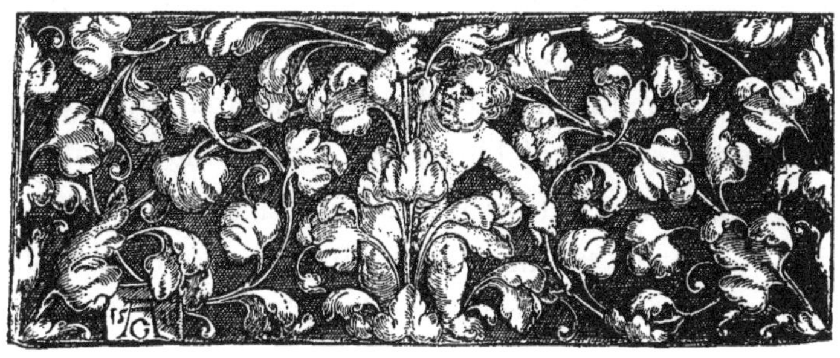

HEAD-PIECE, BY HEINRICH ALDEGREVER

plates of the last-named subject, satirizing the vices and immoralities of the monastic orders. Of his engraved portraits the most interesting are those of John of Leyden, leader of the Anabaptists, and his lieutenant, Knipperdolling, whose wild theories and fanatical enthusiasm attracted multitudes to Münster, among them probably Aldegrever, who left a drawing, afterwards engraved by Virgil Solis, showing the ideal life of this remarkable sect. There are fine copies of the two portraits by the Dutch engraver, Jan Muller. There are also portraits of Luther, and Melancthon, and two portraits of himself. Aldegrever was the most prolific ornamentist of the Little Masters, and of his more than 300 plates nearly one-third are vignettes and ornamental designs for gold and silver work, some of rare beauty.

It will not be necessary to mention the works of Jacob Binck, Hans Brosamer, Virgil Solis, Theodore de Bry, the Hopfers, and other engravers who followed the example of their more renowned contemporaries without rendering any distinguished services to their art. About the middle of the century the Little Masters passed from the scene, and the works of their successors are far less important and interesting. Following the example of Barthel Beham and George Pencz, many of them journeyed into Italy, and upon their return hastened the transition already well under way, so that by the close of the century the school of Dürer had lost its individuality. Nor in the seventeenth century is there anything especially attractive or important in German engraving, if we except Hollar and the mezzotint engravers who went to England, and who will be mentioned in a subsequent chapter. It was not until the second half of the eighteenth century that the German engravers again became important. In the meantime the engravers of the Low Countries were beginning to attract attention by the superior excellence of their works, and to these we will now turn our attention before mentioning the German engravers of more recent times.

CHAPTER IV

DUTCH AND FLEMISH ENGRAVERS

Varied character of Dutch and Flemish Engraving — Early Dutch Engravers; Lucas van Leyden, Goltzius, and their followers — Influence of Rubens — The Rubens Engravers; Vorsterman, the Bolswerts, Pontius, and De Jode — Etchings by Van Dyck; the *Iconographia* — Dutch Line Engraving; Suyderhoef and Visscher — Rembrandt the Typical Painter-etcher — The Dutch Etchers; Ostade, Potter, Berghem, Du Jardin, Waterloo, Zeeman, Bakhuisen, and others — Houbraken — Decline of Dutch and Flemish Engraving, and ascendency of the French school.

AT the beginning of the sixteenth century, engraving in Italy and Germany was rapidly approaching its maturity. In the Netherlands the art was still in its infancy; its career had scarcely commenced; but if less rapid in its growth and development, it became most important at a time when the schools of Italy and Germany were at their lowest ebb. As the engravers of those countries had their peculiar points of excellence, so the Dutch and Flemish engravers excelled in qualities lacking in the works of their predecessors. They practised almost every form of the art, and their prints are of the most varied character, both from original designs and interpretations of works by eminent painters.

The earliest of the Dutch engravers whose works are important, either artistically or in point of technic, was Lucas Jacobsz, called from his birthplace Lucas van Leyden. A contemporary of Dürer and Marc Antonio, his career extended from 1494 to 1533, covering the most brilliant period of the Italian Renaissance. As a painter, he was a disciple of Massys; but, like Dürer, he was by preference an engraver, although his engraved works lack the vigor, lofty sentiment, and inspiration of Dürer, and are without the masterly ease, graceful drawing, and elegance of the Italian. But it must be remembered that he was a pioneer, without a Schongauer or a Mantegna to prepare the way.

Lucas was remarkable for the early fertility of his genius. It is said that he commenced to engrave when scarcely nine years old, and one of his most celebrated prints, 'The Monk Sergius killed by Mahomet,' was engraved at the age of fourteen, before which time he had achieved distinction as a painter. He engraved in the quaint, semi-Gothic manner prevalent in the North, and his prints show the peculiar feeling for realism emphasized in the works of his successors. His faults were those common to the Northern artists of his time. He had little regard for beauty of form or expression, and chose his models from the peasant types around him, seemingly indifferent to anachronisms in features and costume which render some of his figures almost ludicrous in appearance; but there are many instances in which the attitudes and expression are faithful and lifelike. His style is wonderfully neat and precise, and the extreme delicacy of his technic accounts for the scarcity of good impressions of his prints, from which, only, a just estimate of an engraver's powers can be formed.

Lucas was one of the first engravers who had correct ideas of rendering atmospheric distance and perspective, qualities in which the works of Dürer are noticeably deficient, and which the Italian engravers seem either to have misunderstood or to have purposely neglected. According to Vasari, "whatever portion of the picture recedes into the distance has precisely the degree of force required, each being less clearly made out as the distance increases, exactly as we find it in nature, becoming

DAVID PLAYING BEFORE SAUL

A portion of the Engraving by Lucas Van Leyden

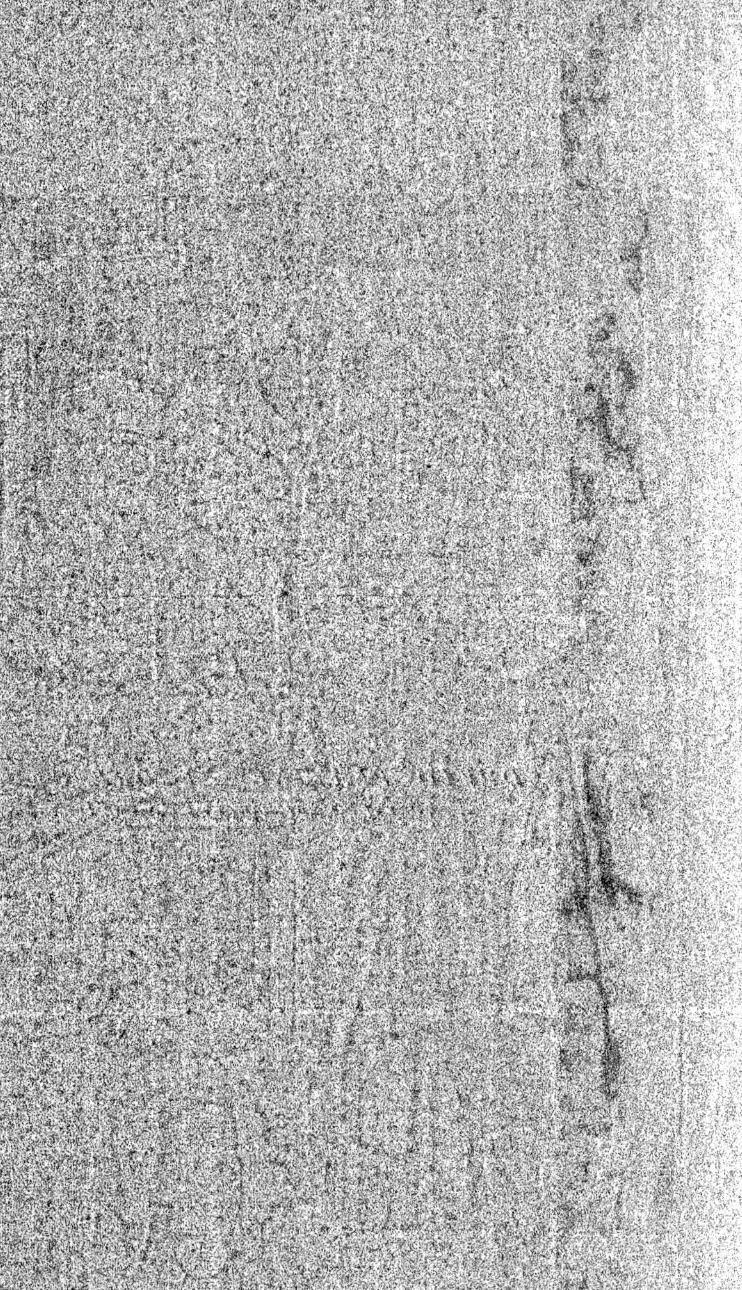

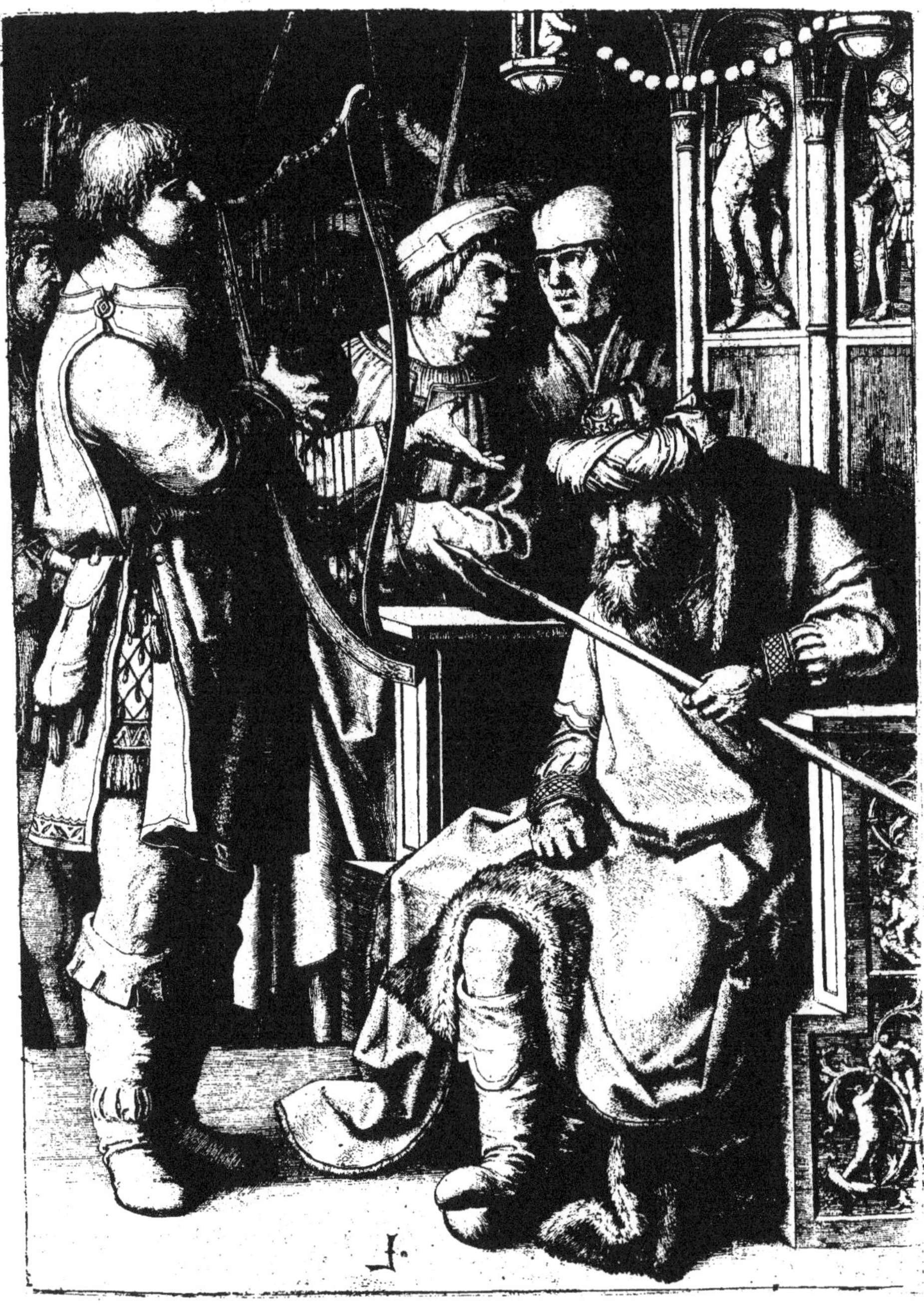

gradually lost to the sight, as it is known that natural objects become less and less clear to the eyes of the observer with increased distance." But we can scarcely agree with Vasari in attributing such perfection to Lucas, whose knowledge of perspective is remarkable chiefly in comparison with the ignorance of his predecessors. The best examples of his manner of rendering perspective are to be found in the two prints, 'Sergius killed by Mahomet,' and 'Calvary.' Of his numerous other prints may be mentioned 'David playing before Saul,' and 'Mary Magdalen Dancing,' or enjoying the pleasures of the world, extremely fine, and considered his masterpieces; the famous 'Uylenspiegel,' of greater rarity than merit; the 'Crucifixion;' a series of fourteen prints of the 'Passion;' an etching called the 'Wedding Ring;' a fine portrait of Maximilian I.; and a portrait of himself. There are also a number of woodcuts and chiaroscuros, but of inferior merit.

Lucas worked in various parts of the Netherlands, principally at Leyden, Middleburg, and Antwerp, and achieved great distinction in his own time. He was a friend of Dürer, with whom he exchanged prints, and who describes him as "a little man who was born in Leyden." He lived to enjoy fame and affluence beyond most artists of his time, and is said to have led an exemplary life, aiding those less fortunate than himself with a tender charity disguised under the pretext of requiring assistance. He died at Leyden in his thirty-ninth year, having won during his short career a high place in art as well as in the affections of his countrymen.

As Lucas of Leyden greatly surpassed his predecessors in the Low Countries, so his works, like those of Dürer, became models for imitation; but he had no successors worthy of particular mention until the second half of the century, when Hendrick Goltzius, of Mülbrecht (Cleves), gave to Dutch and Flemish engraving a new impulse and direction. Goltzius was born in 1558, and was the son and pupil of an eminent glass-painter. He learned the art of engraving from Dirk Cuerenhert, a man of many accomplishments, poet, author, religious controversialist, and statesman, as well as engraver, but now best known as the reputed author of the *Wilhelmus.*

Goltzius, like Dürer, is said to have married unhappily; but, unlike the German artist, he fled from domestic discord. He travelled through Germany into Italy, where he studied the works of the Italian masters, particularly Raphael, Michael Angelo, and Caravaggio, whose manner of drawing he attempted to imitate, but with a result generally extravagant and often grotesque, although his works engraved in the styles of Dürer and Lucas van Leyden are remarkably successful. After residing for a time at Rome, he returned to his native country and settled at Haarlem, where he died, 1617.

Goltzius possessed great technical skill, but with a tendency to extravagance and exaggeration. His genius was of the familiar kind that is said to need the curb rather than the spur. He often prolonged his lines to a most unreasonable extent, affecting an ease and mastery of drawing which often led to somewhat startling results. Some of his attempts to imitate the drawing of Michael Angelo are almost ludicrous in their exaggeration; we see distorted figures in violent action, but none of the grandeur of the Italian artist. But although many of his prints have this air of exaggeration, or, to use Mr. Ruskin's expression, "attitudinizing," there are others almost free from mannerism which will always hold a high place in art.

Goltzius had a high opinion of his own powers, to display which he engraved a series of six large plates, imitating the styles of Raphael, Parmigiano, Bassano, Barocci, Dürer, and Lucas van Leyden. These plates are known as the "Masterpieces of Goltzius," but, notwithstanding the paradox, they are by no means his best works.

The principal works of Goltzius are the famous 'Dog of Frisius,' 'The Virgin Weeping over the Body of Christ,' the 'Passion,' a series of twelve prints, 'The Standard Bearer,' 'Venus and Cupid,' and the portraits of Cuerenhert, William, Prince of Orange, in armor, and a life-size portrait of himself. These masterpieces belong in the choicest collection of the amateur. The superb print of the 'Boy and Dog,' dated 1597, enjoys a deserved celebrity. The boy, believed to be the son of the Venetian painter, Theodore Frisius, to whom the print is dedicated, sits astride a large hunting-dog and holds on his right hand a falcon. The life-like attitude and expression of the dog, and his entire sympathy with his young master, are altogether admirable. The beautiful landscape background also comes in for its share of praise. 'The Virgin Weeping over the Body of Christ' is engraved in the style of Dürer. His large portraits are remarkably free and bold in treatment—in striking contrast to the miniature-like work in some of his smaller prints. The other prints of Goltzius exceed 500 in number, comprising all sorts of subjects; in many of these he was assisted by his pupils. He also engraved a number of wood-cuts, of which the seven cuts of the 'Heathen Divinities,' from his own designs, are the best examples. There is a fine portrait of Goltzius engraved by Suyderhoef.

The example and influence of Goltzius were not entirely beneficial, for many of his disciples, instead of imitating the great qualities which he undoubtedly possessed, were dazzled and misled by his affectation of ease and his great mechanical facility. Some of these engravers possessed remarkable technical skill, among them Jan Muller, whose portraits of Isabella, Infanta of Spain; Albert, Archduke of Austria, and Christian IV. of Denmark, are striking examples of the peculiar and extravagant technic of this school. Muller also engraved a number of fine subjects in the same general style. The works of Joannes Saenredam, and of Jacobus Matham, the son-in-law of Goltzius, also present the same characteristics.

Some of the followers of Goltzius, however, avoided the mannerism and extravagance of their master's style, notably Pieter de Jode the elder, who belonged to an Antwerp family for three generations distinguished in the history of engraving. Gerrit, the head of the family, engraved in the style of Cornelis Cort, and was the early instructor of Pieter "the elder" before he entered the school of Goltzius, and he in turn transmitted his skill to Pieter the younger, who was especially successful in his portraits after Van Dyck.

The brothers Wierix, voluminous engravers, disciples of Dürer, also belonged to this period. They engraved many prints, including a number of fine copies after Dürer, remarkable for neatness and precision.

The numerous followers of Goltzius produced very little of real importance. Their accomplishments were chiefly of a technical order; they neglected their own art for that of Italy, which in the latter half of the century was extremely popular throughout the Netherlands, many artists even going to Italy to reside, like Cornelis Cort, who became Titian's engraver, and his instructor Hieronimus Cock, who assisted Vasari in compiling his biographies of the Dutch engravers. The true character of Dutch and Flemish art did not appear until the following century, when Rembrandt and Rubens and their pupils and followers gave to the respective schools their national characteristics.

We now come to an important era in the history of engraving: the period of transition to the modern schools. We have mentioned the services rendered to the art by Marc Antonio, Albrecht Dürer, and Lucas of Leyden, and now come to the school of engravers who drew their inspiration from Rubens. These engravers abandoned the clear, simple methods of their great predecessors, and by a multiplicity of lines and elaborate cross-hatchings endeavored to give to their prints the breadth and richness of their master's works. They engraved chiefly from the works of contemporary Dutch and Flemish painters, principally Rubens and Van Dyck, and produced brilliant and striking contrasts and effects of light and shade, opening the way for modern engraving which undertakes to represent, with all the resources of the art, the qualities and effects of painted canvas.

As Raphael directed Marc Antonio, so Rubens instructed the engravers of the school which bears his name. After his return from Italy in 1608, he settled at Antwerp, where he built a palace in the Italian style. This he filled with the choice works of art which he had collected, and surrounded himself by his pupils, over whom his influence was almost absolute. He directed many of his pupils to abandon the brush and become engravers, and inspired them with his own enthusiasm, correcting and retouching their proofs, and encouraging them by counsel and assistance. His efforts were rewarded, for no other painter has ever lived to see so many of his important works so finely engraved. The collections in the British Museum and the Bibliothèque Nationale at Paris contain many proofs drawn upon by Rubens with chalk or pencil, suggesting alterations or improvements. Under his leadership all rivalry between the different schools ceased, and both the Dutch and Flemish engravers set out in this new direction with the same aims and methods. Rubens was an illustration of his own saying: "Do well, and people will be jealous of you; do better, and you will overcome their jealousy." He was not only a dictator in art, but also scholar, courtier, and diplomatist, and one of his country's most important men.

Lucas Vorsterman, one of the greatest of the so-called Rubens engravers, was born at Antwerp about the year 1578, and was one of the pupils whom Rubens induced to lay aside the brush and take up the burin. Vorsterman soon achieved great distinction an an engraver, and after leaving his master's studio went to England, where he remained for nearly eight years, enjoying the patronage of the Earl of Arundel and Charles I., and engraving from the pictures in the Arundel and Royal collections, among them a number of subjects after Raphael, Annibale Caracci, Parmigiano, and Caravaggio; but although some of these plates are highly attractive, his style was better adapted to rendering the works of the contemporary painters of his own country. He excelled in his subjects after Rubens and in his portraits after Van Dyck. Of the former 'The Adoration of the Magi' and 'Descent from the Cross' possess great merit, although 'Susannah and the Elders,' the 'Adoration of the Shepherds,' and a number of 'Holy Families,' after the same master, are but little inferior. The print of 'Susannah and the Elders' is said to have been an especial favorite with Rubens. His other subjects, after various Flemish and Italian masters, are numerous.

Vorsterman is chiefly famous for his masterly portraits after Van Dyck, among them a fine portrait of his patron,

THE STANDARD-BEARER

By Hendrik Goltzius

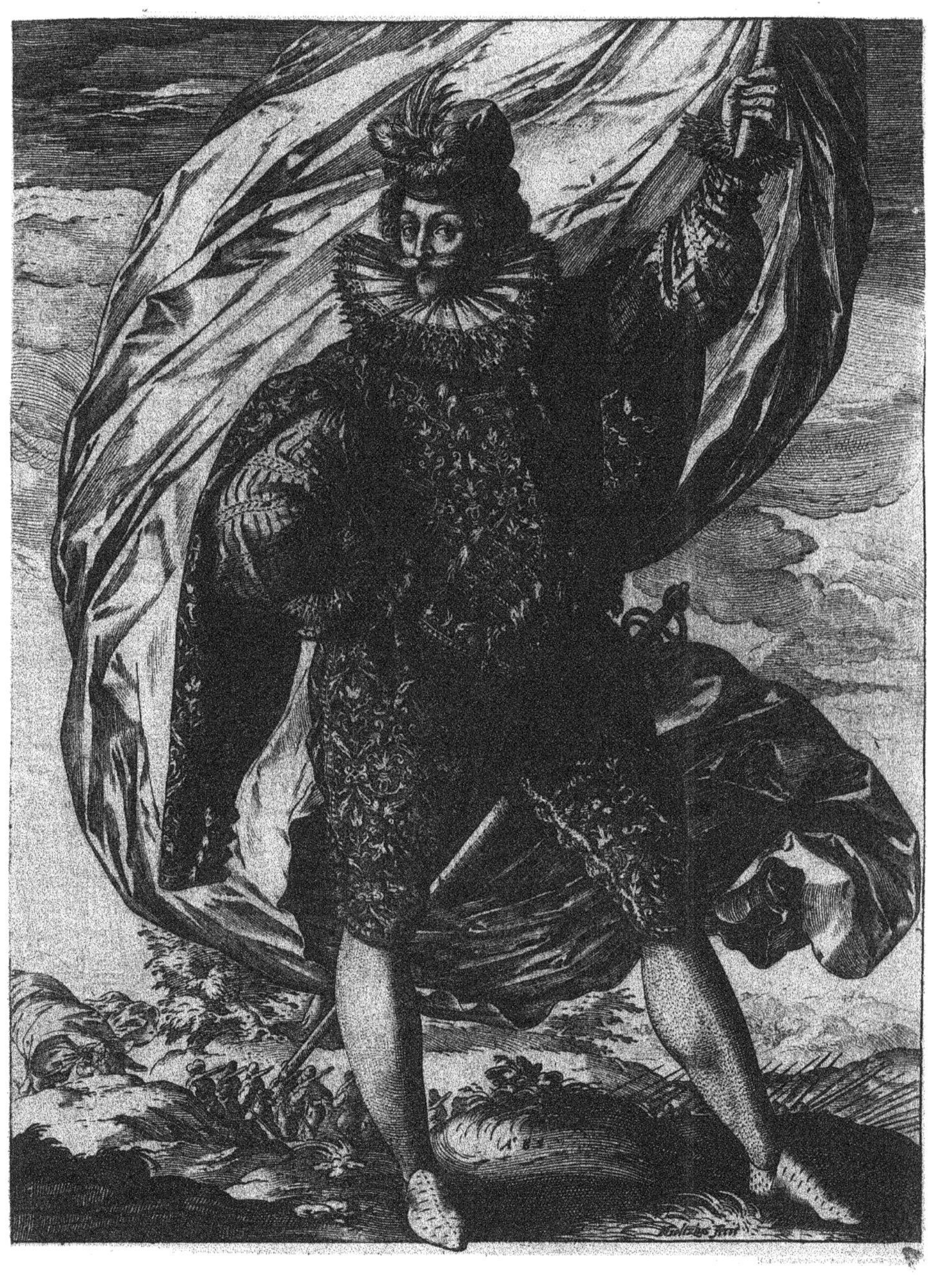

the Earl of Arundel, and upwards of twenty portraits engraved for the famous volume known as the "Centum Icones," which possess more of the characteristics of that great master of physiognomy than can be found in the works of any other engraver. In return, Van Dyck etched a portrait of Vorsterman in the most beautiful and graceful manner, showing a countenance full of character and intelligence.

The ablest and most characteristic of all the Rubens engravers was Schelte à Bolswert, famous for his fine subjects, as Vorsterman was for his masterly portraits. Born at Bolswert, in Friesland, in the year 1586, he settled at Antwerp with his brother Boëtius, also an engraver, and here he died at an advanced age in 1659, after becoming the most famous engraver of the Rubens school. Many of his prints after Rubens and Van Dyck are masterpieces of engraving, possessing in a remarkable degree the characteristics of the originals. Among his numerous works the following may be taken as typical examples of the style of the Rubens engravers at their best: 'The Crucifixion,' dated 1631, 'St. Cecilia' and 'The Rainbow Landscape,' after Rubens; 'Christ Crowned with Thorns,' 'The Crucifixion,' and a number of 'Holy Families,' after Van Dyck; 'Pan playing on a Flute,' 'Pan holding a Basket of Fruit,' 'The Infant Jupiter,' and 'Mercury and Argus,' after Jordaens; and 'Peter Denying Christ,' after Zeghers. As examples of the works of Boëtius à Bolswert may be mentioned his fine prints, 'The Resurrection of Lazarus' and 'The Last Supper,' both after Rubens. Many of the subjects engraved by the Bolswerts have fine landscape backgrounds.

Another engraver who drew inspiration from Rubens was Paulus Du Pont, better known under his latinized name, Paul Pontius, who was born at Antwerp about the beginning of the seventeenth century. Pontius was taught engraving by Vorsterman, and worked much under Rubens, with whom he was a favorite pupil. Although lacking the marvellous facility of Bolswert and the delicacy of Vorsterman, his works are engraved in a bold, clear style, and with rare fidelity to his originals. Pontius is famous for his fine subjects after Rubens and for his portraits after Van Dyck. Among the former are 'St. Roch interceding with Christ for the Plague-stricken,' 'Susannah and the Elders,' 'The Assumption of the Virgin,' 'The Massacre of the Innocents,' 'The Presentation in the Temple,' and 'Thomiris.' Of his portraits, that of his master Rubens, after Van Dyck, is a masterpiece of rare beauty and excellence, one of the finest produced by this school. He also engraved about thirty-five of the portraits in the "Centum Icones," which as a whole are but little inferior to those of Vorsterman.

Pieter De Jode the younger, another principal contributor to the "Centum Icones," also engraved a number of fine subjects after Rubens, Van Dyck, and Jordaens, of which 'St. Augustine adoring the Mystery of the Holy Trinity,' after Van Dyck, is the best example.

The engravers named were the most illustrious of the Rubens school, although Peter Soutman, a Dutch engraver who settled at Antwerp and became a disciple of Rubens, deserves notice as a skilful engraver, although more eminent as a teacher, numbering among his pupils Suyderhoef and Visscher.

Rubens did not confine his encouragement to copper-plate engraving, for he caused a number of his designs to be engraved upon wood, some in the chiaroscuro manner. The best of these cuts were engraved by Christopher Jegher, a German engraver who had settled at Antwerp. His fine cut of 'The Repose in Egypt,' already mentioned, is a good example.

Many of these subjects were drawn directly upon the wood by Rubens, and the engraver followed the outlines and hatchings scrupulously, giving almost exact fac-similes of the originals. The best impressions of these cuts bear Rubens's name as publisher. Rubens is credited with a number of etchings, of which 'St. Catherine,' a bold, picturesque work, is the best example.

While the Bolswerts, Vorsterman, and Pontius excelled in their engravings after the Flemish painters, they were less successful in their subjects after the Italian masters. They lost the spiritual character and exquisite grace of the originals in the naturalism of their own school of art. Their master, Rubens, died in 1640, Van Dyck in 1641, and Vorsterman, the Bolswerts, and Pontius before 1660, after which time Flemish engraving, as well as Flemish painting, declined rapidly in importance. Their successors lacked the inspiration of Rubens, and like the imitators of Lucas van Leyden and Goltzius, subordinated art to mechanical excellence, imitating the faults of their predecessors without their good qualities. But the Dutch engravers had again become important, Suyderhoef and Visscher excelling in portraiture, and Rembrandt and his contemporaries carrying to perfection the art of etching, of which the Dutch and Flemish engravers had made but little use except as an auxiliary to line engraving. But before mentioning the Dutch engravers, one other Flemish artist claims our attention.

As many of the best works of Sir Anthony Van Dyck were beautifully engraved by the Rubens engravers, so that great painter encouraged the engraver's art by example as well as precept, for he left a few etched subjects and portraits, executed with great energy and spirit, and with classical taste and refinement, and the same fine discrimination and idealization of character which he displayed in his paintings. In marked

8

contrast to the powerful and picturesque portraits of Visscher are these by Van Dyck, which are characterized by spirit, refinement of expression, and unaffected simplicity.

Evelyn, in his *Sculptura*, states: "And to show what honor was done to this art by the best of painters, Sir Ant. Van Dyck did himself etch divers things in aqua-fortis, especially a 'Madonna,' 'Ecce Homo,' 'Titian and his Mistress,' 'Erasmus Rotterdamus,' and touched several heads before mentioned to have been graved by Vorsterman." The subjects etched by Van Dyck, however, are greatly inferior to his etched portraits, which are mostly of contemporary painters and engravers with whom he was upon terms of intimacy. Many of these portraits, although slight sketches, are executed in a free and masterly manner, full of vigor and energy, and are brilliant examples of his skill in the use of the free line. Some of these portraits remain as Van Dyck left them; in others, backgrounds and accessories were added by other engravers, which did not increase their attractiveness, but rendered many of them dull and heavy; it is by the pure etchings, before the plates were touched by other hands, that Van Dyck should be judged. The portraits of Lucas Vorsterman, Justus Suttermans, Joannes Snellinx, Paul Pontius, Francis Synders, and Willem de Vos are masterpieces full of expression, and show Van Dyck as an etcher at his best.

The so-called *Iconographia* of Van Dyck comprises the portraits engraved after that master by Vorsterman, Bolswert, Pontius, De Jode, and others, and a few of Van Dyck's own plates. The publications of the artist's friend, Martin Vanden Enden, formed the basis of this work; these portraits had been issued singly as the plates were finished. After the death of Van Dyck, eighty of the plates of Vanden Enden passed into the hands of the famous Antwerp publisher Gillis Hendricx, who erased the name of the former publisher, added his own initials, and changed names and inscriptions. He also acquired the plates of fifteen of the portraits etched by Van Dyck and added six other plates published by himself, and published the whole with a title-page containing the head of Van Dyck as a bust, the pedestal bearing the inscription: "Icones principum virorum doctorum, pictorum, chalcographorum, statuariorum, nec non amatorum pictoriæ artis numero centum: ab Antonio Van Dyck pictore ad vivum expressae ejusq. sumptibus aeri incisæ. Antverpiæ: Gillis Hendricx excudit A° 1645." This beautiful work, known as the "Centum Icones," a tribute of the high esteem of his contemporaries, represents his portraits as those of no other painter were ever represented by the engraver's art. The head of Van Dyck in the frontispiece was etched by the master himself; and it is said that according to the original design, Van Dyck was to etch the outlines of all the portraits, leaving the details to be filled in by the other engravers, of whom Vorsterman and Pontius were the chief. Many editions of these plates have since appeared, and most of the coppers are still preserved in Paris.

As the style of the Rubens engravers was especially adapted to the works of the Flemish painters, so the Dutch engravers Jonas Suyderhoef and Cornelis Visscher are famous for their engravings after the artists of their own country. They combined with great success the work of the burin and needle.

Suyderhoef excelled in portraiture, engraving many interesting portraits after Rembrandt, Rubens, Van Dyck, Frans Hals, Soutman, and other Dutch and Flemish artists, besides a number of fine subjects after Ostade, Terburg, and De Keyser. Among the latter are two famous historical prints, the most important and interesting of his works. One of these represents the four burgomasters at Amsterdam in consultation as to the honors to be shown to Marie de' Medici upon her entry into that city in 1638. In the midst of their deliberations they are surprised and dismayed by the news that she has already arrived. The original painting by Thomas De Keyser is still in the gallery at The Hague. Suyderhoef's masterpiece, however, is the so-called 'Peace of Münster,' a famous historical print containing many figures, and a most exact and truthful interpretation of Terburg's painting of the same size now in the National Gallery. This rare print is a collection of portraits of the representatives of the United Provinces and Spain assembled to confirm by oath the treaty which preceded by a few months the great Peace of Westphalia which terminated the Thirty Years' War, with which treaty some writers have confounded the subject of this print.

Superior to all other Dutch line engravers of the seventeenth century was Cornelis Visscher, the chief of a numerous and distinguished family of engravers. For bold, skilful technic and picturesque effect the works of this eminent master have scarcely been excelled. Born at Haarlem about the year 1610, he removed to Amsterdam, where he became Suyderhoef's fellow-pupil in the school of Soutman. But he soon departed from his master's style and adopted a superior manner of his own, in which he excelled all other engravers of his time. Towards the close of his career he returned to Haarlem, where he died about the year 1670.

Visscher's subjects after the Dutch masters Ostade, Berghem, Brouwer, and De Laer are unsurpassed, although his interpretations of the Flemish painters, particularly Rubens, are inferior to those of Bolswert and Vorsterman. Of his subjects,

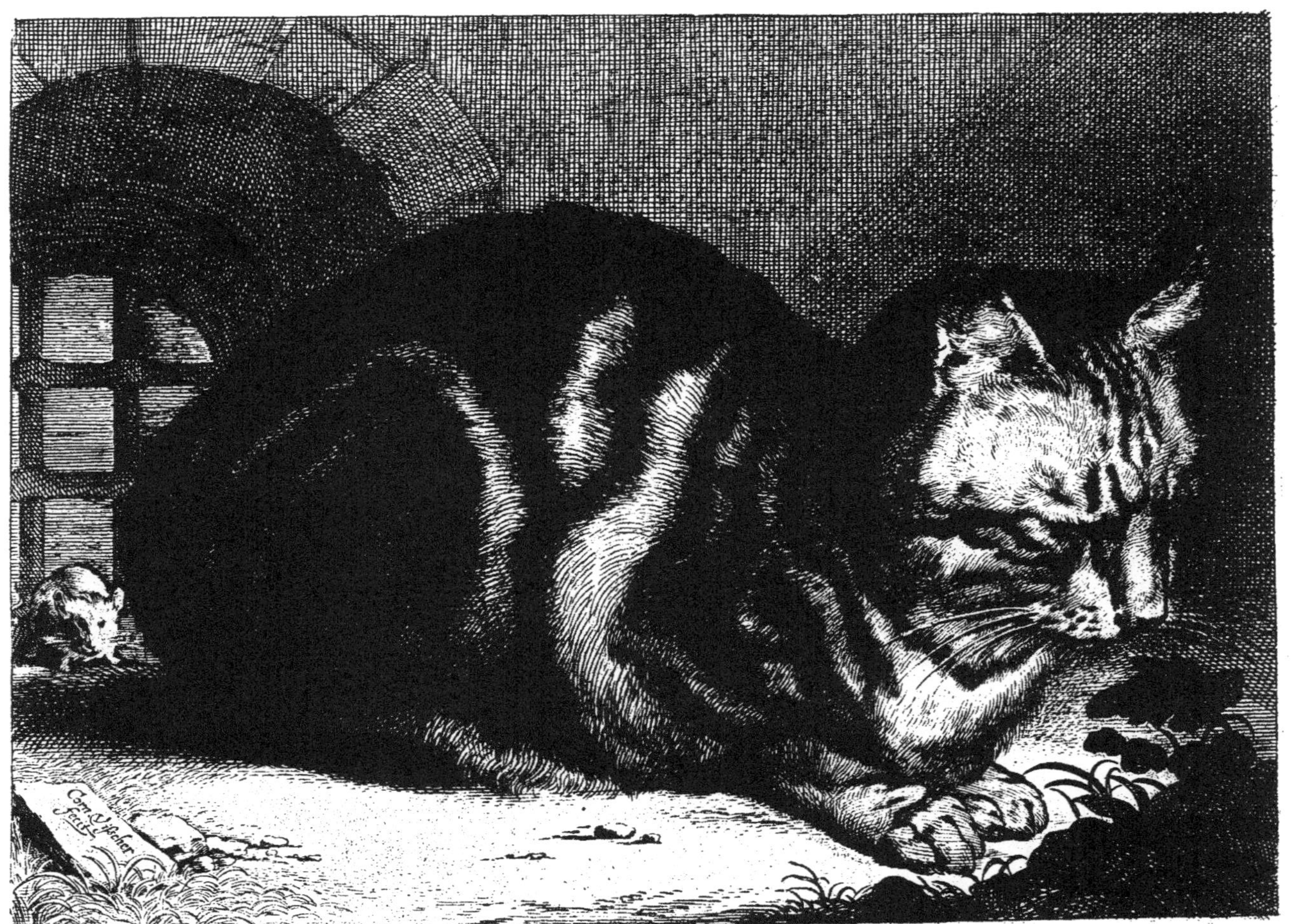
Corn. Vißcher
fecit

the 'Travelling Musicians' and 'Skaters,' after Ostade, and the 'Rat-catcher' and 'Pancake Woman,' from his own designs, stand foremost. These prints are masterpieces of engraving, full of truth and spirit. There are also two prints from his own designs of a sleeping cat, of which the larger is a universal favorite, a family portrait familiar to all.

Visscher's masterpieces, however, are to be found in his portraits, which number more than 100, and represent many celebrated historical characters of his time. Of these the portraits of Gellius de Bouma, the ecclesiast at Zutphen, and William De Ryck, the Amsterdam oculist, both from his own drawings, and known as the "Great Beards," are fine examples. The former is especially remarkable for its bold, picturesque treatment, fine modelling, and vivacity of expression, and shows Visscher's greatness both as designer and engraver. This portrait may be taken as a typical example of Dutch line engraving at its best. Of his other portraits may be named Andreas Winius, called 'The Man with the Pistol,' extremely fine; Petrus Scriverius, Willem van den Zande, Cornelis Vosbergius, and two portraits of himself. In fine, early impressions all of these portraits are rare and valuable.

Chief among the followers of Visscher were Cornelis Van Dalen and Abraham Blooteling. The former engraved admirable portraits of Aretino, Boccaccio, and Giorgione, after Titian, and a number of subjects in the style of the Rubens engravers. Blooteling was a prolific engraver in line, aqua-fortis, and mezzotint, and was also eminent as a designer. Some of his finest plates were engraved in England, whither he went upon the invasion of the French in 1672.

Contemporary with Rubens, Van Dyck, and Visscher was Rembrandt Harmensz Van Ryn, who, from an artistic stand-point, was the most important individual who lived in the seventeenth century. Rembrandt was born at Leyden, July 15, 1607, and was the son of a miller in comfortable circumstances. His first master was the local painter Jacob van Swanenburch, now chiefly known through his illustrious pupil; but his progress was so great that he was soon sent to Amsterdam to enter the studio of Pieter Lastman, famous in his time. After leaving Lastman he returned to Leyden, where he worked for a number of years, but removed finally to Amsterdam about the year 1630, where he passed the remainder of his life. Here in 1632 he painted his first great corporation picture, the famous 'Lesson in Anatomy,' now in the gallery at The Hague. In the year 1634 Rembrandt married his first wife, Saskia van Ulenburgh, who belonged to a distinguished Friesland family, and brought to her husband a substantial dowry as well as influential friends. To Saskia, Rembrandt was devotedly attached; she was a model of whom he never tired, the gentle inspiration of many of his important works. Her features have become familiar through her numerous portraits, many in character, painted and etched by her husband.

Upon the death of his mother in 1640 Rembrandt's fortune was still further augmented, and he purchased the famous house in the Jodenbreedstraat, which, like Rubens, he filled with works of art, and gathered around him his many pupils, among them Gérard Dou, who had been his pupil at Leyden. Rembrandt's art collection was superb, comprising, in addition to many fine works by his contemporaries, paintings by the most celebrated artists of other times and countries, among them works by Raphael, Michael Angelo, Giorgione, and Van Eyck, besides many volumes of the choicest prints of the great Italian, German, and Dutch engravers, and a large collection of drawings, casts, statuary, arms, armor, costumes, furniture, tapestries, rich carvings, porcelains, musical instruments, and botanical, zoological, and mineralogical specimens, making, all together, a collection which illustrated art from its revival. Although Rembrandt never visited either Italy or Germany, this collection sufficiently shows the wide scope of his studies, and that he was an enthusiastic collector as well as dispenser of art.

The year 1642 marks "the strongest light and the deepest shadow" of Rembrandt's career. In this year he finished the grandest of his canvases, the so-called 'Night Watch,' or 'Sortie of the Company of Banning Cock,' now in the Museum at Amsterdam, and familiar through the fine etchings of Flameng and Waltner. In the same year the death of the beloved Saskia cast over the artist's life a shadow which never lifted. From this time Rembrandt's fortunes rapidly declined. Through extravagance and bad management, aided perhaps by the growing preference for Italian art among his patrons, his fortune rapidly disappeared, and some years later he was adjudged insolvent, and his property, including a large portion of his art collection, was sold to pay debts. His works of art, which, according to the sales catalogue, were "collected by Rembrandt himself with much love and care," were sold at an unfavorable time and brought but a small portion of their value, as had also been the case with the renowned collection of Charles I., sold a few years before. In 1665 Rembrandt married his second wife, Catherina van Wijck. After the sale of the house in the Breedstraat he lived for a time with his son Titus, the only survivor of Saskia's four children, in a somewhat obscure portion of the city; but in March, 1669, Titus died, and on the 8th day of October in the same year the great artist followed him to the grave, and was buried in the Westerkerke.

No artist has left more or greater evidences of his wonderful powers than Rembrandt. Upon every branch of art to which he turned his attention he left the mark of his individuality and genius. As a painter his works rival in some respects those of the great masters of Italy, and as an etcher he stands alone in the sum of his great qualities, technical and intellectual. Etching was known and practised before the time of Dürer; but as long as purity of line and modelling of the human figure continued to be the engraver's chief aim, there could be but little competition between the point and the graver. The peculiar province of etching as an autographic art was not understood by the early etchers, most of whom attempted to imitate the pure, clean-cut lines of the graver, as the early printers had endeavored to imitate the manuscript missals, instead of perceiving the true character and independence of their art. Although etching had been practised with various degrees of success, it remained for Rembrandt to develop its resources, and to define its province and limitations. In etching he perceived the natural interpreter of the picturesque, and practised that art in its various branches with a degree of perfection beyond any artist before or since, even printing his own proofs.

Rembrandt followed the natural inclinations of his own genius, untrammelled by the conventional art of his predecessors. The Italian influence had long been supreme in the Low Countries, and it remained for Rembrandt to give to Dutch art its distinctive character and individuality. He was devoted to nature, and represented life as he found it among the people with whom he lived, the scenes and forms familiar to him, but expressed his realism with dignity, simplicity, and picturesque effect. Idealist, as well as realist, his works do not merely attract the eye; they possess an intellectual quality and depth of sentiment which lead us to believe that in many instances only a small portion of his conception is actually expressed, and that beyond this are profound reflections upon humanity, a deeper meaning of which these often insignificant subjects are merely the outward tokens.

The etched work ascribed to Rembrandt forms of itself a collection numbering more than 350 prints, exclusive of "states," of which he created many, sometimes, it is thought, unnecessarily, to suit his ever-ready customers for unique impressions of his prints. He practised etching in its purest form, and used the free line in a manner approached by few artists, ancient or modern. He was a thorough master of light and shadow, and the grandeur and harmony of his chiaroscuro have seldom been equalled. He combined and harmonized dry-point with etching as no else has ever done, and handled the dry-point, a refractory instrument, with such skill that in some of his prints, where he removed the bur, it is almost impossible to distinguish between the work of the point and that of the acid. Many of his prints were also retouched and strengthened with the point and great richness of effect added. Rembrandt never lost sight of the unity of his subject, as was often the case with Dürer; and unlike most of our modern etchings, every line has its distinct function, and there is little attempt at mere embellishment.

Rembrandt is said to have painted his own portrait nearly fifty times. His last work is believed to have been the famous laughing portrait, etched by Flameng and Jacquemart. He also etched more than thirty portraits of himself, of which 'Rembrandt appuyé' and 'Rembrandt with the Sabre and Aigrette' are the most attractive. Taken together, these portraits show the great artist at all periods of his career; at times gay and jovial, with his beloved Saskia upon his knee; again stern and almost fierce in expression; in light and in shadow, and in a variety of attitudes and costumes. Rugged and picturesque in appearance, with sharp, piercing eyes sparkling with intelligence, a more interesting face is scarcely to be found in the whole domain of art. Rembrandt also etched a number of portraits of his old mother; and of his etched portraits of Saskia, the one in character known as the 'Great Jewish Bride' is perhaps the most interesting. Among the most celebrated of his other portraits are those of the Burgomaster Six, his intimate friend; Uytenbogaert, the gold-weigher; Janus Lutma, the goldsmith; the advocate Tolling; the physician Ephraim Bonus; the landscape-painter Jan Asselyn; Clement de Jonghe, his publisher; Janus Sylvius, the cousin of Saskia; the Haarings; and Coppenol. Nothing in art could be more natural than the attitudes in which these persons are represented and the simplicity of their surroundings, each absorbed in his own pursuit or deep in thought.

That Rembrandt, like Dürer and Lucas of Leyden, was indifferent to personal beauty is apparent, even upon a casual examination of his prints. His ideal of beauty was of the mind, and had nothing in common with the spiritual ideal of the Italians or the sensual beauty of the Flemish artists. To him a picturesque beggar or peasant with strong Dutch features was a sufficiently attractive subject upon which to display his art. There is one little print, however, of great beauty and delicacy, a slight sketch representing Youth surprised by Death; but in Rembrandt's prints there is seldom any approach to beauty or elegance of form. Rembrandt etched more than twenty subjects of beggars, most of them mere outline sketches drawn with a few swift but certain strokes of the needle, but expressing with remarkable effect both character and costume. Of these the

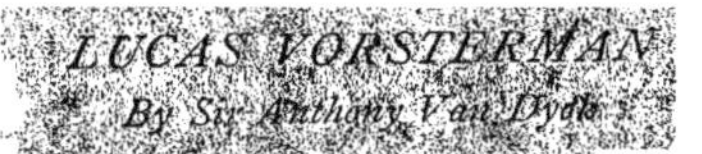

LUCAS VORSTERMAN
By Sir Anthony Van Dyck

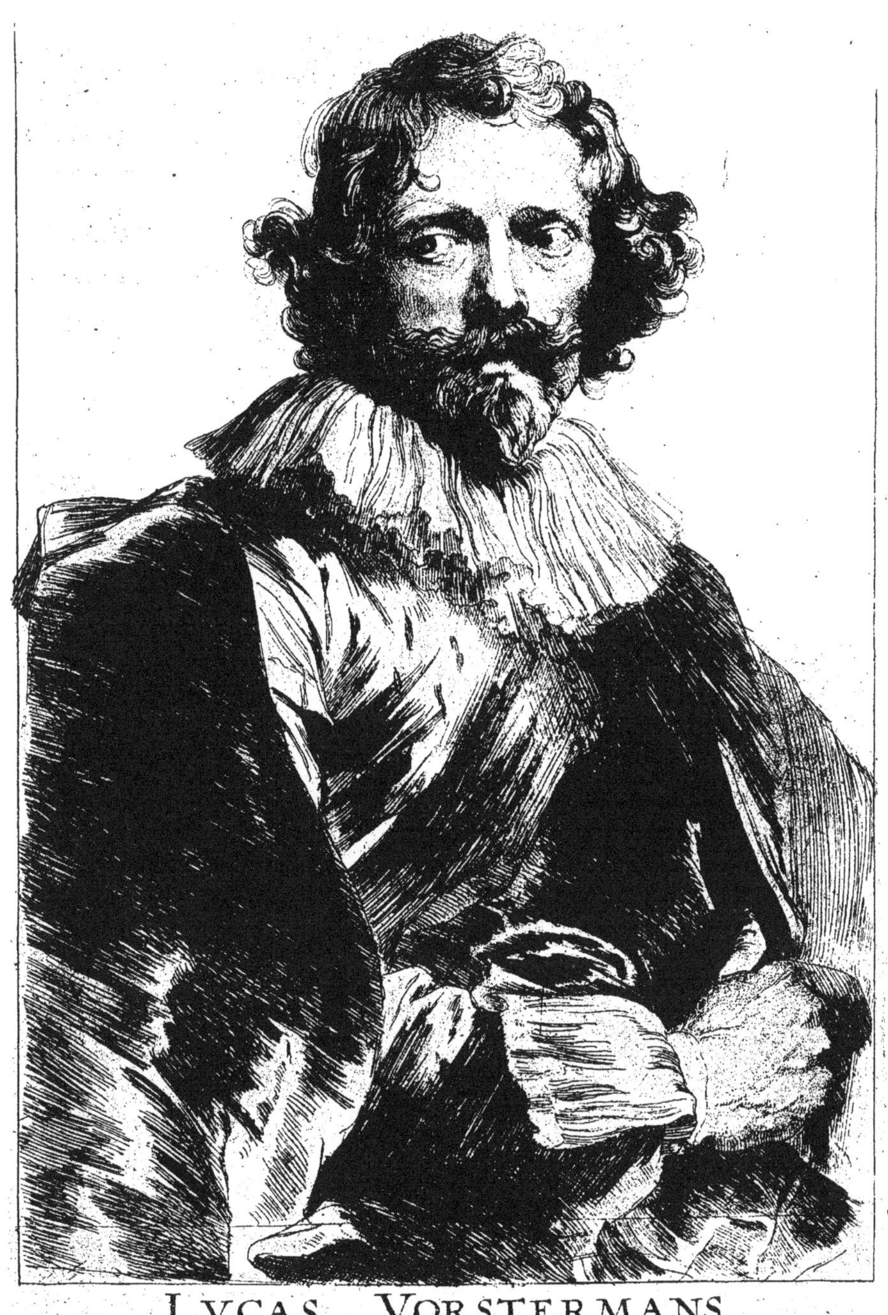

LVCAS VORSTERMANS
CALCOGRAPHVS ANTVERPIÆ IN GELDRIA NATVS.

'Gueux à gros ventre' and the 'Mendiants homme et femme' are the most interesting. Of his subjects of naked figures 'Diana at the Bath' is considered the finest example.

Of Rembrandt's landscapes, which represent his own damp and curious country, with its vast horizons and innumerable canals and windmills, that known as the 'Three Trees' is the largest and most magnificent example. The 'Landscape with the Three Cottages,' which contains rich dry-point effect, the 'Landscape with the Tower,' the 'Cottage with the Great Tree,' the 'View of Omval;' 'The Mill,' and 'Amsterdam' are also notable examples. But the human interest of Rembrandt's works is the quality that chiefly attracts us, and it was in his portraits and figure compositions rather than in his landscapes that his art found its true expression.

Of Rembrandt's religious pieces the 'Christ Healing the Sick' is his principal work, everything considered, and one of the most elaborate pieces of etching ever attempted. This print is marvellous alike for its grandeur of conception, its diversity and delicacy of technic, and the grand harmony of its chiaroscuro. At the right the completeness and delicacy of finish have never been surpassed; while the figures on the left are merely outlined, but with wonderful force and expression. This etching is known as the 'Hundred-Guilder Print,' from the circumstance that a proof of it was sold by Rembrandt for that amount, or its equivalent. A fine impression of this print has since brought the enormous sum of £1180, and still higher prices have been realized for rare or unique impressions from other plates. At this rate a complete collection of Rembrandt's prints, assuming the possibility of making such a collection at all, would not lie within the limits of any ordinary fortune. A wonderful fac-simile of the 'Hundred-Guilder Print' was etched by Léopold Flameng for the great catalogue published by Charles Blanc. Flameng etched almost perfect fac-similes of forty of Rembrandt's etchings for this work. Of Rembrandt's other religious subjects, the 'Ecce Homo,' the largest of all his prints; the 'Crucifixion;' 'Jesus Christ Preaching,' called the 'Little La Tombe;' the great 'Descent from the Cross;' 'Our Lord before Pilate;' and the 'Death of the Virgin,' may be taken as typical examples, although there are others in many respects equally good.

Nearly all of Rembrandt's works are highly esteemed, and only a few representative examples have been given. The student is referred to the catalogues and critical writings of Bartsch, Blanc, Wilson, Dutuit, Vosmaer, Haden, Hamerton, and the host of other writers who have devoted careful study to the works of this indefatigable and many-sided genius. Only of recent years have we known much about this great artist, and by the researches and bold criticisms of a few writers ascertained the true value of his services to art.

Of the numerous disciples of Rembrandt the chief were Ferdinand Bol, Jan Livensz, and Jan Van Vliet, who etched many plates after their master, or in imitation of his style, chiefly remarkable for effects of light and shade. The German etcher Dietrich, and the accomplished amateur Captain William Baillie, may also be mentioned as among the most successful imitators of Rembrandt's manner.

That the works of the Dutch and Flemish engravers should have been little esteemed by the Italian artists, with their traditions of classical art, was, perhaps, to have been expected. It is said that they were considered in Italy only as fit decorations for pot-houses. Even in France and Germany, where the Italian influence prevailed, they at first met with scarcely more favor; but Rembrandt's position as the typical etcher and the importance of his art are not likely to be again assailed.

Although etching had been practised for a long time by individual artists, both in the preliminary work of line engraving and as an independent process, there was no school devoted to this art until the time of Rembrandt. The Dutch etchers, like the Little Masters, appeared in a body, and had the same general tendencies and ideals; but while all were devoted to nature, and represented scenes in every-day life, and the phenomena of sea, sky, and landscape, their works possess characteristics which render them as a rule easily distinguishable. Their prints, almost endless in number, represent rustic and village scenes from Dutch peasant life, fairs, markets, interiors of ale-houses and cottages with peasants drinking, dancing, and often quarrelling, peasants tending their flocks, studies of animals, single and in groups, trees, landscapes, shipping and marine views, and a multitude of similar subjects. Their prints were exceedingly popular, and the plates have been so often and so badly retouched that good impressions are now scarce. Many of these etchers will also be recognized as painters of great ability and reputation. Mr. Ruskin, usually severe in his criticisms upon the Dutch realists and chiaroscurists, includes some of them among the persons "without imagination at all; who not being able to get any pleasure out of their thoughts, try to get it out of their sensations."

Adrian Van Ostade (1610–85) is generally considered the most important of this group of etchers, besides being one of the most celebrated and prolific painters of the Dutch school. His family name was Hendrik; the name Ostade was probably adopted by Adrian and his brother Isaac from the small hamlet which is believed to have been their father's birthplace. Both were men of character and standing as well as artists of high rank. The portrait of Adrian, painted by himself in middle life, represents him in a Puritan costume, and with a grave and somewhat melancholy countenance instead of the jovial features which his works would lead us to expect. In this respect he contrasts strangely with his master Frans Hals, whose features are reflected on his canvases, and who may be taken as a literal verification of the adage, "the painter paints himself."

Many of Ostade's subjects represent peasants dancing or drinking, without any higher thought than the gratification of their animal appetites, and utterly devoid of beauty of character or refinement beneath the surroundings of poverty. Ostade represented little more than the animal natures of his peasants, without seeing the mental or moral qualities which Rembrandt, Millet, or Bréton would have discovered. The irresistible charm of his works consists in the life and sparkle and the humor and piquancy which pervade them; in their remarkable composition and effects of light and shadow; and in the manner in which the figures are relieved from each other and from the background.

Ostade's etchings number about fifty-two, of which there are many states. In early impressions they are rare and costly, although many of them are common enough in inferior impressions from the worn-out plates. The subjects known as 'La Famille,' 'Le Goûter,' and 'The Dance in the Ale-house,' called 'Ostade's Ball,' are important examples of his works which are very even and uniform in quality.

The works of Ostade's pupils, Cornelis Bega and Cornelis Dusart, are inferior to those of their master, although generally resembling them in subjects and technic. Dusart engraved a number of plates in the mezzotint manner. Adrian Brouwer, who belonged to the same school, possessed rare abilities, which he is said to have wasted by participating too freely in the scenes of dissipation which he represented.

Foremost among the etchers who devoted themselves to the representation of the lower animals was the renowned Paul Potter, who was born in 1625, and died in 1654, at the early age of twenty-nine years. Few artists have produced such clever work, or have achieved such great popularity before reaching the prime of manhood. He etched a series of eight plates of cows, oxen, and other animals, and another set of five plates of horses, besides some landscapes with animals, which are executed in a simple, life-like manner, faithful in character and expression, and show his great sympathy for animal life.

In striking contrast to the simplicity of Paul Potter are the elegance and attitudinizing of Nicholas Berghem, or Berchem (1624–83), who, unlike Potter, generally subordinated his figures to his landscapes. Berghem's manual skill was great, and much of the merit of his prints consists in their technical excellence; but many of his works possess an elegance and brilliancy which do not accord with their subjects. His charming groups of peasants and cattle are placed in romantic landscapes, enriched with architectural ruins, and the scene is one of enchantment rather than of real life. His peasants are as elegant and dandified as those of Ostade are coarse and repulsive. The two prints 'Les Trois Vaches au Repos' (B. 3), and 'Le Joueur de cornemuse' (The Piper — B. 4), are fine examples of his peculiar style.

Berghem's most accomplished pupil, Karel du Jardin, also etched a number of plates which, while free from false elegance, are inferior to those of his master and of Paul Potter. Du Jardin was very popular in his own time, not only at home, but in Italy, for which country he is said to have sailed under the pretence of seeing a friend off for Leghorn, and without the formality of bidding farewell to his family. His paintings and etchings are still highly esteemed, notwithstanding many harsh criticisms they have received.

Adrian Van de Velde, Philip Wouwerman, Marc de Bye, Jan Fyt, and Dirk Stoop also etched animals and landscapes with great success, and some of their works are exceedingly clever. Fyt is famous for his dogs, and Stoop for his horses. Jan Both and Jacob Ruysdael, eminent painters, also etched a number of charming landscapes, which are both picturesque and characteristic. Allart van Everdingen, "the Salvator Rosa of the North," loved to etch rocks and the wild and rugged aspects of nature, and many of his prints are highly interesting. His technic is equally characteristic with that of Ruysdael, and some of his prints are finished with a sort of work resembling mezzotint. A few of the etchings of Herman van Swanevelt are also esteemed, especially his 'Satyrs,' although most of his work is monotonous and uninteresting. There are some excellent prints by Jan Visscher, the younger brother of Cornelis Visscher, after Berghem, Ostade, Wouwerman, and other Dutch artists. He did not confine himself to etching, but finished many of his plates with the graver. His plate of 'Berghem's Ball' is an attractive example of these works.

Antoni Waterloo (c. 1618–77), one of the best-known landscape etchers of the Dutch school, loved to represent wild sylvan scenery; the lonely road through the forest, the solitary cottage by the wayside, the picturesque water-mill turned by the mountain stream, or the mighty forest with its "gloomy shades sequester'd deep;" such scenes as that into which Endymion loved to wander. The landscapes, canals, and wind-

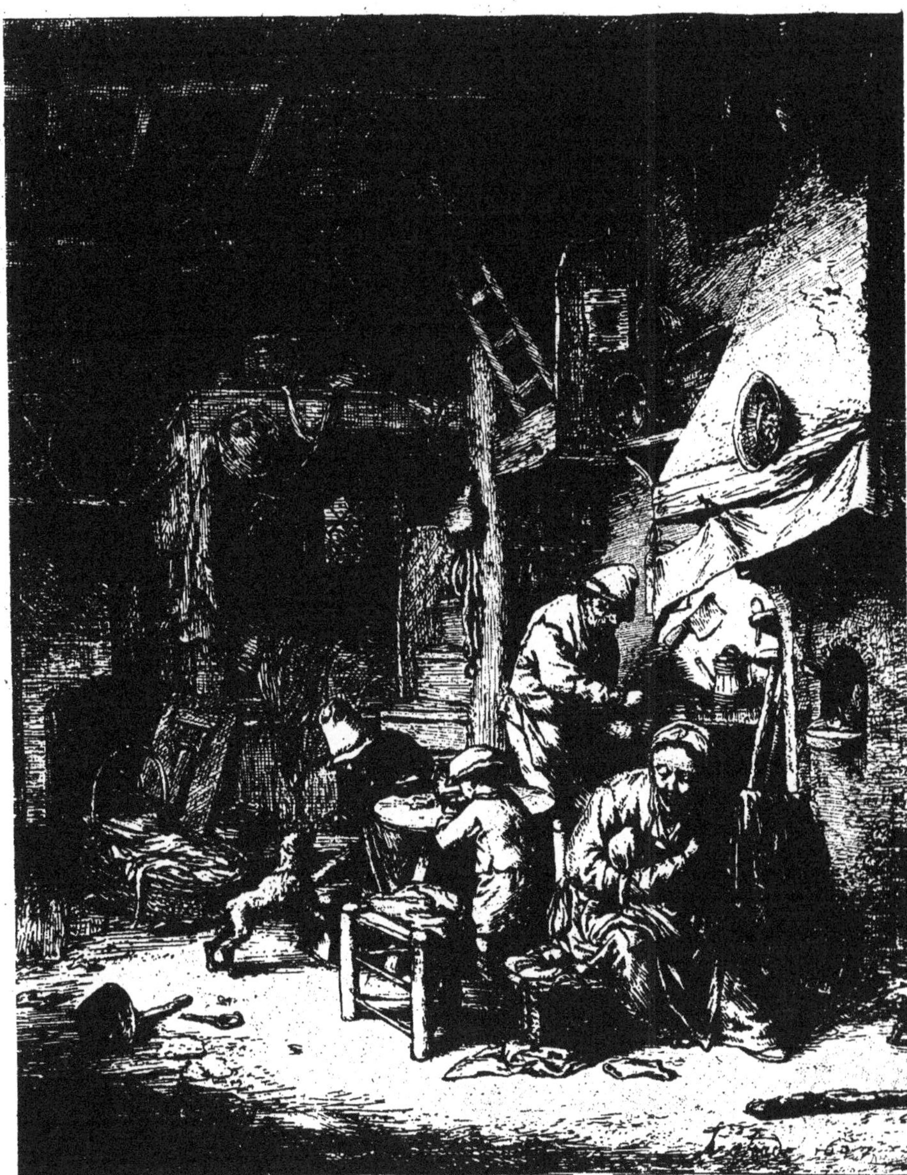

mills of his own country had no attraction for him. Although among the best landscape etchers of his time, he has been far surpassed by later artists.

Of the Dutch etchers who devoted themselves chiefly to marine subjects, Renier Nooms, called Zeeman, and Ludolf Bakhuisen were the most important. Zeeman was "par excellence the etcher of ships, as Potter was of horses." In his youth he was a sailor, as his name implies, and his love for the sea is everywhere apparent in his works. Zeeman expressed his accurate knowledge of shipping and marine subjects with great force and directness, as well as great simplicity and remarkable economy in the use of lines; his distances are expressed in a purely arbitrary manner, the foreground dark, and the receding distance becoming lighter and more delicate in successive planes.

Zeeman worked at Berlin, London, and Paris as well as at Amsterdam. He was in Paris about the middle of the seventeenth century, and painted a number of views of the city, among them his fine view of the Old Louvre. Some of these views, including this masterpiece, were etched by Méryon, who was greatly influenced by the works of the Dutch artist. Zeeman's etchings are numerous, and comprise Dutch landscapes with canals and boats, views of Amsterdam and Paris, and many subjects of shipping, seaports, and naval battles. Among the last are three scenes of the engagements which took place in 1673 between the fleets of the French, English, and Dutch. The flag of the Netherlands is triumphant.

Ludolf Bakhuisen, celebrated as a painter of sea-pieces and storm scenes, when more than seventy years of age turned his attention to etching, and produced some excellent marine subjects; his views on the Y are full of life and movement. He is said to have hired the fishermen to take him out in their boats in the most tempestuous weather, regardless of danger, in order to observe the waves dashing against the rocks and the boats driven before the gales. These scenes he afterwards represented with great fidelity. Bakhuisen is said to have been the instructor of Peter the Great at Saardam. Mr. Ruskin evidently includes him in his tirade against "the van-somethings and Back-somethings, more especially and malignantly those who have libelled the sea."

There were no other Dutch engravers belonging to the seventeenth century worthy of especial attention; and in the following century but a single engraver will be mentioned, Jacobus Houbraken, who was born at Dordrecht in the year 1698, and inherited both the taste and talent of his father Arnold Houbraken, painter and biographer of the Dutch and Flemish artists. Jacobus devoted careful study to the works of the Dutch and French engravers, especially Nanteuil, Edelinck, and the Drevets. His finest works are portraits of celebrated Dutchmen, although his portraits after Holbein, Van Dyck, Lely, Kneller, and others, engraved for Birch's *Heads of Illustrious Persons of Great Britain*, published at London in 1743-52, are now best known.

As the Flemish school of engravers founded by Rubens had rapidly degenerated into insignificance after that master's death, so in the Low Countries the art inaugurated by Lucas van Leyden, and continued with such renown by Goltzius, Visscher, and Rembrandt, and his contemporaries, met a like fate, for in the eighteenth century there was scarcely a Dutch engraver worthy of mention if we except Houbraken. The almost continuous wars which had devastated and impoverished Flanders and the Netherlands had driven many of their best artists to

France, where both painters and engravers were received with consideration, and by their works brought honor upon the country of their adoption. Soon after the middle of the seventeenth century engraving in France, under the royal patronage of Louis XIV., reached the zenith of its glory, and to that country we will now follow the art.

CHAPTER V

ENGRAVING IN FRANCE

French Artists of the Renaissance — Cousin, Duvet, Bernard Salomon — The School of Fontainebleau — Jacques Callot — Claude Lorraine — Portrait Engraving in France — Claude Mellan — Abraham Bosse, Sébastien Leclerc, Claudine Stella, Morin, Poilly, Pesne, Picart, and others — Engraving under Louis XIV. — Nanteuil — Edelinck — Masson — Gérard Audran — The Drevets — Age of Louis XV. — School of Watteau; Boucher and Cars — Illustration in France — School of Wille — Schmidt — Ficquet — The Nineteenth Century — Bervic — Desnoyers — Henriquel-Dupont — Gaillard, etc. — Revival of Etching

DURING the Middle Ages, the golden period of the calligraphers and illuminators, France possessed many clever architects, sculptors, miniaturists, and painters upon glass; but the national character of her school of painting did not appear until the sixteenth century. Jean Cousin, who was born about the beginning of the century, turned from his masterpieces of glass painting to canvas, and inaugurated the school which, under the influence of the masters of Fontainebleau and Simon Vouet, soon became Italianized. Wood-engraving in a rude form was practised in France probably as early as the middle of the fifteenth century; but almost the only known engravings of French origin printed from metal plates previous to the sixteenth century are a series of views copied from the wood-cuts in *Breydenbach's Travels*, printed at Mainz in 1486, and the illustrations in the *Books of Hours*.

Jean Duvet, sometimes called the "Master of the Unicorn," from his mark, was the earliest of the French engravers upon metal plates worthy of the name. Duvet was born at Langres in 1485, and was a goldsmith in the service of Francis I. and Henry II. His prints are somewhat heavy and Gothic in appearance, but are by no means devoid of merit. His series of twenty-four subjects from the 'Apocalypse' and 'The Martyrdom of St. Sebastian' are good examples.

Duvet's versatile contemporary Cousin was also an engraver upon metal, but is now best known through his designs for wood-cuts, some of which he is said to have engraved, and by his fine painting of 'The Last Judgment,' in the Louvre, engraved by Pieter De Jode the elder. Of his designs for wood-cuts, 'The Entry of Henry II. into Paris,' 1549, 'The Entry of Henry II. and Catherine de' Medici into Rouen,' 1551, and the designs for the Bible published in 1596 by Jean le Clerc, generally attributed to Cousin, are the most important. These, together with the illustrations to the Bible, and Ovid's *Metamorphoses* by his contemporary Bernard Salomon of Lyons, known as "*le petit Bernard*," an artist of the Franco-Italian school, are among the most characteristic examples of French wood-engraving in the sixteenth century; of the period preceding its decline and extinction as an art.

Under Charles VIII. and Louis XII. France received inspiration from Italy in all matters pertaining to art. Francis I. summoned Italian artists of the decadence to assist in the decoration of Fontainebleau, of whom Rosso and Primaticcio were the chief, and Catherine de' Medici, by birth a Florentine, was not only a patron of Italian art, but encouraged its imitation by her example. The engravings and book illustrations of the period reflect the popular taste, and are mainly extravagant imitations of the works of the Italian masters of Fontainebleau, abounding in emblems and allegories, and possessing a general air of exaggeration and false elegance.

Of the numerous engravers who reproduced the designs of these masters were Antoine Fantose, René Boivin, Léonard Thiry, Guido Ruggeri, and Etienne Delaune, who engraved with great exactness many of the designs of Rosso and Primaticcio, preserving to the world the beauties of originals, many of which have perished. Delaune was one of the most able and prolific engravers of the French Renaissance, and an eminent designer of goldsmith's work. His prints are mostly of small size, and are beautifully drawn and highly finished. Fantose is believed to have been the same Antonio da Trento who robbed his master Parmigiano and decamped.

Until the seventeenth century, however, French engraving had no essential character of its own like that of Italy, Germany, and the Netherlands, and there is no engraver worthy of particular attention until we come to Jacques Callot, who was born at Nancy, in Lorraine, in the year 1592. We are indebted to his biographer Meaume for most of our authentic information concerning Callot, a man of great industry and ability, who led an adventurous and romantic career, but a unique rather than great artist, and who, exceedingly popular in his own time, still has enthusiastic admirers.

Callot belonged to a noble family, and was intended by his father for the government service, but he preferred the artist's career, a choice which did not meet with the paternal approval. It is said that he ran away several times to Italy before he was sixteen years of age, once with a band of gypsies, whose wanderings he shared, but each time he was captured and sent home. During one of these visits he was for a time a pupil with Della-Bella in the atelier of the Florentine engraver Canta-Gallina. In 1608 he undertook his last journey to Italy, this time with the parental consent. At Rome he became a pupil

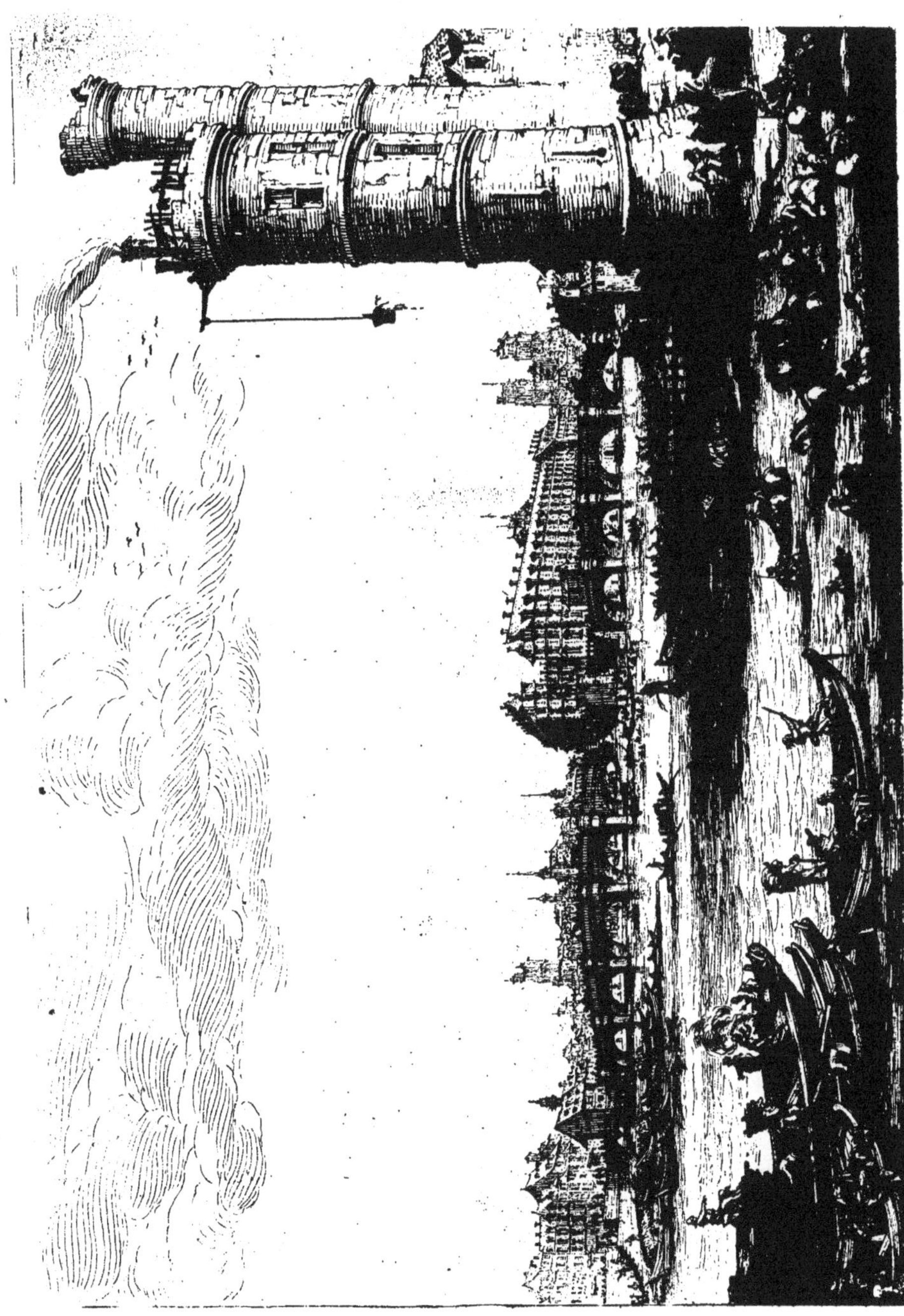

of the engraver Philippe Thomassin; going thence to Florence, he entered the service of Cosmo de' Medici, mingling in the fêtes and gaieties, and renewing his intimacy with his former master; but about the year 1622 he returned to Nancy, to enter the service of the Duke of Lorraine. Here he applied himself diligently to art, and soon gained a wide reputation. His abilities were so highly esteemed that he was called to Brussels, by a royal commission, to design and engrave 'The Siege of Breda,' and was subsequently summoned to Paris by Cardinal Richelieu to represent in a similar way 'The Siege of La Rochelle' and 'The Attack of the Fortress of Saint-Martin.' During this period he also engraved his celebrated views of Old Paris; but by the year 1633 he was again in his native town, and witnessed its siege and capitulation. It is related that the French king requested him to engrave a plate to commemorate this victory, as he had others, but that he declined to use his talents in the humiliation of his own country. Callot determined to return to Florence; but in 1635 he died at Nancy, in his forty-fourth year. He is described as pleasing in appearance, of engaging manners, and a favorite wherever he went. His portrait was painted by Van Dyck, and engraved by Vorsterman.

During the period of Callot's residence in Italy art was in its decadence; affectation and frivolity prevailed, and it is not surprising that his personal eccentricities should have been reflected in abundant measure in his works. He gave free play to his fancy, and his grotesque humor and satire, and his wonderful facility and ready invention, brought him into great popularity. The faults of his work are obvious, and the same may be said of its merits. His excessive mannerism and grotesque invention are everywhere apparent. He cared little for correctness of drawing or proportion, or for unity of composition, and his technic is generally an erratic combination of etching and burin work, often ragged and showing undue haste; but when he chose, he could handle the needle in a masterly manner. The charm of his work consists in his marvellous grasp of the details of a scene, the wonderful variety and lifelike arrangement and grouping of his multitudes of figures, and the touch of life and humor which characterizes them, and in his picturesque rendering of architecture. His prints are of great historical interest, illustrating many features of the reign of Louis XIII. In spite of their shortcomings, many of them possess an irresistible charm and attraction.

Callot's prints, single and in sets, number more than 1400, comprising all sorts of subjects and figure compositions, portraits, costumes, book illustrations, architectural pieces, and landscapes. To the examples already named may be added the series of spirited prints published under the title 'Les Misères et les Malheurs de la Guerre;' 'The Great Fair at Florence,' engraved at Florence in 1620; the 'View of the Old Louvre with the Tour de Nesle,' and its companion, the 'Pont Neuf,' works of great beauty and historical value; 'The Punishments;' the 'Temptation of St. Anthony,' dated 1635, probably his last, and certainly his most fantastic and eccentric work; and the portrait of his artist friend at Nancy, Claude Deruet.

Contemporary with Callot was another artist of Lorraine, of far greater importance, whose influence upon the engraver's art may be compared with that of Raphael and Rubens. Claude Gellée, generally known as Claude Lorraine, was born in the year 1600, in the village of Chamagne, on the Moselle. Our information concerning his life throughout is meager and uncertain. According to his biographer Sandrart, his parents, who were poor, apprenticed him as assistant to a pastry-cook, while the account of the Florentine painter Baldinucci recites that he assisted his brother, a wood-engraver, who taught him the elements of drawing. Both agree, however, that at about the age of fourteen Claude left his native country and went to Rome, where he lived in the house of the landscape and marine painter Tassi, in the capacity of groom, valet, color-grinder, and assistant, and that he became a diligent student of art; it is sometimes asserted that he also pursued his art studies at Naples.

In the year 1625 Claude set out upon a pilgrimage, going to Venice and into Bavaria, and arriving at his native place a year later, whence he proceeded to Nancy, and assisted Deruet, then court-painter to the Duke of Lorraine, upon the decorations of the Carmelite Church at that place. But the attractions of Rome were too strong for him to be contented with life in a provincial town like Nancy; and in 1627 he set out once more for the Eternal City, where, after a serious illness on the way, and after being robbed of all his money, and narrowly escaping death by shipwreck, he arrived in the same year.

After a time we find Claude established near the Church of Santissima Trinità de' Monti, a favorite resort with artists and authors, commanding one of the grandest views in Rome. Nicholas Poussin, the greatest of the French painters, and later Salvator Rosa lived near him, both exceedingly popular, and having large followings, yet neither history nor tradition connects the name of Claude with either of these artists, a silence incomprehensible whether we regard them as friends or rivals. The only artist among the multitude then in Rome with whom Claude seems to have been on terms of intimacy was the German painter and art critic Joachim von Sandrart, whose 'Academia Artis Pictoriæ,' published in 1683, contains a biography of our artist.

Claude possessed a modest, sensitive nature, and was a dreamer by disposition. He seems to have led an isolated life, free from the contentions and jealousies of his contemporary artists, working much in the open air, and making many excursions into the Campagna and surrounding country, often accompanied by his friend Sandrart. Very little, indeed, is known of the details of Claude's life during his residence in Rome, except that his paintings acquired great reputation, and were eagerly contended for by sovereigns and ambassadors, as well as by private purchasers, Cardinal Bentivoglio and Urban VIII. being among his patrons; we may judge of his diligence by the four hundred pictures which he left.

The great esteem in which Claude's paintings were held led to many imitations and plagiarisms; and to his desire to preserve an exact record of his work we owe the famous *Liber Veritatis*. He made drawings in bistre and white of his paintings as they left his easel; these he often inscribed with the date, the name of the person for whom the picture was painted, its destination, and such other particulars of the transaction as he thought worthy of preservation. The precious volume containing about two hundred of these drawings found its way into the library at Chatsworth, and is well known through the mezzotint engravings of Earlom. These sketches were intended, as their name implies, only as pictorial records for future reference, and are not finished drawings, or of any great artistic importance.

Claude is claimed by the French, as his native province, Lorraine, was added to the French possessions during his lifetime; but his entire art education and training were Italian, and many of his landscapes were taken from scenery in the neighborhood of Rome, idealized and changed to suit the requirements of his art. He was inspired by nature in her softer moods, and had no sympathy with the cold, impressive solitudes, the rugged landscapes, and turbulent billows of the Dutch artists. He loved the land of sunshine, with its peaceful bays and havens, and his Arcadian scenes are enriched with picturesque ruins of ancient temples and classic buildings, monuments to the glory of a by-gone age. The figures in these scenes are always subordinate, for, although Claude devoted much study to figures, he was never able to draw them with correctness; and appreciating his own shortcomings in this direction, stated that he "sold his landscapes, but gave away his figures." In many of his pictures the figures were painted by other artists. The applause bestowed upon his works induced a multitude of artists to imitate his style and choice of subjects, which are so eminently characteristic as to be generally unmistakable. His most formidable rival in modern times, J. M. W. Turner, bequeathed to the National Gallery two landscapes of his own, in the style of Claude, with the condition that they should be hung between the famous pictures painted by Claude for his patron the Duc de Bouillon.

Claude also etched about thirty-two plates of similar scenes, besides a series representing the fireworks exhibited at Rome in 1637 upon the election of Ferdinand III. of Austria as King of the Romans. Of these etchings, most of which were executed between the years 1630 and 1640, although a few probably as late as 1663, that known as 'Le Bouvier,' dated 1636, is a most perfect type of landscape etching in tenderness of handling, transparency and soft effects of light, and delicate gradations of distance. A herdsman, seated in the foreground, is playing upon a pipe; his cattle are crossing a pool towards the ruins of a building which is embedded in trees of the most magnificent foliage; far away lie the hills, wrapped in the soft haze of a summer afternoon. Of Claude's other etchings, 'The Sunset' (a seaport), 'The Village Dance,' 'The Brigands,' 'The Campo Vaccino at Rome,' the 'Herd of Cattle at the Watering Place,' and 'The Dance under the Trees' are the most important examples.

Claude's influence upon landscape engraving was accomplished rather through his paintings than through his etchings. The engravers who interpreted his paintings were compelled to devote careful study to atmospheric effects and transparency, delicate distinctions and values, aerial perspective, and the varying conditions of light and shade. The best engravings after Claude were produced in England in the latter part of the eighteenth century, and among many beautiful examples the 'Roman Edifices in Ruins,' engraved by Woollett, is generally accorded the first place. Claude died in the year 1682, and was buried in the Church of Santissima Trinità de' Monti, near the scene of his labors; but in 1840 his remains were transferred to the Church of San Luigi, near the Roman Pantheon, where a memorial bears record of the esteem of his countrymen.

One other artist of Lorraine, a native of Nancy, must be mentioned, Israel Silvestre, who imitated the style of Callot and Della-Bella, and left many remarkable views of landscapes, buildings, and ruins of France and Italy, among them a set of Paris views; his works are chiefly valuable as preserving records of monuments since destroyed.

We leave the characteristic artists of Lorraine to come to the great portrait engravers, whose works are the glory of the

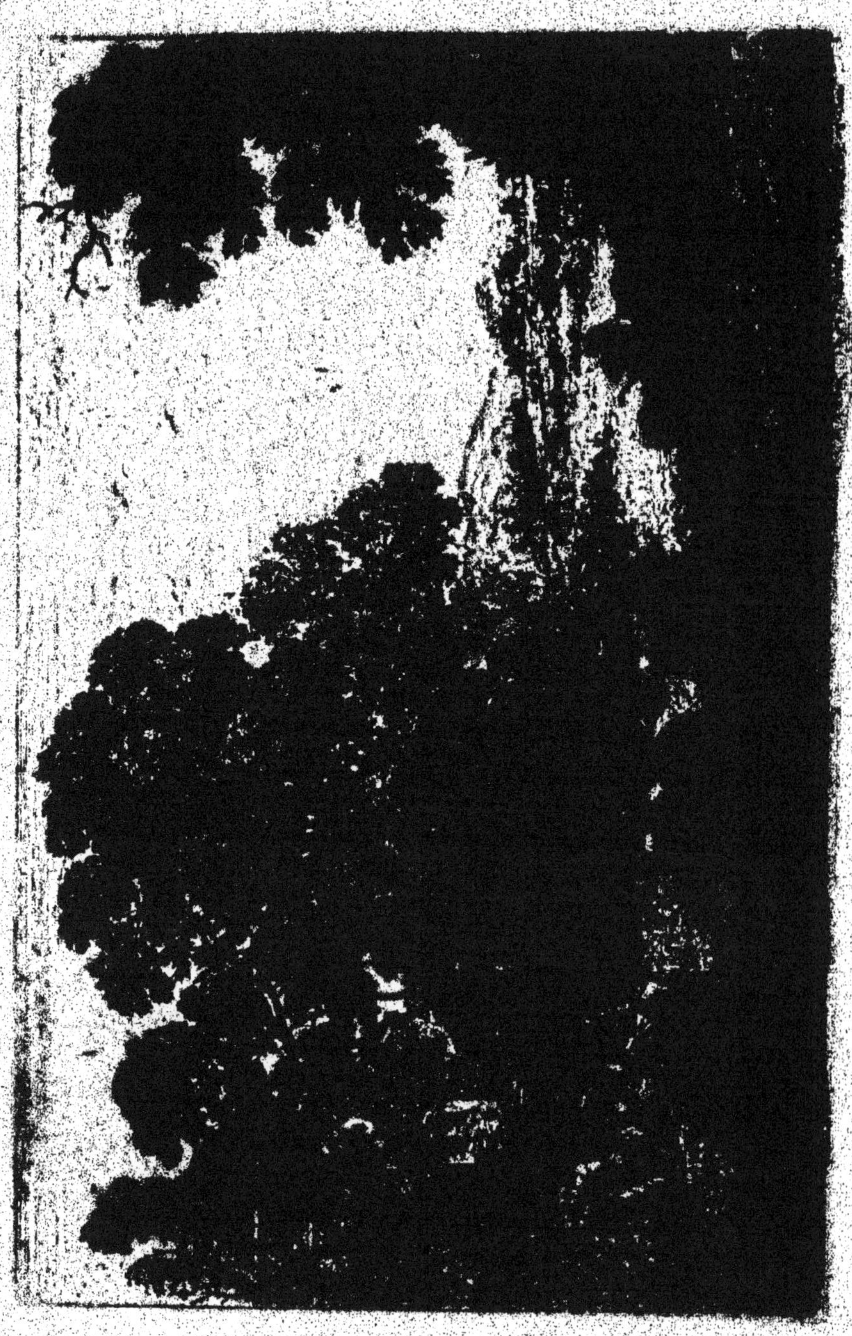

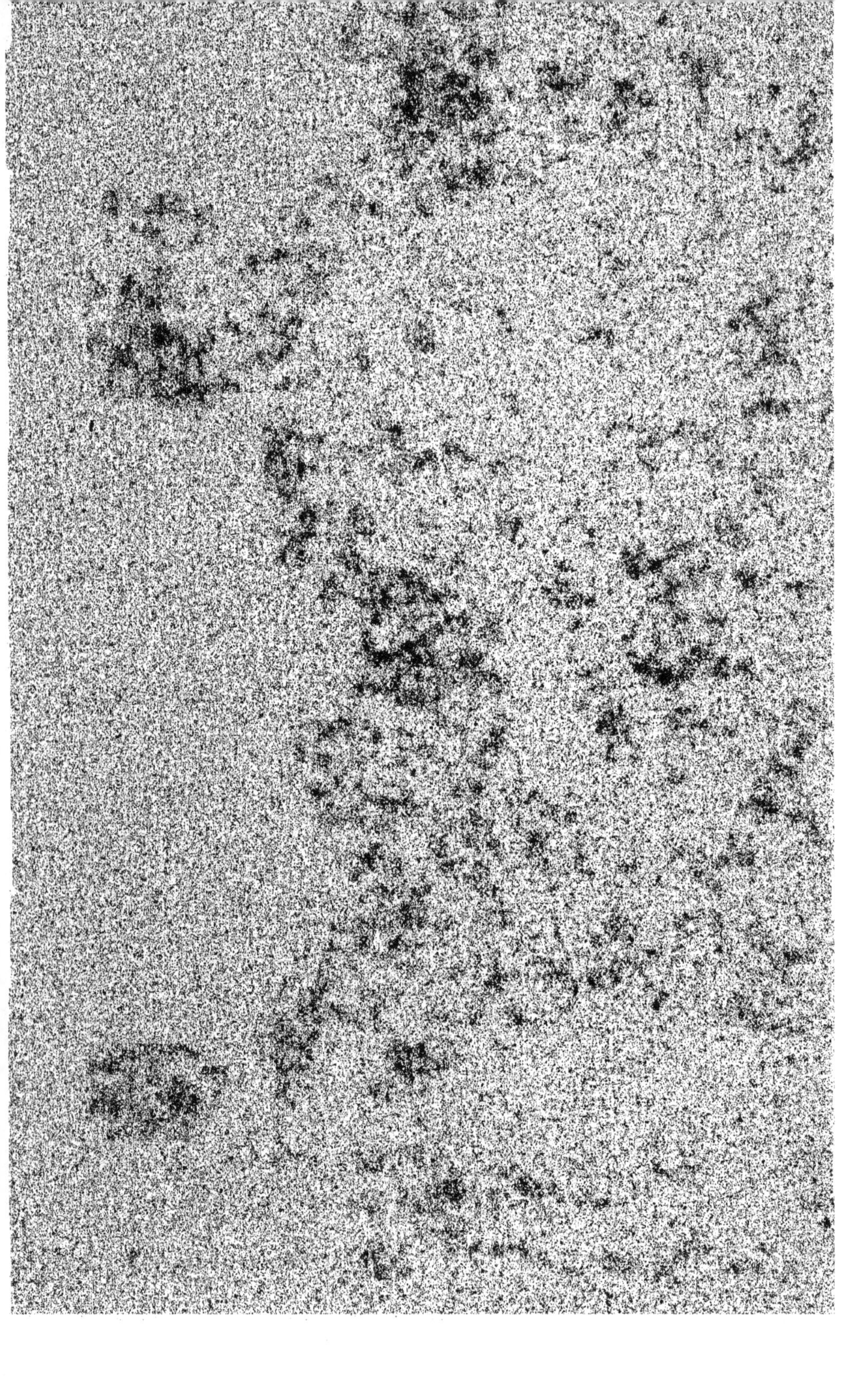

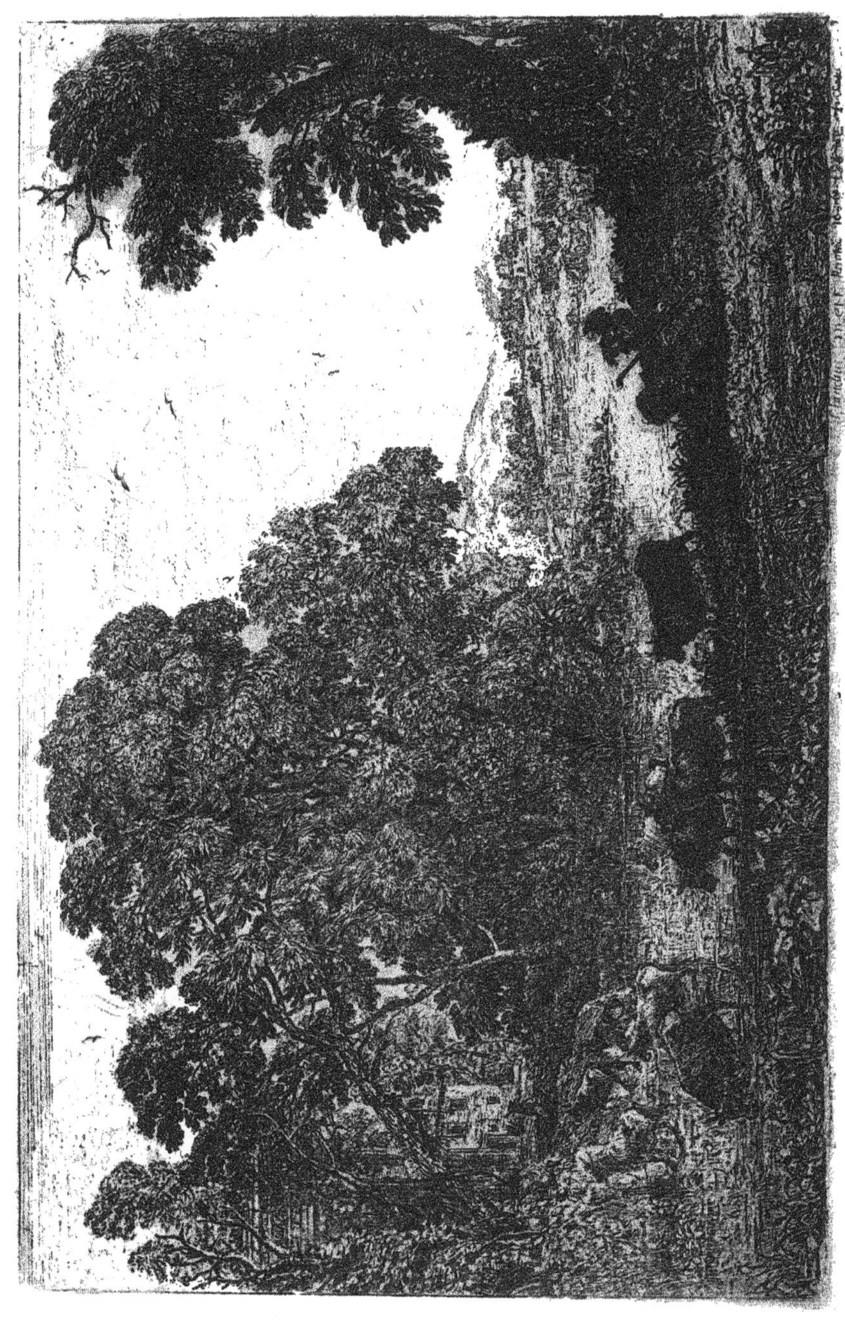

French school. As the engravers of Italy, Germany, Flanders, and the Low Countries had their peculiar excellences, so those of France surpassed all others in the number and excellence of their engraved portraits. The first to appear was Claude Mellan (1598–1688), who in his own time achieved such celebrity that his name appears among the illustrious sons of France in the famous volumes of Charles Perrault, *Les Hommes Illustres*, etc. (published 1696–1701), to the illustration of which many of the foremost engravers of the time contributed their talents. After studying in Paris, Mellan went to Rome, where he engraved in the ordinary manner of the time, crossing and recrossing his lines to produce the required shadings and effects, but upon his return to Paris he adopted a peculiar style, employing single parallel lines without crossing, varying the thickness of the lines to produce the necessary gradations and shadows; a manner more novel than artistic.

Mellan engraved numerous portraits of eminent persons, and a great variety of subjects, besides many plates from ancient and contemporary busts and marbles, and title-pages and illustrations for books. His most celebrated print, the 'Sudarium of St. Veronica,' a subject often represented by early artists, is engraved by a single spiral line begun at the extremity of the nose and continued over the whole plate, the effects being brought out by the varying thickness of the line. Mellan's print was highly praised in his own time, and he is said to have taken to himself great credit in its performance, but it is now regarded only as one of the curiosities of engraving. Mellan also engraved a fine plate after Tintoretto of 'Rachel meeting Jacob at the Well,' and there is a highly esteemed print of 'St. Peter Nolasque' borne by two angels. Of his portraits those of Cardinal Bentivoglio Peiresc, and Urban VIII. are fine examples.

Thomas DeLeu, who flourished in France 1560–1612, Abraham Bosse (1602–76), Cornelis Bloemaert (1603–80), Jean Morin (1609–66), François de Poilly the elder (1622–93), Jean Pesne (1623–1700), Claudine Stella (1636–97), Sébastien Leclerc (1637–1714), and Bernard Picart (1673–1733) were among the foremost engravers of their time, and deserve more attention than the limits of this work will permit. Morin engraved with a difficult and peculiar, although pleasing, combination of strokes and dots, in imitation, it is believed, of Van Dyck's manner. His portraits of Cardinal Bentivoglio, after Van Dyck, and the abbé Richelieu and the printer Antoine Vitré, after Philippe de Champaigne, are justly celebrated. Poilly and Picart belonged to eminent families of engravers highly esteemed in their own time. Picart, like Goltzius, had an exalted opinion of his powers, and engraved a series of seventy-eight prints, in which he imitated the styles of the old engravers. These were published after his death in the volume known as *Les Impostures Innocentes*. Picart and Leclerc also designed charming frontispieces and vignettes for books. Abraham Bosse, besides being a designer and engraver of ability, was also the author of a number of important and interesting works upon art, among them a treatise upon engraving, one of the earliest published in France, *Traité des manières de graver en taille-douce*, etc., first published in 1645. Bosse was the author of many interesting prints showing the various costumes worn in his time. He is also famous for his graceful vignettes, ornaments, and illustrations for books. He engraved a number of curious prints showing the interiors of the bookseller's shops of the Palace, the studios of copper-plate engravers, interiors of printing offices, etc. His works, like those of Callot, illustrate historical features of the reign of Louis XIII. Jean Pesne excelled as the interpreter of Poussin. He engraved two fine portraits of that master, besides many of his finest subjects, among them the 'Testament of Eudamidas' and the 'Entombment.' Claudine Bouzonnet, called Claudine Stella, one of the most famous female engravers, also excelled in her engravings after Poussin. Her print of 'Moses striking the Rock' is a fine example of her skill. Of the multitude of engravers who interpreted the works of Poussin, the chief were Pesne, Gérard Audran, and Claudine Stella.

While the works of the early schools show the gradual development, and the successive stages of advancement of the engraver's art from rudeness towards perfection, we now come to the age of Louis XIV., when all the resources and qualities of the various schools were first combined.

The France of Louis XIV. was especially favorable to literature and the arts. When Louis ascended the throne the literary glory of France was fast approaching its zenith. In no other country could be found such a brilliant array of orators, dramatists, moralists, and philosophers as Bossuet, Fénélon Corneille, La Rochefoucauld, La Bruyère, Pascal, Descartes, and their contemporaries; and notwithstanding the frivolous tendencies of the age, we find the names of Molière, Racine, Boileau, and La Fontaine also shedding lustre on the reign of Louis, and the arts encouraged as never before or since. The King gathered around him the brilliant society so graphically described by Madame de Sévigné, embodying in himself the tastes and opinions of the age, raising a false Olympus whose object of worship was himself. His minister Colbert and his painter Le Brun shared his enthusiasm, and to their untiring efforts was due much of the brilliancy of the "grand reign." Colbert founded for Louis the Institute and various academies of art, architecture, and music in different towns, reorganized the Academy of Painting and Sculpture, encouraged literature, pensioned eminent writers, both French and foreign, and induced many foreigners of genius to settle in France. The famous establishment which that eminent family of dyers, the Gobelins, had founded in the fifteenth century in the Faubourg St. Marcel, and to which in the following century was added the world-renowned manufactory of tapestry, Colbert purchased for Louis, who transformed it into a royal manufactory of tapestry, upholstery, and furniture, and placed it under the superintendence of the royal painter Le Brun. To this establishment was afterwards added a school for the cultivation of engraving, which, by the edict of 1660, Louis had decreed a "liberal art," according to its professors the privileges possessed by other artists. In this school Sébastien Leclerc was a professor, and such masters as Nanteuil, Edelinck, and Gérard Audran supervised the works of pupils and beginners. It is not surprising that great results should have flowed from such encouragement as this.

The great body of French artists withdrew their allegiance from Italy and hastened to assume their places in the grand era inaugurated by Louis. The influence of the court at Versailles soon became everywhere apparent in the art, literature, language, manners, and dress of the period; everything was elaborate and picturesque, dedicated to effect and display. The popular tendencies and ideals of the age are typified in the palaces built by Mansard and profusely decorated with the creations of Le Brun, and in the gardens laid out in stiff designs by Le Nôtre. The art of the period was often meretricious, abounding in theatrical grandeur and bombast, although by no means devoid of dignity and originality. It found its type in the paintings of the popular artists Le Brun and Hyacinthe Rigaud, in stupendous allegories, and in portraits with gorgeous accessories. Never was such ingenuity displayed in designing and arranging complicated folds of drapery and costume, and never were the accessories multiplied to so extravagant an extent, "bringing down on their school the censure of frippery and flutter;" but Sartor Resartus was yet to appear, and art merely reflected the popular tendencies of the age, rendering homage to the King instead of to nature.

Notwithstanding the splendor of accessories and embellishments in these portraits, they were subordinated to the features which are full of life and spirit. Never in the history of engraving have portraits of such a high, uniform standard of excellence been produced, nor has the technic of engraving ever been carried to greater perfection. The reign of Louis has been called the classic age of portrait engraving, as it was the Augustan age of French literature, and although many of the most skilful engravers of this period delighted in mechanical difficulties, and revelled in the sheen of metals, the lustre of silks, brocades, laces, ermine, and in all manner of gorgeous backgrounds and surroundings, yet they were not merely ingenious artisans, clever in the manipulation of the graver, but consummate artists and men of great genius, many of whom are forever associated through art with their immortal contemporaries. There were a few engravers, as well as painters and authors, who rose above the general tendency towards extravagance and display, and whose works are models of moderation and good taste. There were few men of consequence belonging to this period whose portraits were not engraved in a masterly manner, nor are the instances few of men, important in their own time, whose very names would long ago have been forgotten had not the engraver's skill perpetuated them with his own fame.

Robert Nanteuil, the most eminent of the French portrait engravers, was born at Rheims about the year 1623. To a natural inclination for art was added a classical education and refinement of taste which enabled him to resist the popular tendency towards elaboration, and his portraits are almost wholly free from the meretricious ornament which overloads most of the works of this period. Although intended for the law, while still a student he devoted much attention to drawing and engraving, rather as an amusement than as a serious occupation, and with little thought of the brilliant career in art which awaited him. Owing to a variety of occurrences, among them the ruin of his family and a scandal in which he had become involved, he abandoned the law for engraving, and set out for Paris in 1647, where he arrived unknown and without means. Curious stories are told of his methods of obtaining work at this time. It is related that he once took one of his crayon portraits to a wine-shop where some divinity students were assembled, and asked their assistance in identifying his sitter, who, he pretended, was one of their number, whose name and address he had forgotten. Although naturally unsuccessful in recognizing the original, they were attracted by his work, and prices, and gave him a number of orders. He applied himself diligently to his work, gained influential friends and patrons, and pursued his studies meanwhile under the eminent painter Philippe de Champaigne. At last his reputation attracted the attention of Louis XIV., who gave him a number of sittings for a portrait, and appointed him designer and engraver to the royal cabinet, with a pension. His future assured, he sent to Rheims for his wife, a sister of his early instructor, Nicholas Regnesson, and established himself permanently in Paris. He soon became a success in social circles, and one of the set which gathered about Mlle. de Scudéry, famous for her interminable romances; but although diligent and severely exact in the practice of his art, he seems to have immediately squandered in dissipation the large sums which he received for his work, and at his death, in 1678, left scanty provision for his widow.

In his early portraits Nanteuil followed the style of Claude Mellan, engraving in single parallel lines without crossing; but he soon abandoned this unreasonable manner, and through his own genius worked out a style of his own, which for beauty and distinctness has never been excelled. Nanteuil's engraved portraits number nearly two hundred and twenty, most of which are represented in an oval about 7 × 9 inches, although there are upwards of thirty of life size. These are mostly from his own drawings, and represent many notable persons of the reign of Louis XIV. Although in a few individual instances others may have surpassed him, no other engraver has ever produced so large a number of portraits of such high and uniform excellence. His portraits combine great clearness and individuality with a softness and beauty altogether remarkable, and were printed upon paper of such excellent quality that most of the impressions which have been properly cared for are in about the same condition as when printed more than two hundred years ago.

As examples of Nanteuil's earlier portraits, engraved in the style of Claude Mellan, may be mentioned that of the abbé Molé and a portrait of Cardinal Mazarin. His best manner is shown in the portraits of Pompone de Bellièvre, after Le Brun, Colbert, Servien, Anne of Austria, Le Tellier, Loret, Gilles Boileau, Turenne, Le Vayer, Steenberghen, Cardinal Bouillon, several portraits of Cardinal Mazarin, and about a dozen portraits of Louis XIV. There is also a portrait of John Evelyn, who, under date June 13, 1650, wrote, "I sate to the famous sculptor Nanteuil, who was afterwards made a knight by the French king for his art. He engrav'd my picture in copper. At a future time he presented me with my own picture, done all with the pen; an extraordinary curiosity." There is also a fine large print of 'Moses holding the Tables of the Law,' after Philippe de Champaigne, which, being unfinished on Nanteuil's death, was completed by Edelinck, the latter engraving the face and hands.

Of Nanteuil's numerous portraits, there is none more attractive or beautiful than that of Pompone de Bellièvre, engraved about the year 1657. Mr. Sumner, whose essay on the 'Best Portraits in Engraving' has given great impulse to the study and collection of prints in this country, mentions this as a singular instance of a man esteemed great in his own time, whose many virtues, and even whose very name would long ago have been consigned to an undeserved oblivion but for an engraved portrait. Of ancient and illustrious family, Pompone was himself a magistrate of high rank, the first president of the Parliament of Paris, and an eminent philanthropist, who endowed a great hospital with wealth. He is described as a model of manly virtues, generous, just, and incorruptible, the embodiment of all that was knightly and gentle. Nanteuil's portrait, engraved in the year of Pompone's death, like the narrative of the Loyal Servant, rescues from oblivion "the memory of a good knight almost buried beneath the ingratitude of years."

Nanteuil's pupil, Pieter van Schuppen (1623–1702), Flemish by birth, followed his master's style, and engraved both subjects and portraits; among the latter are some of the portraits in Perrault's *Illustrious Men.* He is known as "*le petit Nanteuil*," and some of his works possess considerable merit.

Although for the number and excellence of his engraved portraits Nanteuil stands at the head of all portrait engravers, yet in a few individual instances, and in particular qualities, he has been surpassed by other engravers. Among those who in this way excelled him was Gérard Edelinck, who was born at Antwerp in 1640, and was one of the numerous artists attracted to France during the reign of Louis XIV. Edelinck at first followed the picturesque manner of the Rubens engravers, but after his arrival in Paris his style was greatly improved and refined by the influence of Nanteuil and Poilly. He was taken into the King's service, given a pension and a studio at the Gobelins, naturalized, made a knight of the Order of St. Michael, elected a member of the council of the Academy, and appointed "Premier Dessinateur du Cabinet." He passed the remainder of his life in Paris, where he died in 1707. He survived Nanteuil, Audran, Masson, Poilly, and Pesne, and was almost the last of the great engravers whom Colbert had assembled at the Gobelins. Edelinck's character contrasts strongly with that of his companion Nanteuil. Instead of following the gay life of his associate, he preferred seclusion and practised economy, and left at his death a considerable fortune. It is said that his highest aspiration was to become churchwarden of his parish—a gratified ambition. Edelinck engraved about three hundred and thirty-nine prints, executed wholly with the graver; of these about two hundred are portraits.

The admirers of Edelinck have proclaimed him the king of engravers, claiming for him the perfection of every quality which goes to make a great engraver. Of his numerous portraits, that of Philippe de Champaigne, from that painter's portrait of himself, is one of the masterpieces of the art; indeed, in general excellence, it is often placed at the head of all engraved portraits. This high standard, however, is not maintained, and it must be acknowledged that, aside from a few masterpieces, his portraits do not possess the charm or interest of those of Nanteuil. Edelinck's works are characterized by vigor, force of expression, and remarkable effects of chiaroscuro. To these qualities Nanteuil did not aspire, but endowed his works with a surpassing softness and beauty, avoiding a certain hardness or metallic quality which pervades some of the works of Edelinck.

Other important portraits engraved by Edelinck are those of Colbert, Bogaert, Mansard, and Mouton, respectively minister, sculptor, architect, and musician to Louis XIV.; the painters Le Brun and Hyacinthe Rigaud, La Fontaine, Pascal, Dilgerus, Madame Helyot, called "La belle Religieuse;" numerous portraits of King Louis, and some of the best portraits in Perrault's *Illustrious Men*, including the equestrian statue of Louis which appears as the frontispiece to that work. Edelinck also engraved with great success numerous subjects after Raphael, Leonardo da Vinci, Guido Reni, Carlo Maratti, and various other Italian masters. Of these the 'Holy Family,' after Raphael, and the 'Battle for the Standard,' from Rubens' drawing from Leonardo's famous cartoon, are fine examples. There are also a number of excellent subjects, chiefly historical, after Le Brun, among them the last of the 'Battles of Alexander,' which completed the series undertaken by Gérard Audran. Another fine print of large size, 'Alexander entering the Tent of Darius,' after Mignard, which remained unfinished at the time of Edelinck's death, was completed by Pierre Drevet.

A worthy companion of Nanteuil and Edelinck was Antoine Masson, who was born at Louri, near Orleans, in 1636, but passed most of his life in Paris, where he died in the year 1700. Although inferior to his great contemporaries as an artist, in point of technical ability he was but little, if indeed any, below them. Masson was educated as an armorer, and his earliest work with the graver consisted in ornamenting gun-barrels and metal plates. When he turned from this harder metal to copper, he is said to have "played with his tool as with a pencil." He handled the graver with firmness and precision, and yet with a delicacy which is amazing. But this facility sometimes induced him to make an undue display of mere mechanical proficiency. The large portrait of Henri de Lorraine, Comte d'Harcourt, called 'le Cadet à la perle,' from the pearl in the ear, exhibits to perfection Masson's wonderful skill in representing the hard, shiny surfaces of metals, with their peculiar qualities, sheen, and reflections, and the texture of silks, laces, brocades, feathers, and a multitude of other substances and accessories. For the surpassing quality and harmony of such representation this portrait, after Mignard's overloaded painting, ranks among the foremost in the art. Masson's undoubted masterpiece, however, from an artistic as well as technical stand-point, is his beautiful portrait of the Queen's secretary, Brisacier, called the 'Gray-haired Man,' a masterpiece of engraving, and a worthy companion to Nanteuil's 'Pompone' and Edelinck's 'Philippe de Champaigne.' This portrait is as soft and tender as that of Harcourt is vigorous and metallic, and the remarkable representation of the hair has long been a model for other engravers. It was followed by Longhi in his portrait of Washington. This portrait of Brisacier, and the rare and almost equally fine portraits of Gaspar Charrier, Oliver d'Ormesson, and Maria de Lorraine, Duchesse de Guise, exhibit Masson as the artist apart from his mere caprices and exhibitions of manual skill, and without the meretricious ornamentation which characterizes the portrait of Harcourt. Masson also engraved a number of life-size heads, of which the portrait of Louis XIV. is a good example; but his large portraits are inferior both in interest and merit to those of Nanteuil. Of his subjects, the 'Supper at Emmaus,' after Titian, sometimes called 'Masson's Table-cloth,' is a masterpiece of great merit, and but little below this is his engraving of the 'Assumption of the Virgin,' after Rubens. Judged by the masterpieces named, the works of Masson are certainly worthy of the high estimation in which they are held. But his attainments were rather of a technical than intellectual character; he had not the advantage of a thorough art education like Nanteuil, whose great natural genius and taste had been refined by education and study of classic art, and who was seldom led away from his high ideals by the florid art of the period with which he was everywhere surrounded.

Contemporary with Nanteuil, Edelinck, and Masson was Gérard Audran, who belonged to a Lyons family famous in the history of engraving. Of this family, which numbered nearly a dozen engravers, Gérard was the most important. While the French boast of their great portrait engravers, they reserve their unlimited eulogy for Gérard Audran, whom they worship as a second Marc Antonio, attributing to him every great quality which an interpreter of the creations of others can possess: the drawing of the great Italian, the vigor and expression of Visscher, the technical skill of Edelinck, and the chiaroscuro of the Flemish engravers, together with unerring taste and striking originality of methods. He engraved chiefly from the works of the French painters, and was the especial interpreter of Le Brun, as Pesne was of Poussin. Some of his works after Raphael lead us to wish that he had devoted more attention to that master—at least, to a purer type of art than the works of Le Brun and Mignard, although under the magic of his burin many of the defects of his originals disappeared.

Gérard Audran was born at Lyons in 1640, the year of Edelinck's birth. He learned the rudiments of his art from his father and uncle, both engravers of great ability, continued his studies at Paris under the royal painter Le Brun, and also studied in Rome, it is said, under Carlo Maratti. While at Rome he engraved a portrait of Pope Clement IX. which gained for him such reputation that Louis XIV., ever jealous of the absenteeism of his countrymen of genius, recalled him to Paris, and appointed him royal engraver, with a pension and apartments at the Gobelins. Here (1672–78) he engraved his superb masterpieces of historical engraving, the 'Battles of Alexander,' from the paintings by Le Brun, then just completed, and now in the Louvre, his prints consisting of thirteen large sheets making four subjects, viz.: 'The Passage of the Granicus,' 'The Defeat of Darius at Arbela,' 'Porus brought before Alexander after his Defeat,' and 'The Triumphal Entry of Alexander into Babylon.' To this series was afterwards added a fifth, engraved by Edelinck, whom Audran is said to have recommended to the painter Le Brun, known as 'The Family of Darius.' These magnificent prints were published at the expense of the King, who presented many of the choicest impressions to sovereigns and ambassadors of other countries. Gérard Audran also engraved after Le Brun five sheets from the paintings on the ceiling of the chapel at the royal chàteau at Sceaux, destroyed during the Revolution, and after Poussin a fine plate of the beautiful 'Triomphe de la Verité' and 'St. John baptizing the Pharisees in the Jordan.' There are also many other beautiful pieces after Raphael, Poussin, Mignard, Le Brun, and others.

Gérard Audran was one of the most skilful draughtsmen of the French school, and his works are characterized by good taste, truth, sentiment, and originality, as well as by great technical skill and remarkable effects of chiaroscuro. He combined with the greatest success the work of the burin and needle in a broad, original style especially suited to his subjects. In his battle-pieces he improved upon his originals in many respects, and in his own time acquired a reputation greater than that of either Nanteuil or Edelinck. It was his intention to embody in a treatise upon his art the results of his experience and observation, but his death, in 1703, prevented its fulfilment. Certainly no engraver has been better qualified to transmit to us the traditions of the early schools, writing from a time when the qualities of all were first united—from the golden period of his art.

To the encouragement which Louis XIV. gave to the engraver's art we owe many of our great collections of ancient and modern engravings. During his reign that eccentric and indefatigable collector, the abbé de Marolles, formed the extensive collection of fine and curious prints which Colbert purchased for the King, and which forms the basis of the great collection in the Bibliothèque Nationale at Paris.

Towards the close of the reign of Louis XIV. Hyacinthe Rigaud, the French Van Dyck, had become firmly established as the fashionable portrait-painter of royalty and the nobility. Although in most respects a representative of the preceding age, his career extended far into the reign of Louis XV. He painted the portraits of no less than five kings, besides a varied array of princes, ministers, ambassadors, prelates, authors, artists, and other distinguished persons. He generally represented his figures at full length, with gorgeous surroundings, and endowed with an air of grandeur which must have been extremely gratifying to the vanity of his patrons. His famous portraits in the Louvre, the eloquent Bossuet, his masterpiece, and Louis XIV., made famous by Thackeray, are striking examples of his skill. His portraits with their superabundance of accessories had been successfully rendered by the engravings of Edelinck, but it remained for the Drevets to give to the world the most astonishing examples of technical skill in rendering and harmonizing these marvels of complicated arrangement and textures.

The famous family of Drevet consisted of Pierre, his son Pierre Imbert, and nephew Claude. Pierre Drevet (1663–1738), at first a pupil of Germain Audran at Lyons, removed to Paris, where he received instruction from Gérard Audran, and rose rapidly into prominence; he received the appointment of court engraver in 1696, and academic honors in 1707. His son and pupil, Pierre Imbert Drevet, was born in Paris in 1697, and became an engraver of rare excellence, overshadowing his father in nearly every branch of his art, which he practised until his death in 1739, notwithstanding a period of insanity, dating from about the year 1730. Claude Drevet, the youngest and least important of these engravers, was born, probably at Lyons, about the year 1705, and was a pupil of his uncle at Paris, where he died in the year 1781. An interesting account of these engravers will be found in the Catalogue raisonné, by M. A. Firmin-Didot.

These engravers worked entirely with the burin, over which they acquired a wonderful command; the splendors of their technic, in richness and delicacy, have rarely been equalled. If their portraits lack the vigor and freedom which characterize the works of Edelinck and the simplicity and clearness of those of Nanteuil, they possess a subtilty of expression and a refinement of technic quite their own. Their representations of the draperies, laces, silks, ermine, carved wood, and all the other accessories and redundancies which characterize the portraits of Rigaud, De Troy, and Le Brun, are as near perfection as any engraver ever attained; yet all these are carefully subordinated to the features, which are engraved with great delicacy and minuteness, and preserve in a remarkable degree the expression, transparency, and warm flesh tints of the originals. On account of their extreme delicacy of technic, these portraits should be seen in early impressions before the plates became worn in printing.

In the qualities which have been mentioned, no other engraver has ever quite equalled the best works of Pierre Imbert Drevet. His famous full-length portrait of Bossuet, after Hyacinthe Rigaud, engraved in the year 1723, when the engraver was but twenty-six years of age, is the most perfect type of these engravings, full of life and vivacity; one of the exquisite masterpieces of the art. But little inferior is the portrait of the rich counsellor and financier Samuel Bernard, after the same painter, while the portraits of Cardinal Dubois, Fénélon, and Louis XIV. when young, are likewise works of great merit. Equal in interest, if not in point of art, is the portrait of the beautiful actress Adrienne Lecouvreur. This portrait, engraved from the painting by Charles Coypel, represents Adrienne in the character of Cornelia in Corneille's tragedy "La Mort de Pompée," although there is a striking anachronism in the costume. We read in the annals of the period of the beautiful and noble, but impecunious, adventuress

Aurora of Königsmarck, who, travelling about from court to court, "found favor in the eyes of Augustus of Saxony and became the mother of Marshal Saxe," whose own relations with the unfortunate actress Adrienne form the subject of the popular drama by Scribe, bearing her name, which portrays her romantic life and untimely death. Adrienne's expression in this portrait is beautiful and sweet, although sad, and the inscription recites that she died in Paris at the age of thirty-seven years. Her talents were highly extolled by Voltaire, who deplored her early death. There is a fine portrait of Marshal Saxe engraved by Wille. The last work of Pierre Imbert Drevet, engraved in the year of his death, and while he was insane, is a portrait of the magistrate René Pucelle.

Pierre Drevet, the elder, engraved a number of fine portraits after Hyacinthe Rigaud, among them that master's own portrait of himself, and the full-length portrait of Louis XIV. from the painting in the Louvre. He also completed the plate begun by Edelinck, 'Alexander entering the Tent of Darius,' after Mignard. Of the works of Claude Drevet, the portraits of Count Zinzendorf and Vintimille, Archbishop of Paris, after Rigaud, are the best examples.

François Chereau (1680–1729), a pupil of Pierre Drevet the elder, also became famous for his fine portraits after Rigaud, particularly that of the Duke of Antin. But we must leave these engravers to come to the school which most faithfully reflects the manners and sentiment of the reign of Louis XV., that of Watteau.

The eighteenth century opened inauspiciously for France. The "Grand Monarque" had outlived his popularity. The bright luminaries of his reign had faded away, and France found herself with a depleted treasury and a discontented people. The era of extravagance and frivolity ushered in by the Regency was destined to end in revolution. Art reflected the tastes and fashions of the hour; contemporary society became the painter's theme. Le Brun "had tainted French art with the wig of Louis XIV;" but Le Brun already belonged to the past, for a new school of art had arisen in France, inaugurated by that fantastic genius Claude Gillot; brought to perfection by Antoine Watteau. The public taste had wearied of the stupendous allegories and historical pieces of the preceding century, and welcomed the new school, whose works were characterized by attractiveness of subject and a general air of grace and elegance, piquancy and prettiness. The artists of this school represented idyllic landscapes, *fêtes-galantes*, pastorals, with coxcomb shepherds and court shepherdesses, beautiful women in fancy costumes, nymphs, cupids, love-scenes; everything festooned and garlanded with roses. Their works are in striking contrast to the homely scenes of Teniers, Brouwer, and Ostade. "The eighteenth century," says Fontenelle, "was favored with a mild sun and laughing sky, and earth covered with roses. France was a universal garden rich with the sweetest and most enervating perfumes. Then were born two delicate children destined to give spirit and color to their age; they were Voltaire and Watteau, the representative poet and painter of the eighteenth century."

Of the multitude of clever artists who reproduced the characteristic designs of Watteau and his followers, the chief were François Boucher (1703–70) and Laurent Cars (1699–1771). Their plates were mostly etched, and finished and strengthened with the graver. In this way Boucher engraved many of Watteau's designs; he also became himself a prolific designer for others. Laurent Cars, the greatest of all these engravers, possessed rare abilities, and represented the old as well as the new school. He is famous for his 'Hercules and Omphale,' after Lemoyne, 'Fêtes vénitiennes,' after Watteau, and his series of exquisite illustrations to the comedies of Molière, from Boucher's designs. Other engravers of this school were Aveline, Chedel, Moyreau, Le Bas, Cochin, Benoit Audran the younger, Larmessin, Aubert, Scotin, Baron—but the list is almost endless. A collection of representative engravings after Watteau and his followers is of great interest—grace, beauty, and spirit predominating. But the school of Watteau rapidly degenerated. "The debasement of painting followed step by step on that of morals." Lancret, Pater, Boucher, Fragonard, and other painters of *fêtes-galantes*, misusing the abilities which, well directed, would have produced great results, soon represented little more than the follies and indecencies of the age. Many of the engravings of this period are also of objectionable subjects, *pièces à surprise*, and show a public taste sufficiently corrupt. With the Revolution came the reaction. David rescued French art from the debasement into which it had been led by the imitators of Watteau, and in turn established a despotism almost as great as that of Le Brun, which lasted until the rise of the Romantic school and the supremacy of Géricault and Delacroix.

Never were engravers more numerous in any country than in France during the reign of Louis XV. Engraving had become a sort of universal craze affecting all classes. In addition to the multitude of professional engravers, the art was practised by a host of amateurs, among them Madame de Pompadour, whose skill was not inconsiderable. Besides the engravers already mentioned, there were many others whose characteristic works are still highly esteemed. Those witty and ingenious artists, the younger Cochin, Gravelot, Eisen, Choffard, and

Moreau le jeune designed charming vignettes, ornaments, and illustrations for books which are unrivalled in their way; while of the engravers who devoted themselves to more serious works were Le Bas, Le Mire, Augustin de St. Aubin, Chereau, Daullé, Baléchou, Beauvarlet, and Porporati, all more or less famous in their time, although, aside from a few masterpieces, their works are of secondary importance. Baléchou is still widely known through his portrait of Augustus III. of Poland, after Rigaud, 'Ste. Geneviève,' after Vanloo, and 'The Storm,' 'Calm,' and 'The Bathers,' after Vernet; Porporati by his masterpiece, 'Susanna at the Bath,' from Santerre's painting in the Louvre, and by a number of subjects after Correggio. But in the meantime appeared an engraver whose advent marks the beginning of a new era in the history of his art: a German by birth, but French by education and adoption, and whose best works are from Dutch originals.

John George Wille was born in a little Hessian town near Königsberg in 1715. In his early years he was apprenticed to a gunsmith, and, like Masson, became a skilful engraver of ornamental work. About the year 1736, in company with his countryman George Frederick Schmidt, he went to Paris to devote himself to engraving, an art which he greatly influenced. He soon received the favorable notice of Hyacinthe Rigaud, some of whose portraits he engraved, and, directed and advised by that master, rose rapidly into eminence, becoming the foremost engraver of his time. With the exception of a short visit to Germany in 1746, he resided thereafter in Paris until his death in 1808, in his ninety-third year. His prints bear dates ranging from 1738 to 1790, after which time he became blind and impoverished during the Revolution. His *Memoirs*, edited by Duplessis, were published in Paris in

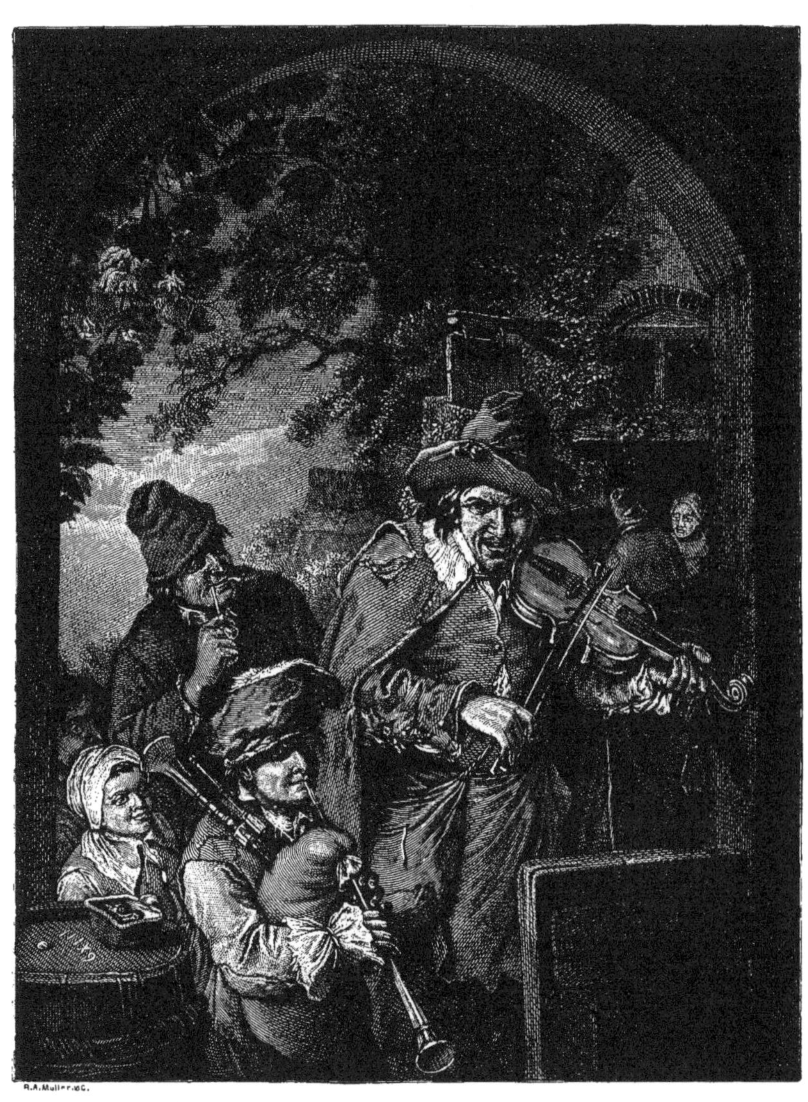

THE TRAVELLING MUSICIANS

Wood-cut by R. A. Muller, from the engraving by Wille

1857, and there is a catalogue of his prints by M. Charles le Blanc.

Wille possessed great mechanical skill, which he was fond of displaying. The railleries about the "lozenge with a dot in the centre" are properly applied to many of his works, which parade his technical skill at the expense of his originals. His best works are subjects after the Dutch masters and portraits after the French painters Rigaud, Tocqué, and La Tour. His superior skill in representing the silk and satin draperies of the Dutch painters is shown to great advantage in his two prints, 'L'Instruction paternelle,' called 'The Satin Gown,' after Terburg, and the 'Mort de Cléopatre,' after Netscher, while his masterpiece, 'Les Musiciens ambulans,' after Dietrich, and 'Le Concert de Famille,' after Schalcken, are full of life and spirit. There are also some fine prints after Gérard Dou, among them 'La Liseuse' and 'La Devideuse,' studies of the artist's mother, and there are a number of plates from paintings by his son P. A. Wille. Of his portraits may be mentioned those of Marshal Saxe, a vigorous piece of work; St. Florentin, Count Aumale, Boullongne, Massé, Cardinal Tencin, Berregard, Berryer, Poisson, and Madame Rigaud, wife of the painter.

As a teacher, Wille was even more successful than as an engraver, although the school of engraving of which he was the founder often sought to conceal its artistic weakness in an undue display of mere mechanical skill. During a life of over ninety years, a career equalled in length only by that of Henriquel-Dupont, he lived to see the descendants of his school established in almost every country on the Continent. He was the teacher of Bervic, J. G. von Müller, Tardieu, and other eminent engravers, who, in turn, transmitted his instructions to their pupils, among whom were Desnoyers, Longhi, Toschi,

Anderloni, J. F. Müller, and many other engravers who flourished in France, Italy, and Germany towards the close of the last and at the beginning of the present century, and whose beautiful engravings after the Italian masters are universally admired. Many of these engravers, while owing much of their mechanical skill to the teachings of Wille, did not, like him, neglect the higher qualities of art, but following their great predecessors, endeavored to enter into the spirit of the artist whose work they interpreted, rather than to make a display of their own technical powers. Of Wille it may be truly said, in the modest words of the late Léon Gaucherel, that his "best works were his pupils." He was appointed engraver to the King of France, the Emperor of Germany, and the King of Denmark, and was a Knight of the Legion of Honor, and a member of the academies of Paris, Vienna, Berlin, Dresden, and other cities.

Wille's companion, George Frederick Schmidt, was born in Berlin in 1712, and was the son of a weaver. After serving for six years in the German artillery he was dismissed on account of his small stature, and at once, following his natural inclination, became an engraver. After receiving instruction at the Berlin Academy he went to Paris, and, like Wille, soon acquired great reputation. He was received into the Academy at Paris in 1742, in which year he engraved his famous laughing portrait of the painter La Tour, and for his reception engraved, in 1744, his fine portrait of the painter Mignard, both masterpieces worthy of the graver of Edelinck. But Schmidt was by nature a wanderer, and two years later he returned to Berlin, where he was appointed engraver to the king. Here he remained until 1757, when he was invited to St. Petersburg by the Empress Elizabeth I., and assisted in establishing there the Academy of

Engraving. At this time he engraved some of his finest plates, among them his famous large portrait of the Empress Elizabeth, after the painter Tocqué, whom the Empress had also invited to the Russian Court, and, after the same painter, the portraits of Counts Esterhazy, Rasoumowsky, and Woronzow, and many portraits of the Russian and Polish nobility. But Schmidt soon again became restless, and in 1762 he returned to Berlin, where he etched some portraits and subjects in the manner of Rembrandt; but his works in this direction are deficient in breadth and freedom, and are less highly esteemed than his works engraved with the burin. He died in Berlin in 1775. His prints exceed 200 in number, and some of them possess great merit, although the greater portion are lacking in taste and intellectual qualities. His own features are preserved to us in his well-known portrait of himself "with the spider in the window."

Etienne Ficquet (1719–94), a pupil of Schmidt and Le Bas, is famous for his small portraits, among them those of La Fontaine, Madame de Maintenon, Rubens, Van Dyck, Voltaire, Molière, Corneille, Rousseau, Boileau, Montaigne, Descartes, Fénélon, and Crébillon. These portraits, engraved with the aid of a strong magnifying glass, possess marvellous spirit and delicacy, and are correct in drawing and facial expression. Some of his portraits are reductions from larger prints by other engravers.

Ficquet, whose follies and dissipations kept him forever in debt and difficulties, seems to have produced some of his best works under compulsion. It is related that his creditors sometimes took him into their own houses until he discharged his obligations by engraving a plate. At St. Cyr he undertook to engrave for the order the portrait of Madame de Maintenon, after Mignard, but having received his pay he had no further inclination to work. He was thereupon confined in the convent, but his life in the society of the nuns was not such as to inspire him to diligence, and it was only after great delay and difficulty that they succeeded in obtaining this portrait of their benefactress, now an extremely rare print. This portrait and that of La Fontaine were considered by Longhi to be the engraver's finest works, although the portraits of Rubens and Van Dyck, engraved for Decamps' *Vie des Peintres Flamands et Hollandais*, are scarcely inferior. As an engraver of small portraits Ficquet stands unrivalled, although approached in some instances by his contemporary Augustin de Saint-Aubin, and by Gaillard and a few other engravers of our own century.

Two other engravers of great ability and reputation, Charles Clément Bervic (whose family name was Balvay), and Auguste Boucher-Desnoyers, although direct descendants of the school of Wille, gave to their works greater breadth and freedom, although they cannot be classed with such masters as Edelinck and the Drevets. Bervic was born in Paris in 1756. At the age of fourteen he entered the studio of Wille, and thereafter rose rapidly into eminence. He was soon received into the Academy, and given apartments in the Louvre. In 1790 appeared his first work of importance—the famous full-length portrait of Louis XVI. in his coronation robes, after the mediocre painting by Callet, now in the Trianon, at Versailles. Bervic's print bears the inscription, 'Roi des Français, Restaurateur de la Liberté.' Soon afterwards appeared the large portrait of the King engraved by the German engraver J. G. von Müller, who had been Bervic's fellow-pupil in the studio of Wille. This portrait, after an original by Duplessis, engraved in the same brilliant manner, bears the significant inscription "Il vou-

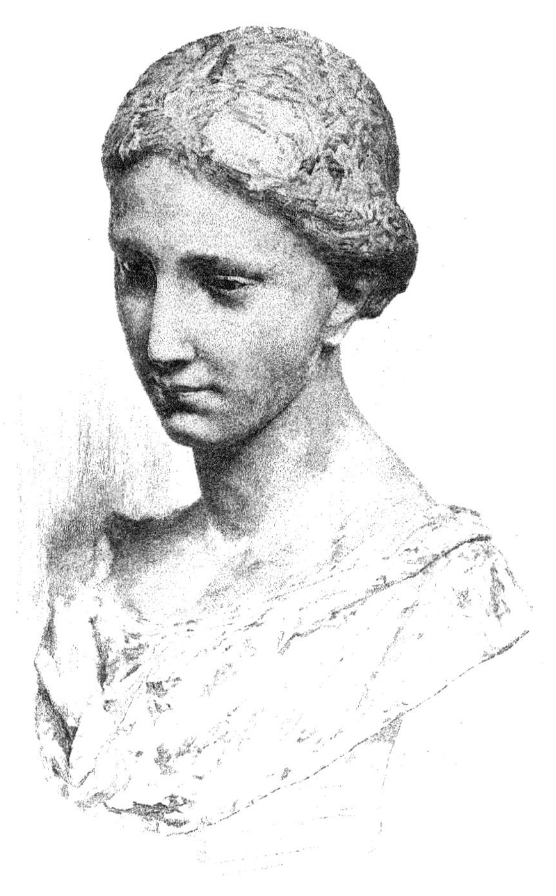

TÊTE DE CIRE

GRAVURE DE F. GAILLARD, D'APRÈS LE BUSTE DU MUSÉE WICAR

Imp. A Salmon Paris.

lut le bonheur de sa nation, et en devint la victime." The "restorer of liberty" was no more. Bervic's plate, which is still preserved in Paris, bears the mark of the terrible Revolution. After the first impressions were taken Louis XVI. was beheaded on the guillotine, and Bervic, who had become an enthusiastic revolutionist, broke his plate, and destroyed all the remaining impressions at a meeting of the "Société Populaire des Arts," of which he was a member. The plate was afterwards repaired, and later impressions printed from it; but these show the crease where it was injured. This portrait, with its gorgeous accessories, recalls the works of the Drevets, although inferior in point of art to such portraits as the Bossuet, Bernard, and Louis XIV.

Bervic's next important works were the companion prints, 'The Education of Achilles,' after the painting by Regnault, in which the painter Carle Vernet, at the age of twenty, is said to have served as the model for Achilles, and the 'Rape of Dejanira,' after Guido. The original paintings are now in the Louvre. The latter plate was awarded the prize offered by the Institute for the best engraving executed during the first decade of the present century. Bervic was an artist of the classical school, and these two prints, his masterpieces, contrast strongly with the works produced by the school of Boucher and Le Bas, so universally popular, and show that the best traditions of his art survived the tempestuous times of the Revolution.

Another celebrated print, the 'Laocoön,' engraved for the Musée Robillard, is an important example, as showing the extreme limits of Bervic's technical skill; but as a work of art it is inferior to the preceding.

Towards the close of his career, Bervic was loaded with honors. He was made a member of the Institute of France, and of most of the Academies of Europe, and in 1819 the Legion of Honor was conferred upon him. It is said that he cautioned his pupils, among whom were Toschi and Henriquel-Dupont, against the vices of the mechanical school, and advised them to avoid servile imitation of others, and to cultivate originality. He died in Paris in 1822.

The whole career of Auguste Boucher-Desnoyers was a succession of triumphs, and seems to have been but little affected by the wars and changes through which he passed. Born in Paris in 1779, he commenced to engrave before he was ten years old, and at the age of twenty his engraving in the dotted manner of Robert Lefevre's 'Venus disarming Cupid' gained for him a prize of 2000 francs at the Salon of 1799. He now entered the studio of Alexander Tardieu, a pupil of Wille and Bervic, best known as an engraver by his masterly portrait of the Earl of Arundel after Van Dyck. Here Desnoyers studied line engraving and etching, and rose so rapidly in his art that in the year 1804 he engraved for the Musée Français his beautiful print, 'La Belle Jardinière,' from the painting by Raphael in the Louvre. At this time Bervic and Desnoyers were the ablest, and by far the most famous engravers in France, and were honored and patronized to an extent almost unprecedented. In 1806 Desnoyers gained a gold medal for his engraving from the drawing by Ingres from the antique cameo of Ptolmey II., "Philadelphus and Arsinoë," then the property of the Empress Josephine, and now at St. Petersburg; and two years later he engraved his famous portrait of the Emperor Napoleon.

Notwithstanding the fall of the empire, Desnoyers, like the painter Gérard, continued to enjoy the favor of the Court, and was in succession elected to the Institute, appointed engraver to the King, created a baron, and decorated with the Cross of the Legion of Honor. He continued his work until about the middle of the century, when age and failing sight compelled him to lay down the graver. He died in Paris in 1857.

Desnoyers is best known as the engraver of Raphael's Madonnas. Both his engraved works and writings show that the "divine painter" was constantly in his thoughts, and that he had made a profound study of drawing to qualify him for the great undertaking which extended over the entire useful period of his career. The series commences with 'La Belle Jardinière,' from the painting in the Louvre, engraved in 1804, and includes, chronologically, 'La Vierge au Donataire,' 'La Vierge au Linge,' 'La Madonna della Sedia' (also finely engraved by J. G. von Müller, Raphael Morghen, Garavaglia, Calamatta, Mandel, and Burger), 'La Madonna del Pesce,' 'La Madonna della Casa d'Alba,' 'La Vierge au Berceau,' 'La Belle Jardinière de Florence,' and 'La Madonna di San Sisto,' the last engraved in 1846. The last of these Madonnas has been beautifully engraved by J. F. Müller, and more recently by Steinla and Mandel, and will be mentioned again in connection with those engravers. A collection of such engravings of Raphael's Madonnas is a choice possession. Desnoyers also engraved in a similar manner the 'Visitation,' 'St. Catharine,' 'Ste. Marguerite' and the 'Transfiguration,' after Raphael, and 'La Vierge aux Rochers,' after Leonardo da Vinci. The last-named print ranks with the famous 'Belle Jardinière,' these two plates being generally considered his masterpieces.

Next to Desnoyers engravings after Raphael and Leonardo come those which he engraved after the baron Gérard, among them the famous large portrait of the Emperor Napoleon in his coronation robes. This portrait, engraved in 1808, was exhibited at the Salon of 1810, and Desnoyers received for it £2000, with the return of the plate after an edition of 600 impressions had been printed. These impressions bear the eagle stamp, and were intended for presentation to foreign princes and ambassadors and distinguished persons of the Empire. His print of 'Belisarius' is also a masterpiece, and there are fine portraits of Talleyrand and Humboldt, the latter an etching. Of his engravings in the dotted manner, his portrait of Thomas Jefferson, President of the United States, engraved in 1801, is the most interesting example, and is now rare. In many of Desnoyers large plates the background was engraved by Frederick Giessler, of Nuremberg. The subjects engraved by Desnoyers are not only more interesting than those of Bervic, but his works show less of the defects of the mechanical school of Wille.

Desnoyers found a worthy successor in Louis Pierre Henriquel-Dupont, who rose into prominence towards the middle of the century, and whose fame has since become universal. Born at Paris in 1797, his career extended over even a longer period than that of Wille. Both as engraver and teacher, his name stands foremost among the masters of our own generation. At first a pupil of the painter Pierre Guérin, he afterwards devoted himself to engraving, and entered the atelier of Bervic. Upon the appearance, in 1822, of his fine plate, after Van Dyck, 'Une Dame et sa fille,' he established a reputation which was confirmed a few years later by his engraving 'L'Abdication de Gustave Wasa,' after Hersent, exhibited in the Salon of 1831. From this period success and honors awaited him, and during a long life of over ninety-four years he engraved many excellent works, both from his own designs and after various masters, mostly his contemporaries. His plates number 115, according to the catalogue of M. Beraldi. He was a member of the Institute, professor at the École des Beaux-Arts, and a commander of the Legion of Honor. He continued the noble traditions of Nanteuil and Edelinck to our own time, and his death, which occurred January 20, 1892, deprived the art of its last great representative.

The style of Henriquel-Dupont differs greatly from that of his master Bervic, and is strikingly original and expressive. He was an artist of varied resources and of the greatest versatility, proficient in nearly every branch of his art. He was also a designer of great ability, and produced many excellent works in pastel and crayon with a genius approaching that of Nanteuil.

Henriquel is best known through his engravings after Paul Delaroche. Of these the 'Hémicycle du Palais des Beaux-Arts' is a masterpiece of exceptional merit and interest—one of the famous engravings of the century. This great work, unique in style and subject, is composed of three sheets united together, making a print about eighteen inches high and more than seven feet long, containing about seventy-five figures. In the centre on a throne are Apelles, Ictinus, and Pheidias, the great artists of antiquity; around them are the genius of the arts, and allegorical figures representing Greek, Roman, and Gothic art, and the Renaissance; the sides represent the world's great painters, sculptors, and architects, nearly all taken from authentic portraits, to procure many of which Delaroche journeyed to Italy. In 1855 the original painting was greatly injured by fire, but was restored after Delaroche's death by Robert-Fleury. Both painting and engraving are valuable for their many portraits delicately and faithfully rendered.

The portraits engraved by Henriquel-Dupont are exceptionally fine, and many of the early impressions are printed in a superb manner on China papers. Among the most interesting examples are those of Peter the Great, the Earl of Strafford, Mirabeau, Pope Gregory XVI., and the Marquis de Pastoret (the last two etchings), all after Delaroche; Louis Philippe, after Gérard; Bertin and Tardieu, after Ingres; and, after his own designs, the portraits of Sauvageot and Brongniart. There are also fine prints of 'Moïse Exposé sur le Nil,' after Delaroche; 'Christus Consolator,' after Ary Scheffer; 'Pilgrims of Emmaus,' after Paul Veronese; 'The Mystical Marriage of St. Catherine,' after Correggio; and 'La Vierge d'Orleans,' after Raphael.

Many other French engravers have achieved renown. J. J. de Boissieu (1736–1810), who belongs rather to the last century, deserves notice chiefly for his great technical skill as an etcher, and for his remarkable powers of imitation. Joseph Théodore Richomme (1785–1849) is best known for his engravings after Raphael, particularly 'The Triumph of Galatea;' Jules François (1809–61) by his masterpiece, 'Le Galant Militaire,' after Terburg; and his brother Alphonse François by his engravings 'Coronation of the Virgin,' after Fra Angelico, and the 'Mystic Marriage of St. Catharine,' after Memlinc. Ferdinand Gaillard (1834–87) possessed rare and peculiar abilities. For delicacy and precision of technic some of his small prints rival those of Ficquet. His most important plates are 'L'Homme à l'œillet,' after Van Dyck, and a wonderful portrait of the abbé Dom Guéranger. Other remarkable works are 'L'Œdipe,' after Ingres; 'La Vierge de la Maison d'Orleans,' after Raphael; 'Tête de cire, musée de Lille;' 'Le Crépuscule,' after Michael Angelo, and the portraits of Pius IX., Leo XIII., and the charitable Sister Rosalie. He left unfinished a large plate of the 'Last Supper,' from Leonardo's painting. Some of his best works were engraved for the *Gazette des Beaux-Arts.* Blanchard, Rousseaux, Huot, Levasseur, Jacquet, and others have also produced works of exceptional excellence. A catalogue of the prints of these engravers will be found in Beraldi's *Graveurs du XIXe Siècle.*

Etching, practised with such enthusiasm in the time of Rembrandt, declined as an original art after that master's death. The story of its revival in France in our own time has been so often told that repetition is unnecessary. For nearly two centuries a slave to its classic companion, the needle has at last superseded the burin, and the followers of Charles Jacque, Charles François Daubigny and Léopold Flameng, pioneers in the movement, are so numerous that an account of their achievements cannot be attempted in the present volume. In a subsequent chapter, however, a few modern etchers, not living artists, will be mentioned on account of the exceptional character and importance of their work.

CHAPTER VI

ENGRAVING IN ENGLAND

Early Engraving in England — Faithorne — Hollar — Mezzotint Engraving — Ludwig von Siegen — Smith and Faber — MacArdell, Earlom, Green, J. R. Smith, Reynolds, Cousin, and others — Stipple Engraving — Ryland, Bartolozzi, Walker, and others — Vertue — Line Engraving — Sir Robert Strange — William Woollett — John Hall — Landscape Engraving; influence of Vivarès and Baléchou — Browne, Mason, and Peak — William Sharp — Publishers of Prints; the Boydells — Raimbach — Wilkie — Turner and his Engravers — The *Liber Studiorum* — Versatility of the English School

THE history of engraving in England presents little of interest before the middle of the seventeenth century. The schools of Italy and Germany had reached maturity and declined; the Dutch and Flemish engravers were at the zenith of their success; and the great school in portraiture had arisen in France before England could boast a single great artist of her own. The success achieved by Holbein was repeated by Rubens and Van Dyck, and many foreign artists, engravers as well as painters, visited England during the reign of Charles I. Stimulated by these illustrious examples, the native art soon asserted itself and came rapidly to maturity.

The first of the English copper-plate engravers whose name has reached us was Thomas Geminus, who published, in 1545, his first edition of Vesalius's *Anatomy*, with illustrations copied from the wood-cuts in the original edition printed in 1542 at Padua. Geminus also published a *Prognostication* and other works rudely illustrated, and his plates were among the earliest printed from a roller press in England.

The age of Elizabeth, so brilliant in literature, saw a great improvement in English engraving, although the real importance of the school dates from the reign of Charles II. The most important of the engravers who practised their art in England during the reign of Elizabeth and her successor were Remigius and Franz Hogensberg, two Flemish engravers who went to England about the year 1560, the Dutch family of De Passe, William Rogers, Reginald Elstracke, Francis Delaram, and John Payne. Remigius Hogensberg engraved, in 1573, a portrait of Archbishop Parker, a conspicuous art patron of the time of Elizabeth, which Vertue considered to be the first portrait engraved in England. He also engraved the portraits of the English kings from the Conquest. Franz Hogensberg engraved a portrait of Queen Mary I., dated 1555, but he was not in England at that time. William Rogers engraved a portrait of Queen Elizabeth, after Isaac Oliver, whose picture was painted at the Queen's command as an authentic likeness to counteract the effect of the unflattering portraits in circulation. John Payne was the first of the English engravers whose works show any considerable ability, but he wasted his opportunities in dissipation; had he applied himself with diligence his name, instead of Faithorne's, would have been the earliest of importance in the English school.

The works of the engravers named contain the only authentic portraits of many eminent persons of the time, and to many of these portraits curious histories are attached; but however important they may be historically, they are of little interest as works of art. We therefore come at once to the first of the English engravers whose works compare favorably with those produced on the Continent, and mark the beginning of successful engraving in England.

William Faithorne, the elder, was born in London in 1616, and was a pupil of Sir Robert Peake, painter, engraver, and print-seller, knighted by Charles I. Upon the breaking out of the Civil War, Faithorne followed his master and fought with the Cavaliers, but was made a prisoner at Basing House and confined at Aldersgate. While in prison he engraved a number of small portraits, among them a portrait of the Duke of Buckingham. Upon the solicitation of his friends he was finally allowed to retire to France, where he employed the period of his exile to great advantage. He found a friend and patron in the abbé de Marolles, and became a pupil of the eminent engraver Robert Nanteuil, in whose best manner he worked; but although he acquired much of the excellence of the French school, his works remained English in character. Soon after the middle of the century he returned to England, and established himself in London as an engraver and print-seller. Here he died in 1691. His engraved portraits possess great richness and color, and represent many eminent persons of his time. As examples may be named those of Viscount Mordaunt, Sir William Paston, Lady Paston, Robert Bayfield, Lady Herbert, Thomas Killigrew, a large emblematical print of Oliver Cromwell, and a portrait of John Milton, aet. 76, engraved from life in 1670. Faithorne engraved many excellent frontispieces and title-pages for books, and was also famous for crayon portraits. He published, in 1662, his *Art of Graving and Etching*, dedicated to his early master. His studio was a fashionable resort for the art dilettanti who, like Pepys, often called to buy "a head or two," and to learn the latest art gossip. There is a poem by his friend Thomas Flatman, a poet who is said to have done "ample justice" to his name, which concludes:

"A 'Faithorne sculpsit' is a charm can save
From dull oblivion and a gaping grave."

Faithorne had many imitators, but none of importance. The only other important engraver of the century who practised his art in England was Wenceslaus Hollar, one of the most unfortunate artists who ever lived, whose great ability, honest endeavor, and indefatigable industry met with no return but poverty, neglect, and sorrow.

Hollar was born at Prague, in Bohemia, in 1607, of an ancient family, and was intended for the law; but in the taking of Prague, in 1619, his family was impoverished, and, thrown upon his own resources, he went to Frankfort and became an engraver. Soon afterwards he travelled through Germany, making drawings and engraving views of cities, particularly Frankfort, Strasburg, Mainz, and Cologne; but although these were greatly admired, they procured for him only the bare necessities of life. At Cologne he formed the acquaintance of the Earl of Arundel, then the English ambassador to the Court of Ferdinand II., and in 1637 accompanied him to England, where he engraved from pictures in his patron's collection, and also etched plates for the published account of the journey of Marie de' Medici to her daughter Queen Henrietta Maria. At this period he also engraved his portrait of the Earl of Arundel on horseback, and several series of plates representing costumes worn by the women of different European countries.

Upon the outbreak of the Civil War, Hollar sided with the Royalists, and, like Faithorne, was made a prisoner at Basing House. He obtained his release with great difficulty, and at once followed his patron to Antwerp, and engraved from his pictures until the death of the latter, which soon occurred.

Hollar now found himself in a strange country, without friends, money, or employment, and with great difficulty made his way back to London in 1652; here he became a print-seller's hack, and was compelled to perform work utterly unworthy of his great talents. Upon the Restoration his prospects were brightened by the return of his Royalist friends, but the Plague, and then the great fire of London, deprived him of employment, and he was once more reduced to extreme poverty. He accompanied Lord Howard to Tangiers to make drawings for the king of the town and fortifications, and on his return, after narrowly escaping capture by corsairs, he succeeded, after great delay, in obtaining from that impecunious monarch a pittance barely sufficient to meet the expenses he had incurred. He now travelled through England, as he had a few years before in Germany, making drawings and engraving views of cities, cathedrals, and ruins, and doing such other work as he could obtain, but returned to London in great poverty. He had at last reached "the dark level of adversity." After struggling bravely on for a time he died in 1677. His last hours were disturbed by the bailiff's officers, who even threatened to seize the bed upon which he lay. When at last death mercifully came to him, it took away "only a crown of thorns."

Hollar is described in the catalogue published by the Burlington Fine-Arts Club, the latest and best catalogue of his prints, as "the most accurate delineator and most ingenious illustrator of his time, and as to technic, the most able etcher." Many of his plates were finished with the point or graver, which he also handled with the greatest facility and lightness of touch. He represented with rare taste and spirit, and with marvellous delicacy and precision, the texture of hair, feathers, and wings of insects, the transparency of glass, reflections of metals, and furs, shells, vases, jewels, and all manner of still-life. He also engraved with great success sets of subjects representing hunting, fishing, and hawking; sets of animals; costumes of different European countries; views of cities, buildings, ruins, and landscapes; and great variety of portraits, both from his own designs and after various masters, principally Holbein and Van Dyck. Among his prints are views of London, showing the city before and after the great fire of 1666, including exterior and interior views of old St. Paul's. Of his many views of buildings, those of Antwerp Cathedral and St. George's Chapel from the Choir are fine examples. For their representations of still-life, Hollar and, among modern etchers, Jacquemart stand supreme. Hollar's prints exceed 2700 in number, a sufficient proof of his industry. Many of these are now exceedingly rare and valuable.

To this period also belong Robert White, Francis Barlow, David Loggan, and Sir Nicholas Dorigny, all engravers of only ordinary ability. Dorigny, a pupil of Gérard Audran, went over from France in 1711 to engrave the famous cartoons of Raphael at Hampton Court; these he completed in 1719, and was knighted by King George I.

The works of Faithorne and Hollar were the best produced in England before the eighteenth century. Much of Faithorne's excellence was due to the instruction which he had received at Paris under Nanteuil, and Hollar belongs to England only by long residence in that country. The English engravers first became important as a body upon the rise of the great school of mezzotint engraving, in which art they have taken and maintained the foremost place. This process was known in France as "La manière noire," the black-manner, or "La manière anglaise," from its prevalence in England. In Italy it was known as "L'incisione a fuomo," or engraving in smoke or black manner; and the Germans called it "Schabkunst," scraping-art, or "Schwarzkunst," black-art. It was also known by a variety of other names in different countries.

The process of mezzotint engraving is in some respects the reverse of line engraving and etching. In the latter, an arrangement of lines and dots is cut into the plate by the burin or acid. In printing, the ink is taken up from the incisions and shows black upon the white surface of the paper. The mezzotint engraver first covers his plate with a fine, even bur, which, in printing, gives a rich, uniform black of great depth. The lights, tones, and gradations are then obtained by removing or reducing the bur. He proceeds from black to white, and by tones instead of lines, his tones ranging from the deepest black to the most tender and transparent tints. In practise, the outlines of the subject are generally etched before applying the mezzotint, a process which imparts greater strength, character, and variety to the work. Mezzotint engravings are prized for their rich, soft tones, and the delicacy and purity of their tints and gradations. The process is obviously not adapted to subjects which require pure, sharp outlines, or great clearness or minuteness of detail and finish, although some astonishing things have been done in this direction by Earlom and others. On account of the extreme delicacy of the work but a comparatively small number of really fine proofs can be taken from a plate engraved in this manner, as the bur soon wears away or becomes reduced by the friction and pressure in printing; as Gilpin has it, "the spirit of a mezzotint quickly evaporates." To obviate this disadvantage, steel plates are sometimes employed, but the work then appears cold and hard, and loses much of its artistic effect. Dry-point work, so extensively used

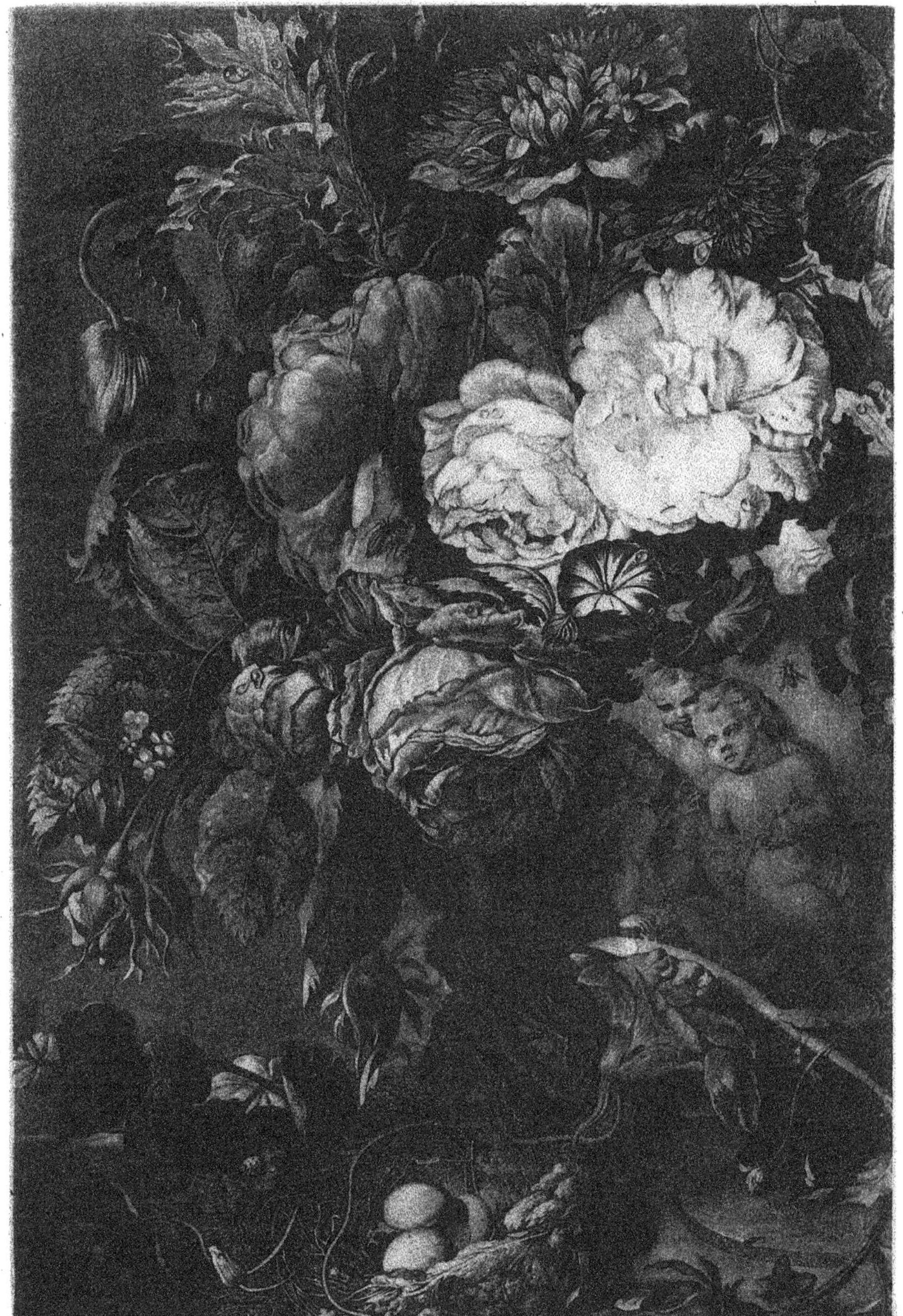

by engravers in finishing their plates, and often as a complete process, has been aptly called "mezzotint in line."

The invention of mezzotint engraving is ascribed to Ludwig von Siegen, a lieutenant-colonel in the service of the Landgrave of Hesse, who engraved in this manner a number of prints, mostly portraits, one of which, a portrait of the Dowager Amelia Elizabeth, Landgravine of Hesse, dated 1642, is the earliest known print engraved in the mezzotint manner.

Ludwig von Siegen was born in Holland in 1609. His mother was a native of that country, and his father, who belonged to an ancient and noble German family, had entered the service of Holland, but returning to his native country in 1619, was taken into the service of the Landgrave of Hesse-Cassel. Ludwig lived alternately in Holland and Germany, and died about the year 1680. While residing in Amsterdam in 1641 or 1642, having already turned his attention to engraving, he invented the process of mezzotint, and in August of the latter year completed his portrait of the Landgravine, probably from a drawing which he had made at Cassel. In a letter which he sent to his master, with a number of proofs from his plate, he wrote, "How this work has been done no copper-plate engraver or artist can explain or imagine, for, as your Grace is aware, only three methods of engraving on copper have hitherto been seen. . . ." In all probability he did not disclose his secret until 1654, when he met at Brussels a kindred spirit, the romantic Prince Rupert, artist and soldier, known in history as the gallant leader of the king's cavalry in the Civil War.

Prince Rupert engraved a considerable number of plates in this manner, some of great excellence, and introduced the art into England, where, for a long time, he was honored as its originator to the entire neglect of the real inventor; curious stories were circulated as to the manner in which his alleged invention had been made. The finest of Prince Rupert's mezzotint engravings is 'The Great Executioner,' after Spagnoletto, a work of considerable artistic effect. He is said to have first communicated the secret of the process to Wallerant Vaillant, a portrait-painter at Amsterdam, who assisted him, and who also engraved portraits in this manner with great success. The names of Fürstenberg, Lutterel, Thomas of Ypres, Abraham Blooteling, and Sir Christopher Wren must also be mentioned, as these engravers were among the very earliest who employed the scraping process. Prince Rupert is also believed to have communicated his secret to William Sherwin, who engraved the first English mezzotint bearing a date (a portrait of Charles II., dated 1669), and also to the famous John Evelyn, author of the *Sculptura*, to whom he gave his small plate of the head of the 'Executioner,' to be published in the first edition of that work. Soon after this time, however, the process became generally known, and within a few years many engravers were working in this manner, but, compared with the masterpieces of a later period, the greater portion of their works possess no great artistic importance, although of interest in tracing the development of the process.

Towards the close of the century a new impluse was given to mezzotint engraving by Isaac Becket and his accomplished pupil John Smith. The latter was taken into the service of Sir Godfrey Kneller, and engraved, after that master, many fine portraits of distinguished persons. The success of the English engravers in this manner soon attracted attention in Germany and other countries, and many foreign engravers came to England to learn the art, which they afterwards brought into favor in their own countries. In the early years of the eighteenth century there were many mezzotint engravers, both native and foreign, working in England. The French engraver J. Simon, a Protestant refugee, and the younger Faber, who came over from Holland, assumed leading positions, and became the rivals of Smith. They engraved many portraits after Kneller, who seems to have been almost as popular with the mezzotint engravers of his time as Sir Joshua Reynolds afterwards became. Faber engraved, after Kneller, the so-called 'Beauties of Hampton Court,' and a series of forty-eight portraits of members of the Kit-Cat Club. There is also a fine print, 'The Guitar-Player,' after Frans Hals. By the middle of the century, however, the art had declined, and the mezzotint engravings of this period are of little artistic importance; but with the appearance of the Irish engraver MacArdell it soon regained all that it had lost, and entered upon the brightest period of its history. In England the great school of portrait-painters had arisen whose portraits, like those of Rembrandt, Rubens, and Van Dyck, were especially suitable for reproduction in mezzotint, and are illustrated by a series of the most beautiful engravings ever produced by this process.

In the latter years of the eighteenth century mezzotint engraving in England had become the national art, and it is reported that at one time more than one hundred mezzotint engravers were employed upon the portraits of Sir Joshua Reynolds, under that painter's supervision. The process, at first confined to portraits, was soon extended to flower and game pieces, and even to historical subjects and landscapes, for which purposes it was often ill adapted. Of the multitude of mezzotint engravers who practised their art in England at this period, the most eminent were James MacArdell and Richard Earlom, although there were many others, both native and foreign, of scarcely less ability, among them Valentine Green, John Raphael Smith, James Watson, Houston, Pether, Frye, Dickinson, Say, and Finlayson, and of the foreign engravers who were attracted to England at this period, the German J. G. Haid, the Viennese Jacobé, and his pupil Pichler.

James MacArdell, who carried the art of mezzotint engraving from the point to which it had been brought by Smith and Faber to comparative perfection, was born in Dublin about the year 1729. At an early age he went to London, where his superior abilities and genial disposition soon made him a favorite with the artists. MacArdell greatly improved upon the technic of his predecessors. He added freedom and boldness by combining strong etching with mezzotint, and his works are characterized by great power and originality. His numerous portraits after Reynolds, Ramsay, Gainsborough, Van Dyck, and other eminent painters have scarcely been surpassed. Sir Joshua Reynolds, appreciating his abilities, remarked that even if the colors of his own pictures faded, yet his fame would be preserved by MacArdell's engravings.

Of the many fine portraits engraved by MacArdell, there are none more attractive that those of George, Duke of Buckingham, with his brother Francis, engraved in 1752, and 'Rubens' Wife,' both after paintings by Van Dyck, and 'Rubens with his wife and child,' from the painting by Rubens at Blenheim. Of his numerous subjects, the 'Finding of Moses,' 'Virgin and Child,' and 'Time Clipping the Wings of Love,' after Van Dyck; 'Christ disputing with the Doctors,' 'The Mathematician,' and 'Tobit and Angel,' after Rembrandt; and the 'Virgin and Angels' and 'St. Jerome,' after Murillo, are all fine examples. MacArdell's early death in 1765 cut short a career of great usefulness and promise, and deprived the art for which he had done so much of one of its ablest exponents.

As MacArdell passed from the scene, Richard Earlom was rising in fame, and proved a worthy successor. As the former is famous for the great number and excellence of his portraits, so the latter excelled in all manner of subjects, and engraved some of the masterpieces of the art. Earlom was born in London in 1743, and was a pupil of Cipriani. Like Valentine Green, he is said to have learned mezzotint engraving without a master, and became so proficient, both as draughtsman and engraver, that he was employed by Boydell to make drawings from the pictures in the Houghton Gallery, some of the finest of which he afterwards engraved. Earlom engraved the 200 plates in the *Liber Veritatis* in the style of the original drawings by Claude Lorraine, together with about one hundred other drawings by Claude; these were published at London in 1777 by Boydell. His principal works are 'A Fruit-piece' and 'A Flower-piece,' after the celebrated flower-painter, Jan Van Huysum. These two prints are among the choicest masterpieces of the art, showing its possibilities in the direction of delicacy of tones, minute finish, clearness and transparency. His engraving of 'Bathsheba bringing Abishag to David,' after Van der Werff, is also a fine example of his skill. The original pictures were at the time in the Houghton Gallery, but are now in the Imperial Gallery at St. Petersburg. The 'Market-scenes,' after Snyders, are also interesting if less important examples. Of his portraits, that of the Duke of Aremberg on horseback may be named. Earlom scraped a multitude of plates, covering a wide range of subjects, and combined etching with mezzotint in a manner equalled by no other engraver.

Valentine Green (1739–1813) and John Raphael Smith

(1752–1833) were also among the foremost masters of the art. The former engraved nearly four hundred prints, including many portraits after Reynolds, and a large number of historical subjects after West. He engraved a large full-length portrait of Washington, from a painting by Trumbull, then in the possession of M. De Neufville, of Amsterdam, according to the inscription. This portrait, published in 1781, is now rare and valuable. Smith is chiefly famous for his fine portraits after Reynolds. There is also a curious portrait, after Romney, of Brant, the Mohawk chieftain.

Since the death of Earlom in 1822 there have been many mezzotint engravers, but few of eminence. His most worthy successors were Samuel William Reynolds, his pupils, David Lucas and Samuel Cousins, and Charles Turner, all famous in their art. To the first of these engravers we owe many fine portraits and subjects after the English painters, chiefly Sir Joshua Reynolds, and a number of beautiful subjects after Horace Vernet, Géricault, Delacroix, and others. Lucas is famous for his English landscapes after Constable, published in 1830–32, and his single prints after the same painter, of which 'The Cornfield,' 'The Lock,' and 'Salisbury Cathedral from the Meadows,' christened by Constable "The Rainbow," are beautiful examples. Charles Turner engraved many fine plates after Sir Thomas Lawrence, J. M. W. Turner, and others, including twenty-three of the plates in the *Liber Studiorum*. The many fine plates engraved by the late Samuel Cousins, after Lawrence, Landseer, Millais, and Reynolds, are widely known and justly admired. The engraver of 'Master Lambton' and 'Pius VII.' well deserves a place among the foremost exponents of his art. In our own day a new interest in mezzotint engraving seems to be awakening. The masterpieces of the art command constantly increasing prices. All this may lead to its revival.

Notwithstanding the great success of mezzotint engraving, another process known as stipple engraving, employing dots, became almost equally popular in England in the latter half of the eighteenth century. In connection with line engraving this process was well known to engravers from an early period. The Italian Campagnola, who worked in the first part of the sixteenth century, had made extensive use of dots to give greater delicacy and finish to his work, and a century later the Roman engraver Ottavio Leoni engraved a number of heads by a mixture of lines and dots; but the first to use the dotted manner as a complete process with any considerable success was the Dutch goldsmith and engraver Jan Lutma, who engraved some portraits by means of dots produced by a punch and mallet. Lutma's process, which he called "opus mallei," was a primitive form of stipple engraving, a process in which the effects are produced by an arrangement of masses of dots, more or less close and delicate as required, made with the graver, dry-point, roulette, and often with aquafortis. As with the "ground" in mezzotint engraving, so in the stipple process the flat tints are often made by a special machine. Stipple engraving was but an improvement and extension of the dotted manner already mentioned. Of its various modifications were the processes known as chalk and crayon engraving, the latter said to have been invented in France by Jean François, and perfected by Demarteau, who engraved in this manner many fac-similes of drawings by Boucher and other artists of his school. The object of this form of engraving was to imitate the effect of chalk or crayon drawings upon paper.

Although of foreign origin, like mezzotint, stipple engraving was perfected in England. While greatly inferior to line engraving, etching, and mezzotint, its novelty, the beauty and softness of the effects produced, and its peculiar adaptation to the works of Angelica Kauffman, Cipriani, and other popular painters of fancy subjects, gave to the stipple process an exaggerated importance. Le Blond, Kirkall, and others had invented various methods of printing in colors from a number of plates and blocks, but after many experiments the results were found more satisfactory where a single plate was used, the colors or tints being carefully rubbed in by the printer. Le Blond printed chiefly from mezzotint plates, but this process was soon abandoned in favor of stipple. The works of Demarteau, Ryland, and others printed in this manner created a sort of craze for stippled prints, and many line engravers abandoned their art to cater to the prevailing fashion. Indeed, the number of engravers who practised mezzotint and stipple engraving in England in the latter half of the eighteenth century far exceeded those who worked in line.

William Wynne Ryland (1732–83) is said to have learned crayon engraving from Demarteau at Paris, and to have inaugurated its practice in England. Upon his return from France, after a five years' sojourn in that country, he engraved many fancy subjects after Angelica Kauffman, Cipriani, and others, and brought the process into great popular favor. Ryland also engraved in line, and held the appointment of engraver to George III. A French writer gravely states that "an accidental circumstance suddenly compelled him to abandon engraving." This "circumstance" was his execution at Tyburn for forging two bills on the East India Company. After this "his name was never heard again."

Upon the coming to England of the Florentine engraver Francesco Bartolozzi, the stipple process attained a popularity never since accorded to it. There are few engravers concerning whose merits there has been so great a diversity of opinion. Since his death in 1815 his works have come successively into favor, and then again into comparatively little repute. Although at the present day his admirers are legion, his works are held in less esteem than formerly by amateurs and collectors. That he engraved some masterpieces both in stipple and line is true, but it is also true that the greater portion of his works, and those by which he is best known, are of a trivial character. Although a draughtsman and engraver of unusual skill, he catered to a depraved popular taste, instead of using his powerful influence to correct and improve it.

Of Bartolozzi personally very little is known, considering his great popularity and comparatively recent career. Born in Florence in 1727, the son of a goldsmith, for which pursuit he was also intended, he displayed unusual abilities as a designer and copyist, and was apprenticed to Joseph Wagner, a Venetian print-seller and engraver, who taught him what little he knew of line engraving. He afterwards studied for a time at Rome, but soon returned to Venice, where he rose rapidly into favor through his engravings after the Italian masters.

It was at this time that Dalton, the librarian of King George III., travelling about in Italy with the royal commission to purchase pictures, knowing Bartolozzi's superior abilities, engaged him on his own account for a period of three years, promising him an appointment as engraver to the King. Bartolozzi accordingly arrived in London, the theatre of his success, in the year 1764, and the appointment was soon afterwards ratified. Stipple engraving had already come into great favor, and Bartolozzi soon excelled in this style almost every other engraver of the time. His numerous works in this manner include a large number of "those charmingly beautiful red prints," representing fanciful designs, tickets of admission to entertainments, vignettes, bacchantes, cupids, family portraits, beautiful women and children fantastically attired, and a multitude of similar subjects, in circles and ovals, after Angelica Kauffman, Cipriani, and others. That many of these stippled prints are pretty and graceful must be admitted, but they were mostly of trivial subjects, "the confectionery of art," and as printed in red and brown inks are not exalted models.

Chief among Bartolozzi's numerous portraits are those of Lord Mansfield and Lord Thurlow, after Sir Joshua Reynolds, engraved in stipple with a small admixture of lines. The well-known Holbein portraits, engraved in the stipple manner and printed in colors, were published in 1792 by Chamberlaine, keeper of the King's drawings. These are not fac-similes of Holbein's drawings, for the engraver added much by way of ornament and finish to the often slight sketches of Holbein. Of his prints engraved in line may be mentioned the beautiful 'Clytie' and 'The Virgin and Child,' called "The Silence," both after Annibale Caracci; 'Mary Queen of Scots and her Son James I.,' after Zuccaro; the 'Madonna del Sacco,' after Andrea del Sarto; and the 'Death of the Earl of Chatham,' a large print containing more than sixty portraits, from Copley's painting. Bartolozzi also engraved the Royal Academy Diploma, a much coveted print, especially when properly filled out and signed. There are also many spirited etchings after Guercino, Cipriani, and various other masters. A complete list of Bartolozzi's prints will be found in the excellent catalogue by Mr. Andrew W. Tuer.

For engraving his portrait of Lord Mansfield, Bartolozzi received 500 guineas, and for the Death of Chatham he is said to have received £2000, and to have expended nearly that amount for assistance, much of which proved worse than useless, as a large portion of the work had to be taken out and re-engraved. He worked with great rapidity, and often with great carelessness, frequently engraving a plate in a single day; and if he earned money easily, he spent it even more freely, and lived a gay life when not at work. His studio was the resort of the art idlers, and as a distinguished man and a member of the Royal Academy he was entertained at Holland House. After living in London for thirty-eight years, Bartolozzi removed in 1802 to Portugal, attracted by the offer of a directorship in the National Academy at Lisbon and the promise of a pension and knighthood; here he died in 1815. During his long life of nearly ninety years he engraved an enormous number of prints, said to exceed two thousand, comprising all sorts of subjects and almost every style of engraving.

Bartolozzi rarely forgot himself in his devotion to art. He made everything conform to his own ideas, and is said to have had a notion that he could improve everything he touched. He was the leader of a popular, but inferior, school of engraving, which declined almost as rapidly as it had arisen; and when the craze for stippled prints had subsided, his reputation greatly diminished. Nor do his prints engraved in this manner show the capabilities of the process, for his best works have been surpassed by other engravers of less reputation. His work in line, although in some instances of a high order, is inferior to that of Strange, Woollett, and Sharp; yet he enjoyed a greater reputation than any of those engravers, and upon the foundation of the Royal Academy in 1769, with Sir Joshua Reynolds at its head, he was invited to become an Academician, an honor from which they were excluded. Much of Bartolozzi's success was due to his personal popularity and to his readiness to cater to the public taste. His abilities are now less highly esteemed.

Among the numerous other engravers in the chalk and stipple manner were Thomas Burke, a favorite of Angelica Kauffmann, Bartolozzi's pupils, Schiavonetti and Tomkins, Anthony Cardon, Thomas Gaugain, and Caroline Watson, and, later in the present century, William Walker, to the last of whom we owe some of the finest portraits ever engraved in the stipple manner, notably those of Sir Walter Scott, Hopetoun, and Raeburn. But the stipple manner, once so popular, has declined in importance, and as a complete process is now seldom employed for important works, although used as an adjunct to other processes.

The portraits and literary works of George Vertue, who belonged to the first half of the eighteenth century, are of great historical importance. Vertue was a man of great industry and modesty, and of scrupulous integrity. He belonged to a good family, "more honest than opulent," and numbered among his friends and patrons the most distinguished men of his time and country. He travelled about in England, making drawings of whatever attracted his attention, engraving innumerable portraits and views of buildings, towns and ruins, copying rare and curious pictures, collecting books, prints, and antiquities, and gathering information about matters pertaining to art with as much industry and enthusiasm as the Suffolk Squire displayed in his agricultural investigations.

Vertue engraved a multitude of portraits of distinguished persons, many of them the only authentic likenesses of the persons they represent. He is said to have "rendered most happily the distinguished air of lords and ladies." If his works have been surpassed by others in artistic effect, they have the high merit of scrupulous fidelity to their originals, a quality not

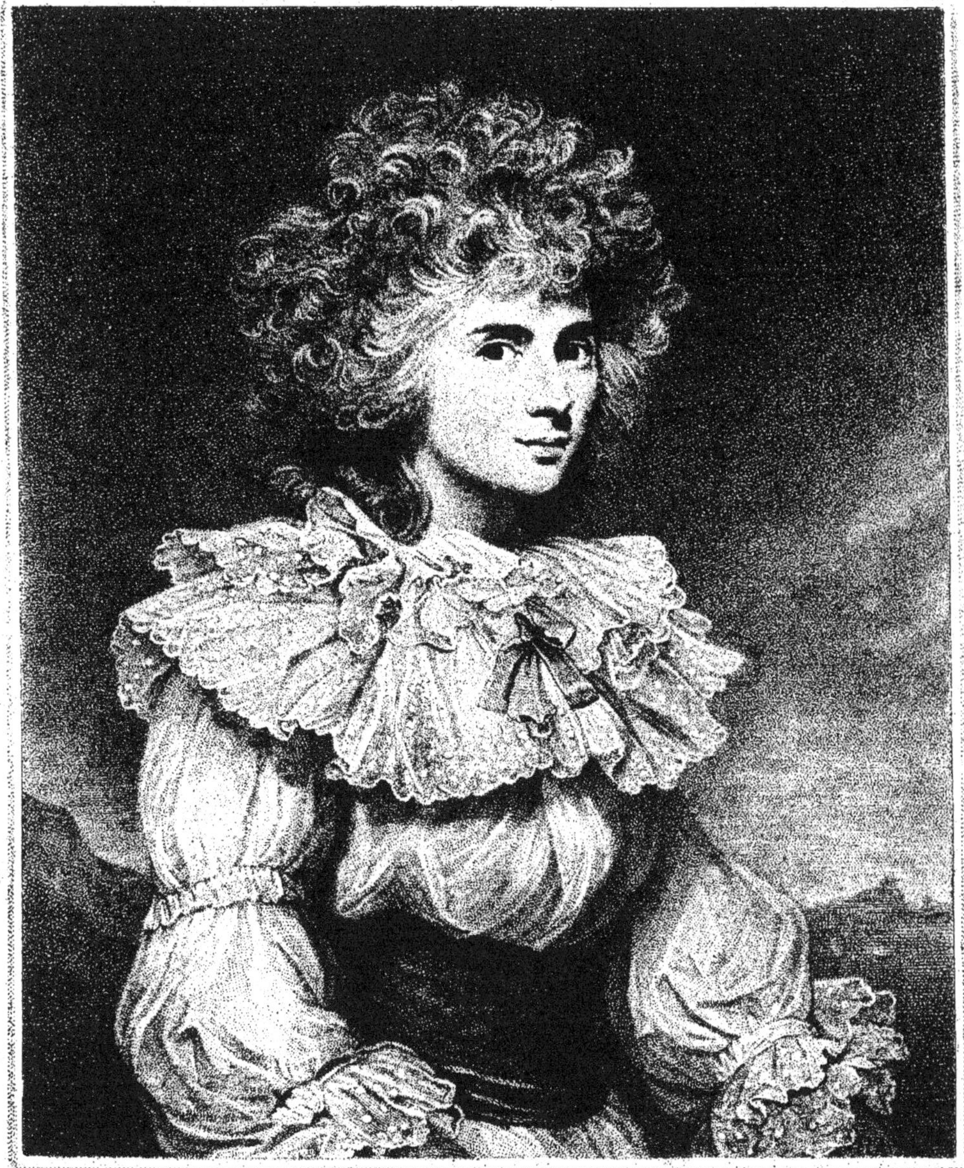

Painted by Sir Joshua Reynolds — *Engrav'd by F. Bartolozzi R.A.*

always found in the works of his contemporaries, some of whom, like Houbraken, did not hesitate to employ their skill upon portraits wholly fictitious.

Vertue left voluminous notes and memoranda, collected during many years of careful research for his *History of the Arts in England.* He even learned French, Dutch, and some Italian in order to consult in the originals his authorities relating to foreign artists. These notes, now in the British Museum, became the property of Horace Walpole, and formed the ground-work of his *Anecdotes of Painting in England,* first published in 1762–71. This work contains Vertue's list of the engravers who were born or who resided in England. Vertue also published, in 1759, a descriptive catalogue of the works of Hollar.

To mention the engraved works of the great Hogarth, or of the caricaturists Gillray, Rowlandson, Doyle, Cruikshank, and their followers seems a digression in a work like the present, for their purpose was moral, philosophical, and satirical rather than artistic. They attempted through art what such masters as Cervantes, Molière, Fielding, and Thackeray accomplished through literature.

The second half of the eighteenth century has been called the Augustan Age of British engraving. The great versatility and excellence of the school are well illustrated in the works of this period. Its landscape engravings, after such masters as Claude and Wilson, are unrivalled, although modern landscape painting requires much more from engravers in the direction of delicacy of tones and subtile transitions of light and shadow. Its engravings of modern historical subjects are unsurpassed; and some of its classical subjects and portraits are in many respects equal to the best of any other school. During this period mez-

13

zotint and stipple engraving were developed and perfected, and the art of wood-engraving was revived by Bewick.

Notwithstanding the great success of mezzotint and stipple engraving, the chief glory of the British school rests upon the works of its three great line engravers, Strange, Woollett, and Sharp. The first of these engravers in point of time was Sir Robert Strange, who was born in the year 1721 on the Island of Pomona, the largest of the Orkneys. Strange belonged to an ancient Scottish family, and was intended for the law, a career which he abandoned in favor of engraving. After serving an apprenticeship in the studio of Richard Cooper at Edinburgh, he practised his art on his own account with fair success until 1745, when he joined the Jacobite forces, and shared their defeat at Culloden. For a time he was a fugitive in the highlands, and it is related that upon one occasion he owed his safety from his pursuers to Isabella Lumisden, "a young lady dressed in the ample costume of the period," who afterwards became his wife. He escaped to France, and in the following year won the prize for design offered by the Academy at Rouen; thence he went to Paris, where he studied under Le Bas.

Upon the restoration of peace, Strange returned to London, in 1751, and soon established his reputation by his engravings of 'The Magdalen' and 'Death of Cleopatra,' after Guido. But he soon lost the royal patronage, and narrowly escaped serious difficulties by refusing to engrave the portraits of King George III. and his minister, Lord Bute, his refusal being attributed to his Jacobite proclivities. The commission was thereupon given to Ryland. Judging it prudent to leave England for a second time, he undertook, in 1761, a long-contemplated journey to Italy, which occupied about five years. He visited Florence, Parma, Naples, Rome, Bologna, and other cities, where he made many drawings, and some of his finest engravings, from celebrated pictures, and acquired a love for the great masterpieces of Italian art which he so well represented. He was received upon the Continent with great courtesy and distinction, and was elected a member of the academies of most of the important cities which he visited. In 1766 Strange was elected a member of the Incorporated Society of Artists, but after repeated applications was refused admission to the Royal Academy as an Academician, whereupon he published his *Inquiry into the Rise and Establishment of the Royal Academy of Arts*, in which he arraigned the managers of that body for excluding engravers from full privileges and slighting their art. Strange was especially jealous of Bartolozzi, who had been elected an Academician, it was said, on account of his abilities as a painter and designer, but more likely through personal popularity and influence. From the year 1855, however, engravers have been admitted to full membership—a somewhat tardy recognition.

Strange possessed technical abilities of a very high order. His style, rich and captivating, expressed warm flesh tints with great truth and delicacy, to which his masterly use of the dry-point, acquired, it is said, from Le Bas, greatly contributed. His works after the Italian colorists are remarkable for breadth, softness, and purity, and possess a peculiar charm and interest. His technical powers as an engraver, however, exceeded his abilities as a draughtsman and designer, and the drawing in some of his works is so weak that his attack upon the Royal Academy was met with the harmless witticism that he sometimes "exhibited Strange carelessness in his delineation of the human figure."

Among the many fine subjects which Strange engraved after Guido, Correggio, Titian, Raphael, and other Italian painters there is none more attractive, or a more faithful translation of the original, than the famous 'Madonna of St. Jerome, with the Magdalen and Angels,' called *Il Giorno*, 'The Day,' from Correggio's painting in the gallery at Parma. The painting by Correggio is one of his most perfect works, renowned alike for its marvellous effects of light and shade, and for the great beauty of the Magdalen. Strange's engraving of this subject, and a number of his other important plates, among them 'Venus' and 'Danae,' after Titian; 'St. Cecilia,' after Raphael; and the 'Penitent Magdalen,' after Guido, were engraved from his drawings made from the originals during his sojourn in Italy.

Strange also engraved a few portraits of great interest and merit. Chief among these are his famous portraits, after Van Dyck, of Charles I. standing by his horse, and attended by the Marquis of Hamilton, a masterpiece of great beauty and interest; its companion, the portrait of Queen Henrietta Maria with her sons; the portrait of Charles I. in his ermine robes; and the three royal children with the King Charles spaniels.

Strange regained the royal favor, and was knighted and otherwise honored. About the year 1790 a magnificent edition of about eighty numbered copies of the finest reserved impressions from his plates was published, with an introductory essay on the progress of his art. For this collection he engraved a small portrait of himself from a drawing by Greuze. Most of these copies have since been separated, but the impressions are identified by the Roman numbers in the margin. Strange died in London in 1792. If in his own time his popularity was overshadowed by that of Bartolozzi, his name is forever associated with the serious and important work of the British school, while his rival has left us few works to justify his greater reputation.

As Strange excelled in his subjects after the Italian masters and in his portraits after Van Dyck, so William Woollett became famous for his landscapes and historical subjects. Woollett was born August 15, 1735, at Maidstone, in Kent, of humble parentage. His father, Philip Woollett, was by occupation a flax-dresser, but having the good-fortune to be part owner of a lottery ticket which drew a large prize, he took a public-house known as the "Turk's Head." We are told that his son William at an early age distinguished himself by scratching a Turk's head on a pewter pot, and otherwise displayed such talent in drawing that he was apprenticed to a somewhat obscure London engraver and print-seller named Tinney, who seems to have had as his pupils a number of eminent engravers. But little is known of Woollett's early life. He is described as small in stature, exceedingly simple and unpretending in manner, very near-sighted, possessing great patience, extremely industrious, and a truly good man. He owed very little to the schools, and was never outside of England; indeed, he scarcely ever left London from the time he entered upon his apprenticeship.

Woollett's early work consisted of shop-bills, views of buildings and gardens, and a few portraits. His important works date from 1761, in which year appeared his famous engraving of 'Niobe,' from the fine landscape painting by Richard Wilson, now in the National Gallery, which had then just arrived from Rome and was the chief topic of discussion in the world of art. This beautiful plate was engraved for Alderman John Boydell, the famous publisher of prints. According to Boydell's statement, Woollett undertook to engrave this plate for 100 guineas, "an unheard-of price" at the time, and this proving insufficient, an additional £50 was allowed to enable him to complete his task. The success of the undertaking justified Boydell's liberality. After taking a few proofs, which are now valuable, the prints were sold at five shillings, and met with such unexpected success, both at home and abroad, that even at that low price they brought in to the publisher about £2000. This engraving established Woollett's fame and brought to him all the work he was capable of performing. In the following two years appeared the landscapes known as the First and Second Premium prints, after the Smiths of Chichester, and in 1772 the great landscape engraving from the painting by Claude Lorraine, 'Roman Edifices in Ruins,' which placed Woollett's name at the head of all landscape-engravers. Up to this time we are told that Woollett was poor, living in upper lodgings, and often in want, a condition of affairs explained, perhaps, by the further information that his wife, Elizabeth Woollett, five times presented her husband with twins, and upon another occasion with triplets.

Allusion has already been made to the great influence of Claude upon landscape engraving. Of the many beautiful engravings of these classic landscapes, Woollett's plate, 'Roman Edifices in Ruins,' stands foremost, both in its technical perfection and beauty, and in its true rendering of the peculiar atmospheric effects and delicate gradations of the original, now at Grosvenor House. This beautiful picture, representing the allegorical evening of the Roman Empire, inspired the engraver to his best efforts. The rich foliage in the foreground, the ruined aqueduct, the winding river, and the sky and distant hills are rendered with rare skill and fidelity. The whole scene is eminently characteristic of Claude, and loses but little of his spirit in the translation. The lines, in the foreground bold and clear, become more and more delicate in the receding distance until lost in the tender and luminous horizon.

Not only is Woollett famous for his engravings of landscapes, but in the more difficult department of historical engraving he is equally renowned. His two plates, 'The Death of General Wolfe' and 'The Battle at La Hogue,' both from paintings by Benjamin West, are among the best engravings of modern historical events.

'The Death of General Wolfe' is a masterpiece of engraving, full of force, tenderness, and expression. The subject is also one of great historical interest. For months the English general lay before Quebec, the strongest place in the possession of the French, baffled by its strength and position, which he could not overcome; but at last, winning by stratagem what he could not take by force, he was stricken down in the moment of victory; unmindful of the mortal injury he had received, he thanked God for his success, and declared that he died happy. The dying general is surrounded by his officers and soldiers, and an Indian chief watches to see if the English soldier is equal in fortitude to the children of the forests, while the French are fleeing before his army. This picture, which brought fame to the painter, as well as fortune to the engraver, was made the subject of much curious criticism. Before this time it had been the custom to represent the heroes clad in classic costume, with spear, shield, and helmet. West substituted the regulation military uniform, musket, and bayonet, insisting upon realism, and claiming that it would be ridiculous to represent English soldiers in the dress of Greeks or Romans. His critics, taking issue upon his claim of realism, thereupon complained that of the important persons represented in the foreground, three at least were not present; for two of them, Moncton and Barré, had been disabled, and Surgeon Adair was at a considerable distance from the scene; the presence of the Indian was also disputed.

This plate has a curious history. After a few proofs were taken, a son of the printer, taking up a hammer in a thoughtless manner, said, in jest, "I could soon be the death of Wolfe," or, according to another account, "General Wolfe is dying, and I'll be d——d if I don't kill him quite." No sooner were these unfortunate words uttered than the hammer fell upon the face of Wolfe, destroying in an instant the finest part of the plate. A detailed statement of this accident is attached to the proof in the British Museum. When Woollett heard of this sad injury which had befallen his choicest work, and to which the best energies of his life had been devoted, he is said to have wept. After great labor the injury was repaired and the printing resumed. While the first proofs were being printed the news arrived that Woollett had been appointed engraver to the King. The press was stopped, and the words "Engraver to His Majesty" were added below Woollett's name, and beneath West's name the words "Historical Painter to His Majesty." The demand for impressions was unprecedented, and Woollett is said to have received more than £5000 as his share of the profits, Boydell and Ryland also being partners in the undertaking. After Woollett's death in 1785 the plate came into the exclusive ownership of Boydell. It was badly retouched, the title erased, and open letters again introduced, and spurious proofs printed and sold. This imposition gave rise to the letter, circulated widely at the time, purporting to have been written by the *late* William Woollett, engraver, to the Right Hon. John Boydell, that worthy having in the meantime become Lord Mayor of London, crying for protection to his memory and revenge upon the wretches who were destroying forever "the only monument desired by the injured." There are ten states of this plate, all of which are represented in the almost perfect collection of Woollett's works in the British Museum, which numbers 123 subjects, besides nearly every state of each plate, from the etched outline to the finished print. There are also many copies of this print, and a parody etched by Gillray, entitled, 'The Death of the Great Wolf,' representing Pitt as the dying hero supported by Dundas and Burke, while the other figures represent well-known leaders in Parliament, the print referring to an attack upon Pitt in the House of Commons.

The 'Battle at La Hogue' represents the naval combat which took place in 1692 between the combined fleets of England and Holland, and the French fleet. The success achieved by these historical prints led West and Woollett to project other similar works, but owing to the death of the latter they were either abandoned or were engraved by other hands.

All of Woollett's works show the greatest originality and the most untiring industry. He was a thorough master of the technical portion of his art. He neglected nothing, however trivial, and would spend weeks, and even months, in making slight alterations and improvements which a less patient and conscientious engraver would scarcely have undertaken. Of a generous disposition, free from jealousy, he duly appreciated and applauded merit in the works of others. After his death there seems to have been a time when his fame greatly decreased, so that in 1821 Bartsch mentions him as having been *formerly* held in high esteem, but again in 1830 Longhi (La Calcografia) speaks of him in the highest terms, attributing to him every good quality, saying that he "was for all contemporary engravers, and is for those of the present day, the marvel and example;" but his great merits are now universally recognized. According to tradition, whenever Woollett completed an important plate, he celebrated the event by firing a cannon from the roof of his house. For several years he was secretary of the Incorporated Society of Artists of Great Britain, and was also highly esteemed on the Continent, where his works had a wide circulation.

Woollett died May 23, 1785, and was buried in the churchyard of Old St. Pancras, where a plain tombstone marked the spot. On this stone was found written in pencil:

"Here Woollett rests, expecting to be sav'd,
He graved well, but is not well engrav'd."

Soon afterwards a subscription was raised, to which West and Boydell were principal contributors, and a memorial was erected in his honor in Westminster Abbey, with the inscription "Incisor Excellentissimus." There is an excellent biographical and descriptive catalogue by Mr. Louis Fagan, late of the British Museum.

Upon the death of Woollett, his companion, John Hall, became his successor as engraver to the King, and continued the projected series of engravings from the historical paintings by West. Among his prints are 'Penn's Treaty with the Indians,' 'The Battle of the Boyne,' and 'Oliver Cromwell dissolving the Long Parliament.'

The antecedents of the great school of landscape engraving which reached its perfection under Woollett may be traced to France, to the painters Claude Lorraine and Joseph Vernet, and the engravers Vivarès and Baléchou. Vivarès, a Frenchman by birth, resided for many years in England, and may be called the founder of the school. In his youth he was a tailor's apprentice, but preferred the etching-needle. His beautiful landscapes after Claude are surpassed only by those of Woollett. Vivarès was an exceedingly industrious engraver, perhaps from necessity, to provide for the wants of a family almost incredibly numerous. Although Baléchou remained in France, his landscapes and marine subjects after Vernet were carefully studied by the English engravers, and contributed greatly to their education. Among the chief disciples of the school of Vivarès and Woollett were John Browne, James Mason, and James Peak, who engraved many beautiful landscapes after Claude Lorraine, Gaspard Dughet, Smith, Wilson, and other eminent landscape-painters. No other country can boast of such an array of talent in this direction.

Scarcely less renowned than Strange and Woollett was their successor, William Sharp, an engraver of varied resources and great originality. Among his works are a number of masterpieces unsurpassed in boldness and picturesque effect. Sharp was born in London, January 29, 1749, and was the son of a gunmaker, who apprenticed him to learn the art of "bright" engraving, to qualify him to ornament fire-arms and plate, a beginning not unlike that of Masson, Schmidt, and other eminent engravers. It is said that he first exercised his skill in decorating pewter pots for the publicans; but he soon turned his attention to the higher branch of his art, and became one of the foremost engravers of his time. If we except two ornamental cards, bearing his name and address, and designed to call attention to his vocation, Sharp's first attempt in this new direction was his portrait of the old lion Hector, who for many years had been an inmate of the Tower—almost as great a public favorite as the late lamented Jumbo. This print, engraved in 1775, and a number of illustrations for the *Novelist's*

Magazine, from Stothard's designs, attracted public attention to his abilities.

Sharp's powers came rapidly to maturity. In 1782 appeared his engraving from West's painting of 'Alfred the Great dividing his loaf with the Pilgrim,' and two years later he engraved his fine print of 'Lucretia,' after Domenichino. To the following year belongs his masterpiece, the famous 'Doctors of the Church,' from Guido's painting, then in the Houghton Gallery, but since removed to the Imperial Gallery at St. Petersburg. This picture, painted by Guido for Pope Paul V., represents the four Latin Doctors of the Church—St. Jerome, St. Augustine, St. Ambrose, and St. Gregory—who, with St. John Damascene and St. Ildefonso, are engaged in a discussion upon the great Catholic doctrine of the Immaculate Conception, which the Pope afterwards confirmed in 1617. This print, boldly and beautifully engraved, is often placed at the head of English engraved subjects.

Mr. Maberly relates that when in Rome, Sharp visited Raphael Morghen, then of great age. The venerable Italian, after exhibiting his choice reserved proofs of his own engravings, at last drew forth from his portfolio an impression of Sharp's 'Doctors of the Church,' saying, "And now Mr. Sharp, I will show you a print which is equal to anything I ever did in my life." Sharp, in relating this anecdote upon his return, added with some enthusiasm, "and indeed the old man was not far from right."

In striking contrast to the 'Doctors of the Church' is 'Lear in the Storm,' after West, characterized by vigor, strong contrasts, and violent action, as the former is remarkable for its atmosphere of repose and contemplation. This print was engraved for Boydell's *Shakespeare*, and is the most important

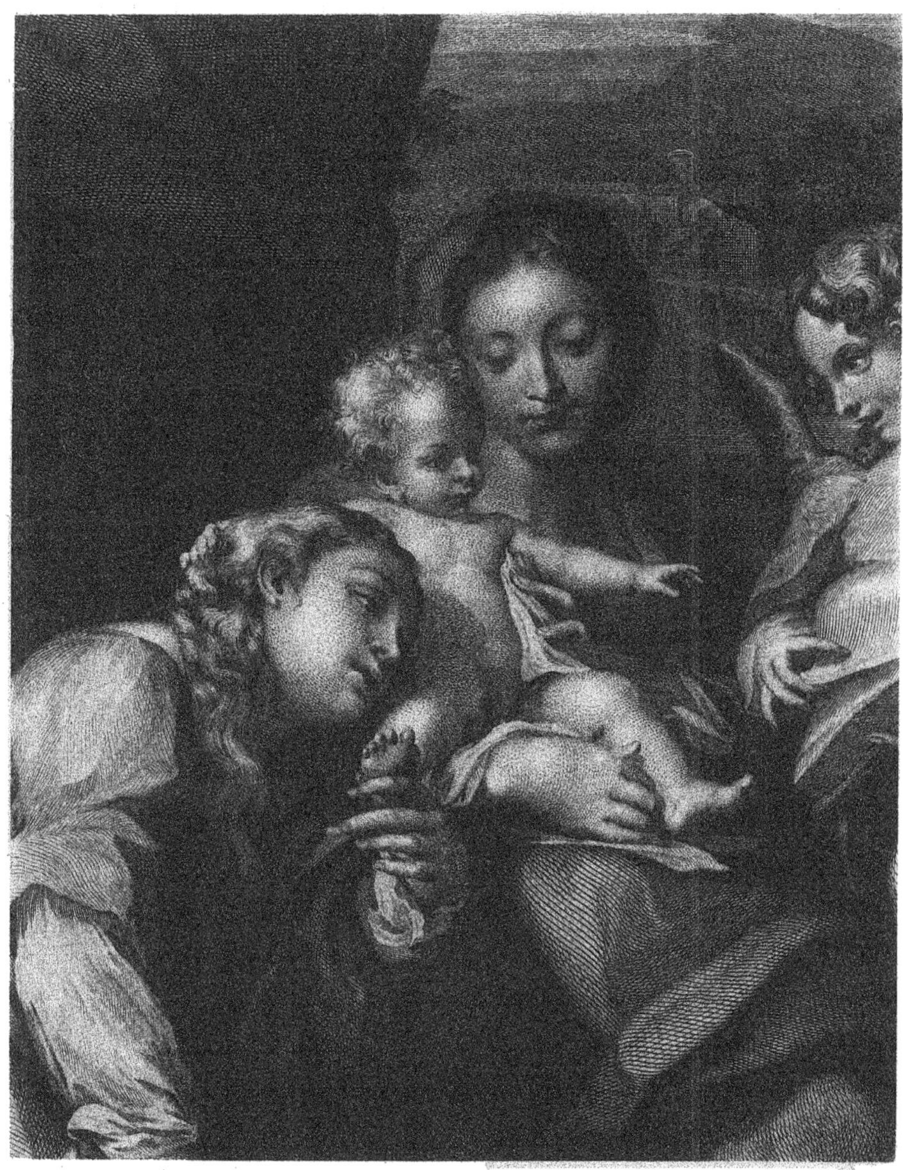

print in the collection. To the masterpieces named must be added the large historical engraving after Trumbull, 'The Sortie made by the Garrison of Gibraltar' on the morning of November 27, 1781, in which many of the heads are authentic portraits. The originals of this and the preceding are now in the Boston Athenæum.

Among other important engravings by Sharp are 'Diogenes in search of an Honest Man,' after Salvator Rosa; 'Ecce Homo,' after Guido; 'St. Cecilia,' after Domenichino; 'The Holy Family,' after Reynolds; 'Infant Christ,' after Annibale Caracci; 'Zenobia,' a profile, after Michael Angelo; 'The Virgin and Infant Saviour,' after Carlo Dolci; and 'The Witch of Endor,' 'The Siege and Relief of Gibraltar,' and 'King Charles II. Landing on the Beach at Dover,' after West. The last of these was etched by Woollett, and finished after his death by Sharp. The well-known print representing the grim old cynic and philosopher Diogenes with his lantern is one of the engraver's most striking works, and may be taken as a typical example of his bold, picturesque style.

As an engraver of portraits Sharp was equally successful. Of his prints, numbering about two hundred and thirty, more than seventy are portraits, and of these nearly one-half are of large size. Foremost among his masterpieces in this direction is his well-known portrait of the eminent surgeon and anatomist John Hunter, from the painting by Sir Joshua Reynolds. This portrait, engraved in 1788, is a worthy companion to the masterpieces of the Dutch and French engravers. To the second place is assigned the portrait of the Birmingham manufacturer and engineer Matthew Boulton, after Sir William Beachy, engraved in 1801; and of scarcely less merit are the portraits of Bishop Seabury, Dundas, Hyde, Home, Burdett, and Sharp's own portrait of himself. Of his small portraits those of Erskine and George, Prince of Wales, from miniature paintings by Richard Cosway, are fine examples.

Sharp's character was a curious combination of opposite traits. His weaknesses stood forth in grotesque relief. No engraver's work could be more true to the conditions of his art; yet we turn from the artist to the man with a feeling of disappointment and humiliation. The illustrious engraver of the 'Doctors of the Church' was weak, simple, and credulous to the point of absurdity, and was a firm believer in all sorts of mysticism and superstitious nonsense. He believed in the "prophecies" of Richard Brothers, who imagined that he had a divine appointment to lead the Jews back to Jerusalem, and engraved his portrait with rays of light descending upon the head, and with the title "Prince of the Hebrews," and the inscription "Fully believing this to be the man whom God has appointed, I engrave his likeness." The "prophet" died in a mad-house. Sharp was also one of the adherents of the notorious Joanna Southcott, and maintained her for a long time at his own expense, besides engraving her portrait. The reveries of Swedenborg were likewise received with perfect credence by the simple-minded engraver. He also for a time espoused the doctrines of Horne Tooke and Thomas Paine, and engraved their portraits, and was once examined before the Privy Council as a revolutionist; but here his simplicity availed him, for, in the midst of the examination, he actually produced the prospectus of a portrait of the patriot Kosciuszko, and asked Pitt and Dundas to become subscribers. He was dismissed as simple and harmless. Sharp imagined that he could trace in the countenance of every person a resemblance to some bird or beast, allied in character, and often frankly named the bird or beast, to the great amusement of his hearers. Like Boswell, his works showed him to decidedly better advantage than his conversation; through these his name will be honored long after the harmless errors and absurdities of his simple life are forgotten.

As an engraver, Sharp's grand powers were recognized throughout Europe. The Imperial Academy of Vienna and the Royal Academy of Munich enrolled him among their honorary members, but he is said to have rejected with disdain the offer of an associate membership in the Royal Academy at London, as he considered his art and its great masters slighted by being excluded from full membership. With the death of Sharp in 1824 passed away the last of the great engravers whose works placed England in the foremost ranks of the art. There is a descriptive catalogue of Sharp's engravings by Mr. W. S. Baker.

Many important engravings of this period bear the address of the famous publisher John Boydell, who, meeting with indifferent success as an engraver, abandoned the practice of his art to engage in publishing the works of others, for which undertaking he was qualified both by his superior mercantile wisdom and by his practical knowledge as an engraver. In this undertaking he afterwards associated with him his nephew, Josiah Boydell. Previous to this time England had been sending abroad large sums annually for the purchase of foreign prints, and the promotion of English engraving soon became a question of commercial, as well as artistic importance. The exportation of English prints was encouraged by bounties, and a duty was imposed upon all French prints brought into England. The balance of trade was turned in favor of the home market, which at one time is said to have received an annual revenue of more than £200,000 from this source. Boydell assisted greatly in creating a market for the English engravers at home and abroad. He aspired to become the greatest patron of British art, and to his liberal encouragement is undoubtedly due much of the excellence of the school. It is said that when he visited Paris, towards the close of the century, he saw his own publications exhibited as leading attractions in the windows of the print-sellers.

After saying this much in praise of Boydell, it must also be recorded that in many instances he consulted only his own pecuniary interests, and employed his engravers upon such works as would command a ready sale, and upon inferior processes, making quantity and novelty, rather than intrinsic merit, the chief consideration, to the demoralization of the public taste, an example which his successors were not slow to follow. Mr. John Landseer, the engraver, while lecturing before the Royal Institution, took occasion to allude in no uncertain terms to what he regarded as the baneful influence of the Boydells; but, to use his own language, he "made false estimates of the comparative strength and influence of those interested individuals," and was dismissed in the midst of his course of lectures.

Boydell published many of the best prints of Woollett, Sharp, Hall, Earlom, Green, Bartolozzi, Vivarès, Browne, Mason, Peak, and other engravers, both native and foreign, his publications amounting to nearly four thousand five hundred plates, a number almost incredible, considering that previous to this time many of the great engravers had published the best of their own works, selecting their subjects and methods of engraving. He soon accumulated a fortune, and aspiring to civic honors, became alderman, and finally Lord Mayor of London. Encouraged by the success of his undertakings, he formed the plan of illustrating the works of Shakespeare on a scale of magnificence altogether unparalleled. He procured pictures to be painted and engraved by eminent masters, and the well-known *Boydell Shakespeare* is a lasting monument to the enterprising alderman. This venture, however, resulted disastrously to its projector, for the French Revolution destroyed his continental market, and, upon his petition, he was allowed by Parliament to dispose by lottery of his gallery of paintings, which, it is said, he had intended to bequeath to the public. Upon the death of Boydell the business was continued by his nephew Josiah until his death in 1817, when it passed into other hands.

Among the multitude of Sharp's successors was Abraham Raimbach, who was born in London in the year of the American Independence, and died at Greenwich in 1843. In the earlier portion of his career Raimbach engraved mostly for the book and print publishers, and also painted miniatures with success, but in 1812 Sir David Wilkie, attracted by the engraver's style, employed him to engrave his painting 'The Village Politicians,' which he did in so admirable a manner that that master thereafter employed him constantly upon his works, for which Raimbach's clear, bold style was especially adapted. His fine plates, 'The Rent Day,' 'Blind Man's Buff,' and 'Distraining for Rent,' have not only forever associated his name with that of the painter, but have also contributed not a little to the latter's renown. Raimbach was an excellent draughtsman and an engraver of great ability. His plates were generally etched, and then retouched and finished with the graver.

Wilkie was one of the forerunners in the modern revival of etching. His superb plate, 'The Pope examining a Censer,' and his dry-point, 'The Receipt,' entitle him to a high place in the history of engraving.

In the early part of the present century arose the school

of engravers who drew their inspiration from that great artist and unique genius J. M. W. Turner. These engravers are well known through their small plates in the "Rivers of France," which are unsurpassed for delicate manipulation, perfection of finish, and marvellous rendering of the tones and subtle distinctions which characterize Turner's water-color drawings. Their exquisitely beautiful vignettes in Rogers' Poems, after drawings by Turner and Stothard, are also unrivalled in their way. They engraved many other plates both large and small, some of great excellence. Turner's influence upon landscape engraving supplemented that of Claude Lorraine, and in these works the perfection of tone engraving appears to have been reached. The individuality of his engravers is so completely lost in his own that, from aught that appears from the prints themselves, the small plates might almost have been the work of a single engraver. The most noted of these engravers were Radcliffe, Willmore, Goodall, Wallis, Miller, Armytage, Brandard, Higham, Allen, Jeavons, Cousin, and Fisher, all of whom contributed to the "Rivers of France."

As Turner had set out to equal or surpass the great landscape-painters in their own respective styles, so, in imitation of Claude's *Liber Veritatis*, he projected his well-known *Liber Studiorum* to illustrate landscape composition. From his original sepia and pen-drawings he etched the main lines of his compositions in a remarkably bold and masterly manner, but relied upon mezzotint to bring out the required tonality and effects. He practised etching and mezzotint as complementary arts, in some of the plates applying the mezzotint himself with great skill, but generally employing for this purpose professional mezzotint engravers, principally Charles Turner. According to the original design, the work was to consist of 100 plates, but, although commenced in 1807, only seventy plates were published by 1819, when the work was abandoned. Of the remainder a few were finished, some were only etched, others merely slight sketches. Although the *Liber Studiorum* was not a success financially, it contains some of Turner's best work, and shows to great advantage his judicious selection of line, vigorous drawing, and sureness of method.

In our brief review of engraving in England we have seen not only the great excellence but the great versatility of the school; its achievements in mezzotint, stipple, and line. Its services in the revival and development of wood-engraving will be mentioned in the next chapter. In our own day that country has furnished to the world an etcher* whose works in many respects rival any which have appeared since the days of Rembrandt, and whose influence in the modern revival of his art has been as salutary as it has been powerful. By the works of her great artists England has forever silenced the claim, once familiar on the Continent, that it was impossible to rear talent in the fine arts amid the fogs of Great Britain.

* Francis Seymour Haden.

CHAPTER VII

REVIVAL OF WOOD-ENGRAVING

Character of Early Wood-engraving — Revival of the Art by Thomas Bewick — The White-line method — Fables, Birds, and other series — Vignettes and Landscapes — Bewick's Pupils; Clennell, Nesbit, and Harvey — Branston, Thompson, and Linton — Wood-engraving in the United States — Anderson — Adams — Anthony and Marsh — The "New School" — Representative American Wood-engravers

AS we have seen in a previous chapter, sixteenth-century wood-engraving owed its immense popularity and success to its perfect harmony with the taste and sentiment of the age; to the designs, which were mainly the work of eminent artists, rather than to the cutting. The actual engravers were, in most instances, little more than mechanics, more or less skilful. In the latter half of the century the art had already degenerated, and by the close of the seventeenth century it had reached its lowest ebb. We find the skill and patience of the engraver, but the designs were no longer furnished by great artists; the process had been superseded by engraving upon metal plates. For an account of

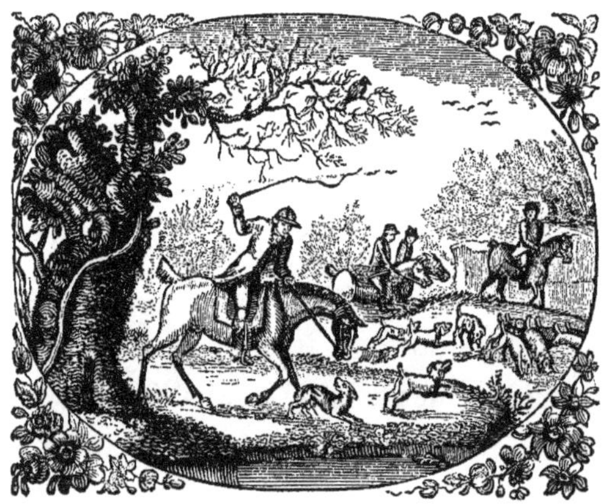

THE HUNTSMAN AND THE OLD HOUND
By Thomas Bewick

the art during the period of its decline the reader is referred to the excellent *Treatise on Wood-Engraving*, by John Jackson. We now come to the time of its revival in the eighteenth century by Bewick, and to the inauguration of the modern school of wood-engraving.

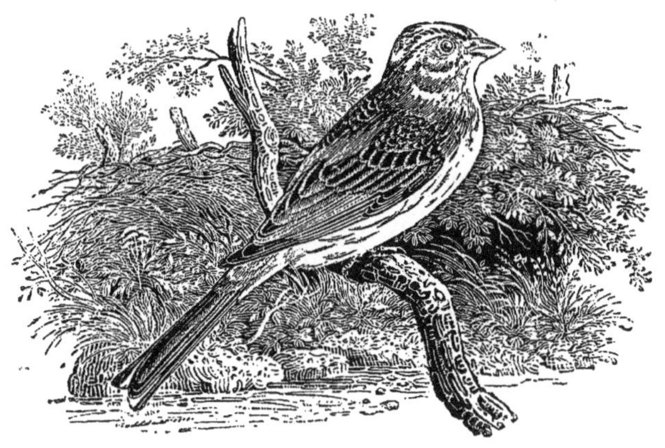

THE YELLOW BUNTING — From Bewick's "Birds"

Thomas Bewick was born near Newcastle-on-Tyne in 1753, and began his career in the studio of Ralph Beilby, a Newcastle copper-plate engraver. During his apprenticeship he engraved a number of wood-cuts for Dr. Hutton's *Treatise on Mensuration*, and, encouraged by his success, determined to devote his attention to wood-engraving, an art which he was destined to revolutionize. By his cut of 'The Huntsman and the Old Hound' he won the prize offered by the Society for the Encouragement of Arts and Manufactures for the best wood-cut engraved in the year 1775. This cut appeared in the edition of Gay's *Fables*, published at Newcastle in 1779. From this time Bewick's career was a succession of triumphs. His *Select Fables*, published in 1784, mark the beginning of the "white-line" method, which he inaugurated and perfected. Other works followed in rapid succession. In 1790 appeared the *History of Quadrupeds*, which gained for him wide reputation; to the year 1795 belong the beautiful cuts which he engraved with the assistance of his brother John, an engraver of much less ability, for Goldsmith's *Traveller* and *Deserted Village* and Parnell's *Hermit;* and in 1797 appeared the first volume of *British Birds*, which was followed in 1804 by the *British Water-Birds*, and in 1818 by a new series of *Fables*. The above contain Bewick's best work, although with the assistance of his pupils he engraved a vast quantity of other cuts of all descriptions. A single volume published in 1870 by the Rev. Thomas Hugo contains impressions from more than two thousand of these blocks, which were brought together for that purpose.

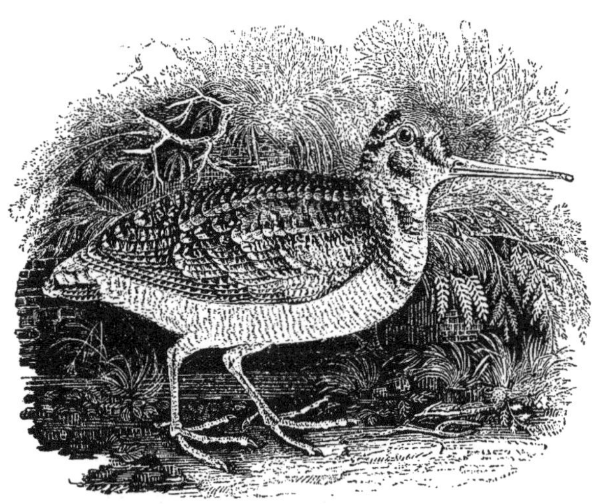

THE WOODCOCK — From Bewick's "Birds"

The wood-engraver of the time of Dürer and Holbein cut away from the surface of his block everything except the lines of his design; these he left untouched, standing in relief. The impressions from his block were therefore fac-similes of his design, more or less perfect, according to the care and skill bestowed upon the work. The lines were not his own, and his work was almost purely mechanical. His process was little more than a convenient method of multiplying the artist's drawings. Although few modern artists can equal the drawing of

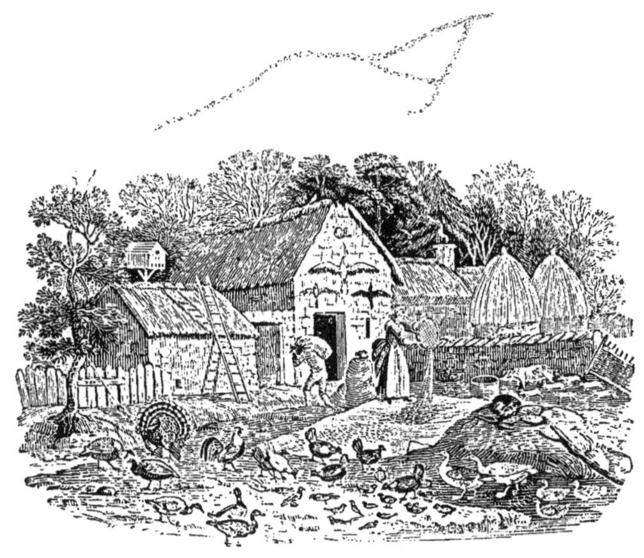

THE FARM-YARD — From Bewick's "Birds"

Dürer or Holbein, there is a multitude of skilful wood-engravers who would find little real difficulty in engraving the same designs in fac-simile, if drawn for them upon the blocks. While Dürer and Holbein furnished the designs, and in many instances undoubtedly drew them directly upon the wood blocks, they were not wood-engravers; the actual cutting of the blocks was left to the professional *formschneiders*, whose work required great skill and patience, but very little originality. Although the artist "never dies," the same cannot be said of the mechanic, for of the multitude of wood-engravers of the six-

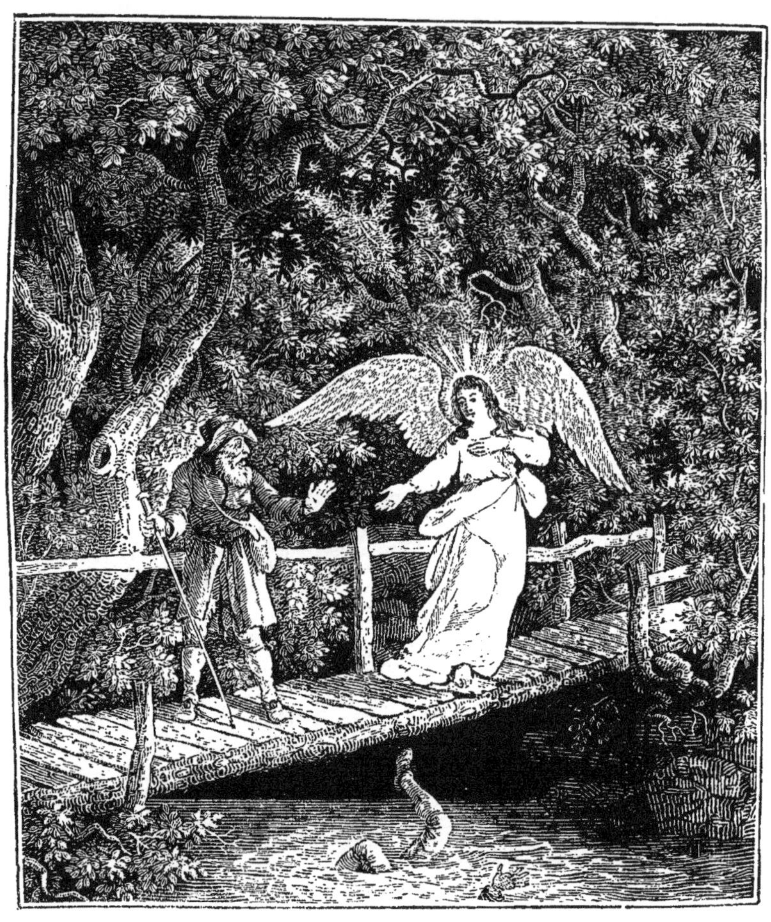

THE HERMIT AND THE ANGEL

Engraved by Thomas Bewick for Parnell's "Hermit"

teenth century only a few names have reached us. Even in the case of Andreae and Lützelberger, whose skill amounted to genius, we know little more than their names, and that they engraved the designs of Dürer and Holbein.

Under Bewick, wood-engraving became a liberal art instead of a mechanical craft, the wood-engraver an artist, instead of a mere mechanic. The "white-line" method which he inaugurated, although imperfectly known to the early wood-engravers, was not practised by them to any extent, owing to the narrow province of their art. This method requires the artist's ability with the engraver's skill. If we take an impression from a block prepared for the engraver and properly inked, but before it has been worked upon, the result is a deep, uniform black. Commencing, then, with black, the engraver cuts out his whites, and by a skilful arrangement of lines, more or less close and delicate, obtains his intermediate shades of gray. His "white lines" are the equivalents of the black lines of the copper-plate engraver. Instead of following the lines of his design, as in the fac-simile process, he creates his own lines, becoming an

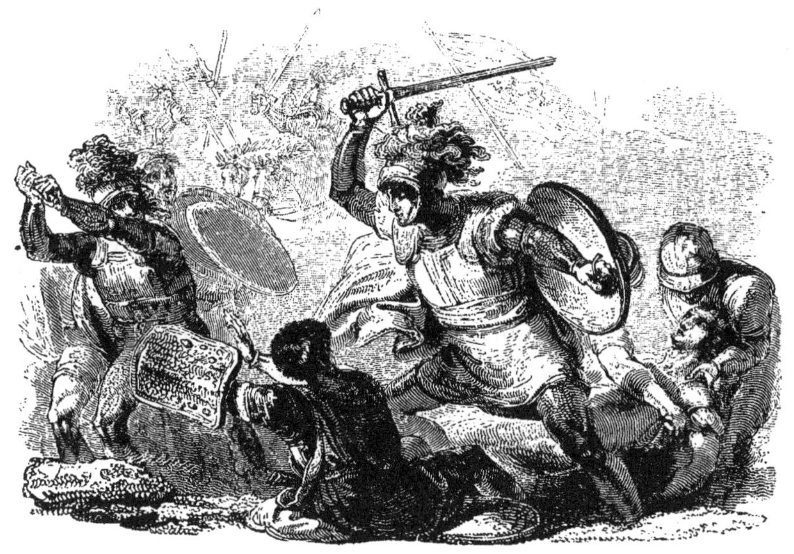

FROM THE "HERMIT OF WARKWORTH"
Drawn and engraved by Luke Clennell

original artist, translating his design into the language of his art. White line, white space, and flat or solid blacks are the means employed, and the natural expression of the art. By this method the engraver's success does not depend upon mechanical imitation, but upon beauty and frankness of line, mental expression and originality, as well as mechanical skill. Cross-hatching, the slavery of wood-engraving, becomes un-

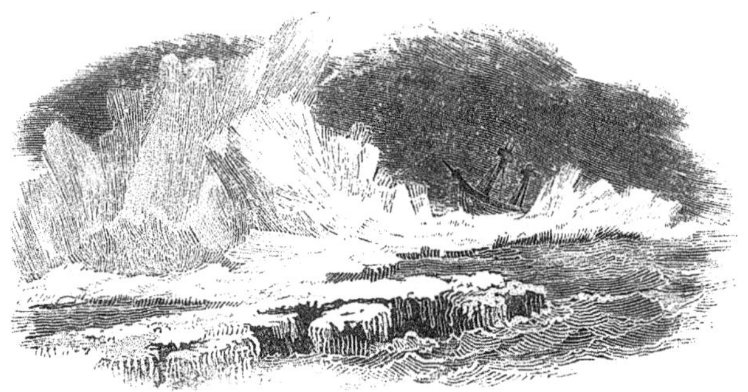

THE STRANDED SHIP — By Clennell

necessary, except in the white lines, as almost every effect can be obtained without it. The white lines are as easily crossed as the black lines in intaglio engraving, being drawn with the burin; the engraver is not compelled to dig out little particles of wood where the lines cross, as in the black-line process. Most of the great wood-engravers, from Bewick, have regarded cross-hatching in the black lines as, in most instances, little more than a waste of time and labor.

Bewick's technical powers were great and varied. His lines were always well chosen; in most instances the best that could be devised, and show the true character of his art. Although other engravers have surpassed him in technical skill, he still remains, by common consent, the great representative master of his art. But he was not a great artist like Dürer or Holbein; he was self-taught, a child of nature. He neither understood nor cared for the subjects of classical art, but devoted himself to the delineation of birds and animals, landscapes and

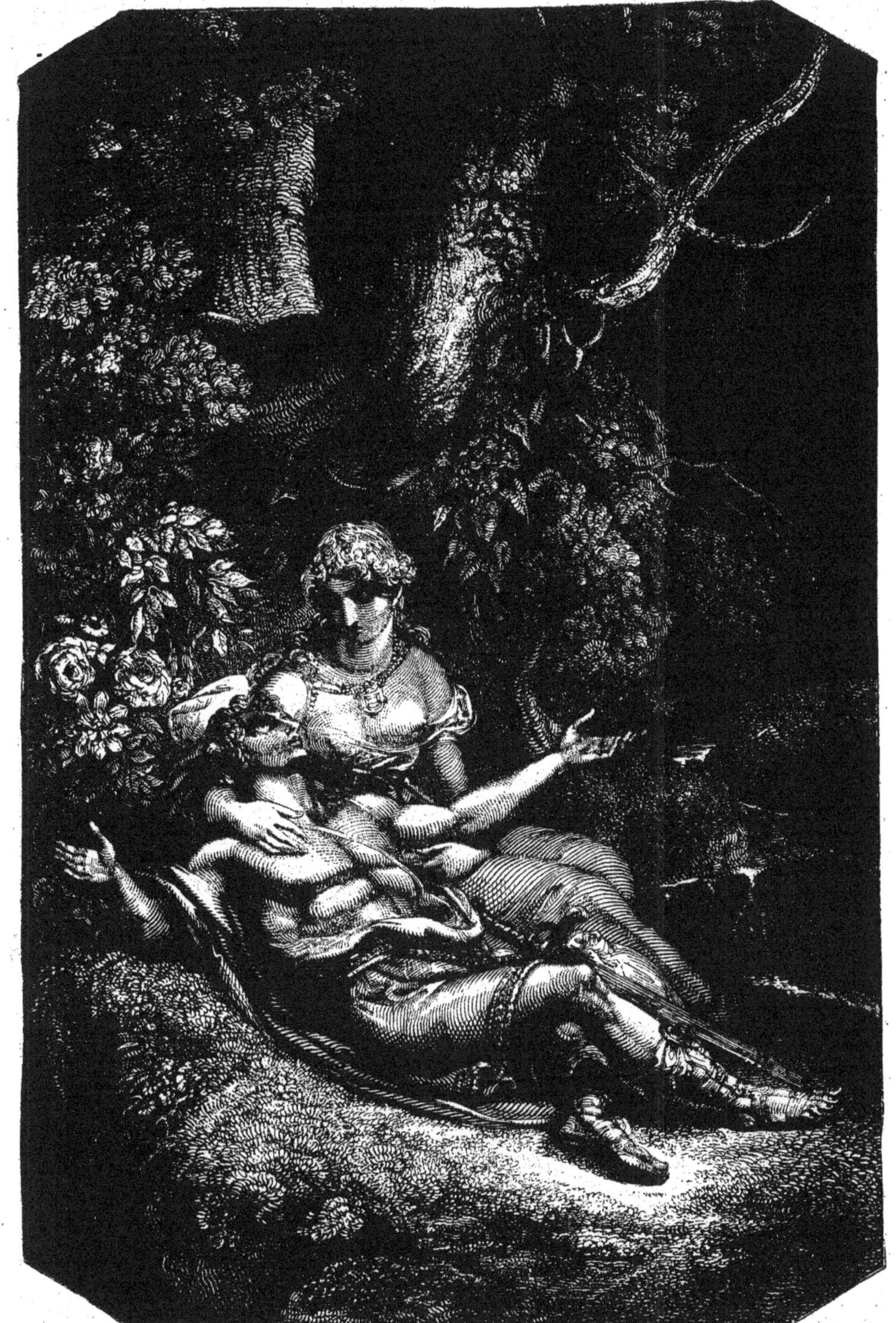

way-side scenes. He was a naturalist with an artist's instincts. To him a water-fowl in its natural surroundings was a far more attractive subject than an Aphrodite. In his Memoirs he states, "I ought also to observe that no vain notions of my arriving at any eminence ever passed through my mind, and that the sole stimulant with me was the pleasure I derived from imitating natural objects (and I had no other patterns to go by). . . ." His landscapes, especially those engraved for the works of Goldsmith and Parnell, are full of poetry and feeling; never were text and illustrations in more perfect barmony. His little vignettes tell their story in a perfectly simple and straightforward manner. While the peasant is saying grace the cat steals his food; a beggar-woman is attacked by a gander; a dog with a tin kettle tied to its tail is pursued by boys; a snarling mastiff attacks a peasant, who defends himself with a stick; a peasant holds on to a cow's tail and fords a stream; a man is caught in a steel trap; an angry woman is trying to drive pigs out of the garden; a child neglected by its nurse is at the heels of a colt, while the agonized mother hastens to the rescue, and so on in great variety. In these scenes his creatures are generally uncomfortable, and his children in mischief; the devil and the gallows are often introduced for moral effect. But

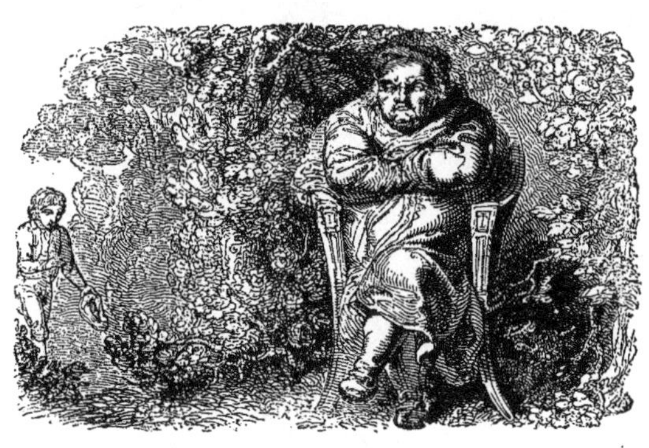

MOROSO

From The Puckle Club. Drawn by John Thurston, engraved by John Thompson

Bewick's best work is to be found in his birds and animals, whose character, expression, and surroundings he represented with rare fidelity and feeling, for he had learned to cherish "what is lovely and human in these wandering children of the clouds and fields."

Bewick possessed a happy, contented disposition, and was

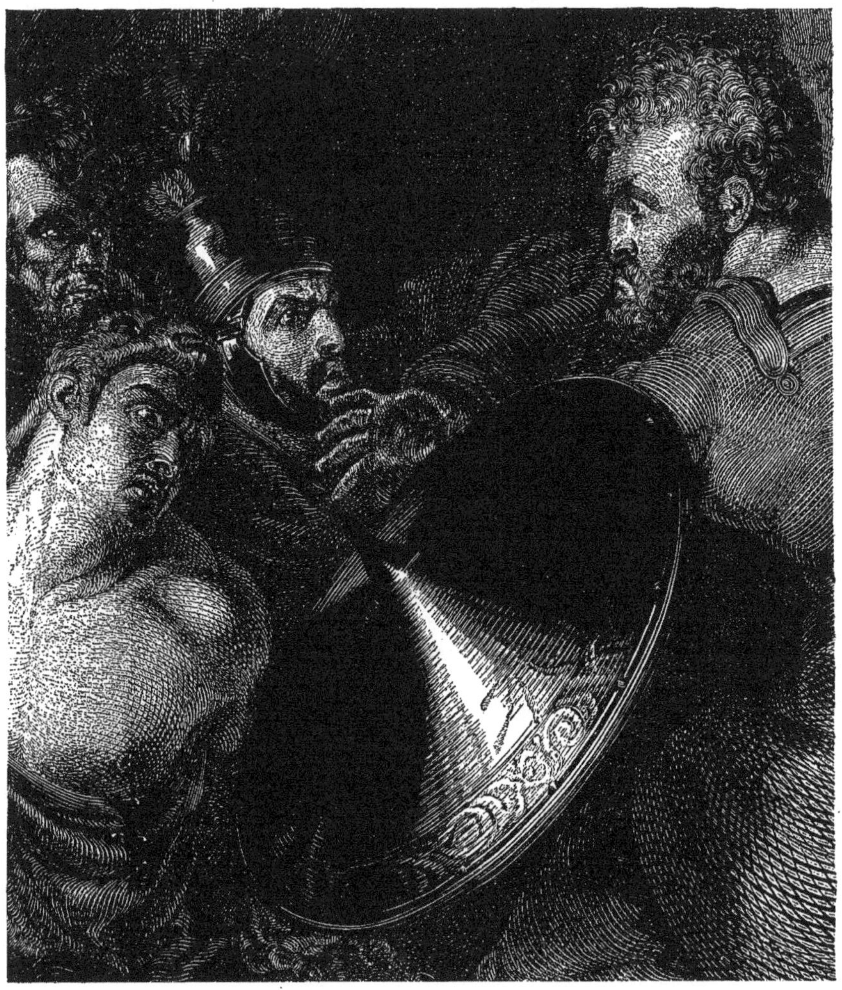

FROM THE 'DEATH OF DENTATUS'

Engraved by William Harvey

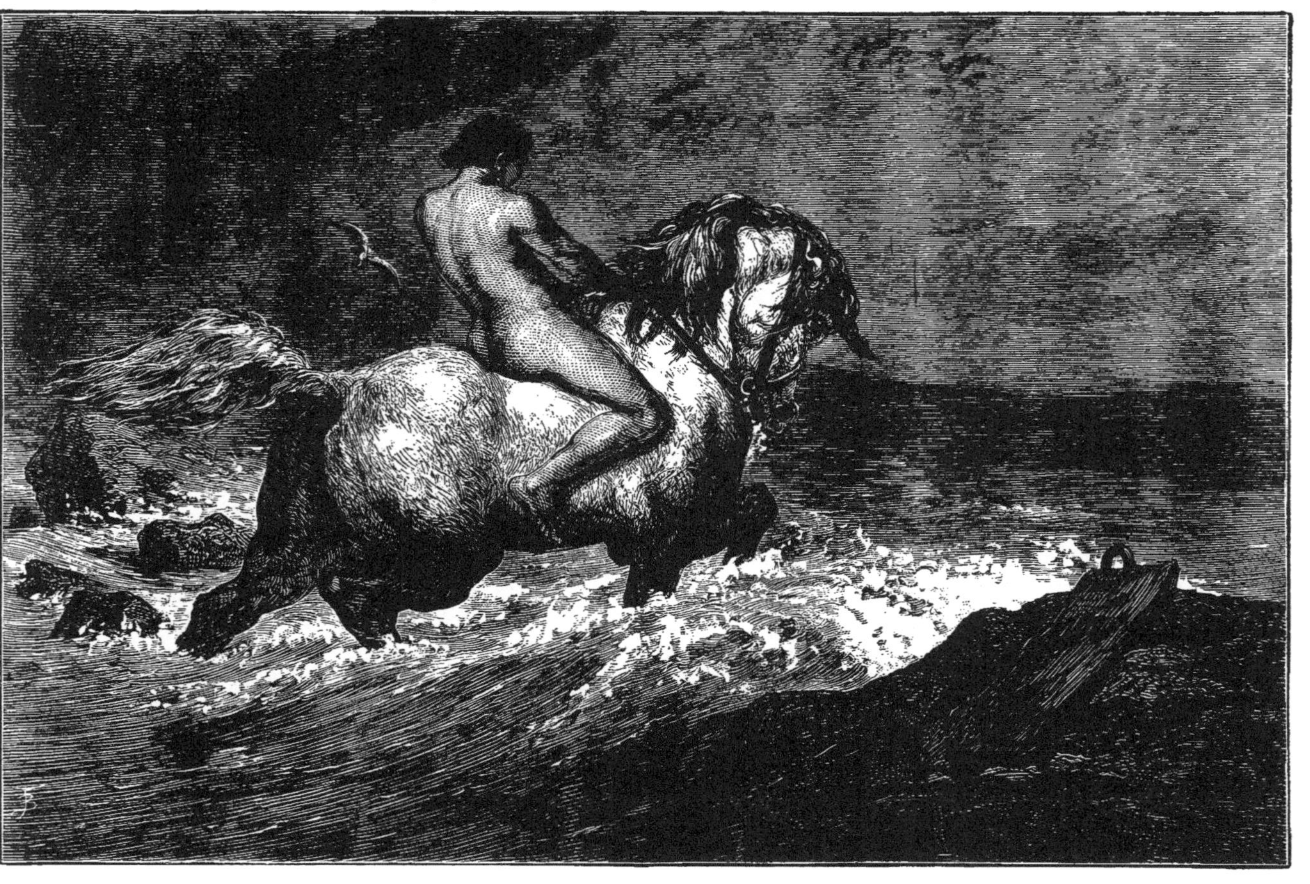

TRAINING THE SURF-HORSE

fond of sports and athletic exercises. He disliked the city, preferring the country, where he "could hear the lark sing." He was a man of considerable wit and many warm friendships, exceedingly popular in his time, and honored alike for his personal qualities and as the leader in his art, which he practised with an energy and enthusiasm unparalleled. He died at Gateshead in 1828, having won an honorable and lasting place in history. In *Blackwood's Magazine* for June of that year occurs the following tribute: "Have we forgotten

'The Genius that dwells on the banks of the Tyne,'

the Matchless, Inimitable Bewick? No. His books lie in our parlor, bedroom, dining-room, drawing-room, study-table, and are never out of place or time. Happy old man! The delight of childhood, manhood, decaying age!—a moral in every tail-piece—a sermon in every vignette. . . ."

The newly awakened interest in wood-engraving also extended into Germany and France, where important schools were established; and in our own country Dr. Anderson and his successors founded a school which has risen to great importance. But we must look to England for the most important examples of its development. Bewick's pupils, Luke Clennell (1781–1840), designer and engraver; Charlton Nesbit (1775–1838), engraver only, and William Harvey (1796–1866), draughtsman and engraver, were inspired by the genius of their master and share his renown. Clennell's 'Diploma of the Highland Society,' Nesbit's 'Rinaldo and Armida,' from Tasso's 'Jerusalem Delivered,' and Harvey's 'Death of Dentatus' are among the notable examples of the art. Clennell's cuts are free and masterly in handling, and show the artist-engraver; in mechanical skill and knowledge of line arrangement Nesbit must be given the first place. Harvey's cut of Dentatus, a large and most elaborate work, engraved from a drawing by the historical painter B. R.

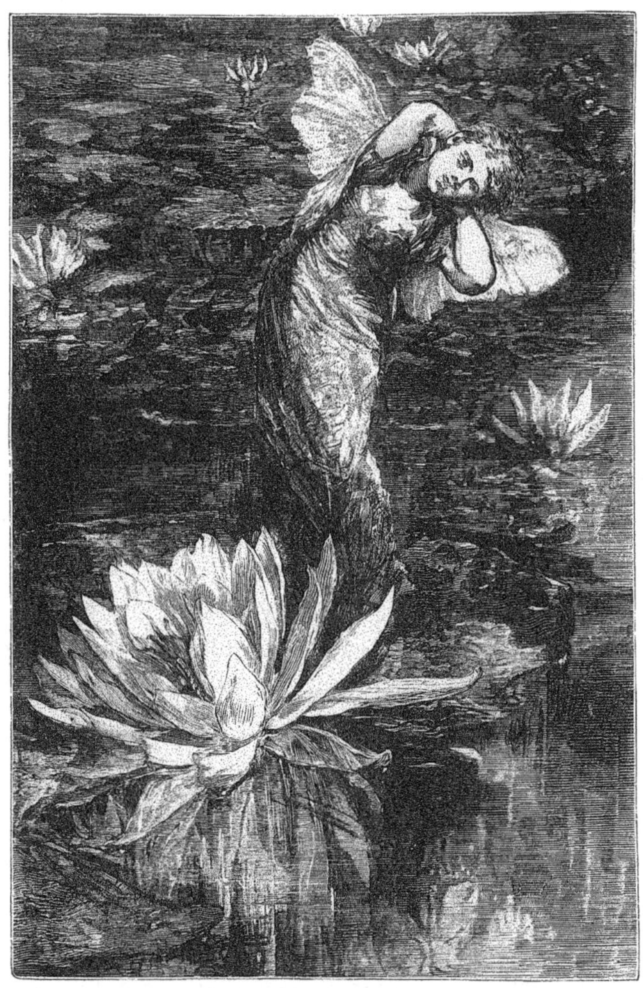

THE WATER-LILY

Drawn by John La Farge, engraved by Henry Marsh

Haydon, cannot be taken as a characteristic example of the works of this school, for it is rather an attempt to imitate copper-plate engraving. As an example of cross-hatching on wood

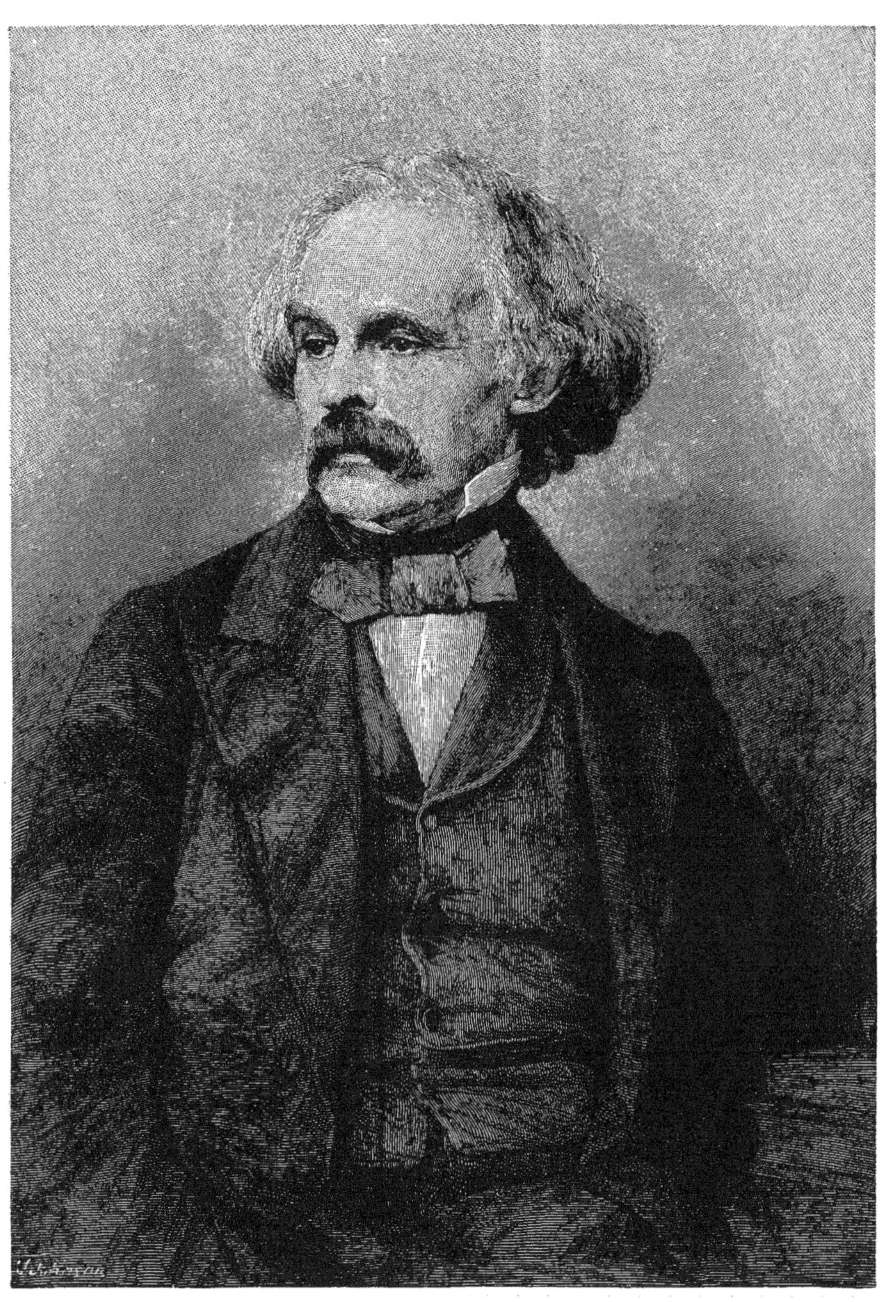

NATHANIEL HAWTHORNE — Engraved by Thomas Johnson

it is unsurpassed. The original block, fifteen inches high and eleven and one-quarter inches wide, and composed of seven pieces joined together, is now in the Department of Prints in the British Museum.

In the latter part of Bewick's career arose a school of wood-engraving which wandered from the teachings of that master, and, while often using the white line in an effective manner, relied chiefly upon the black line. The head of this school, Robert Branston (1778–1827), had served an apprenticeship as a copper-plate engraver, and brought to wood-engraving the traditions of that art. As an engraver he was excelled by his famous pupil John Thompson (1785–1866), whose marvellous skill has scarcely been surpassed. Branston's masterpiece, 'The Cave of Dispair,' published in Savage's *Hints on Decorative Printing*, was engraved in rivalry with Nesbit's 'Rinaldo and Armida,' which appears in the same work. A comparison of these two cuts will show the respective styles of the rival schools. Thompson excelled in his engravings of the human figure, and his work is very uniform in quality. Some of his smaller cuts possess marvellous spirit and refinement, and, of the kind, are unexcelled in general excellence. Many of the best works of Clennell and Nesbit, Branston and Thompson were engraved from the designs or drawings of John Thurston, to whose services the art of wood-engraving owes much. Robert Johnson, also a designer and draughtsman of rare abilities, must be mentioned for his services to the art in the Bewick days. The modern wood-engraver relies but little upon the professional draughtsman; his designs are generally transferred to his blocks by means of photography.

In the work of the successors of Branston and Thompson the distinctive character of wood-engraving was in great part

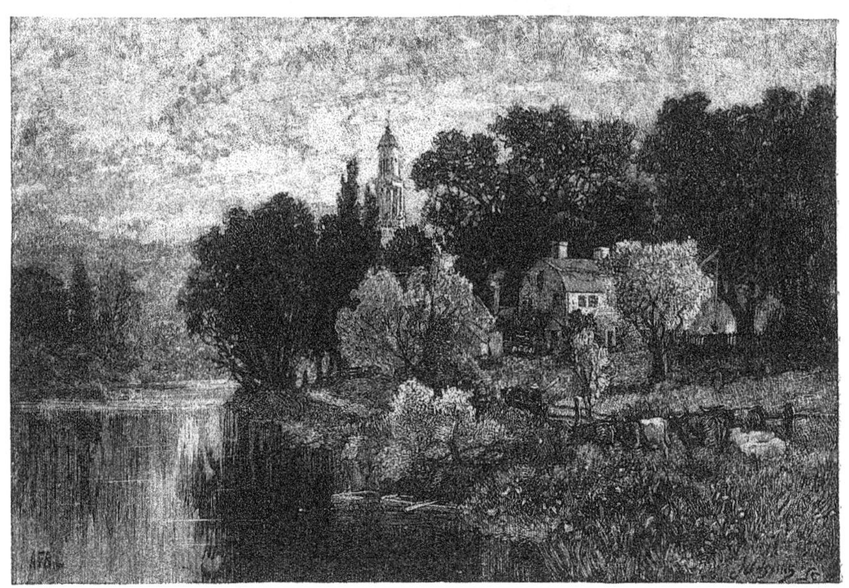

THE PARSONAGE

Engraved by F. Juengling, after A. F. Bellows

lost in the attempt to imitate copper-plate engraving. One engraver, however, the veteran W. J. Linton, remained throughout true to the traditions of his art, insisting upon the importance of the white line, upon "drawing with the graver." For many years Mr. Linton has been a resident of our own country. His work both with the pen and graver is so well known that praise would be superfluous. His *Masters of Wood-Engraving*, a magnificent volume recently published, is a most valuable contribution to the literature of his art.

The subsequent development of wood-engraving may be traced in the works of the engravers of our own country. Dr. Alexander Anderson, the father of American wood-engraving, was born in 1775, the year in which Bewick received the prize for his cut, "The Huntsman and the Old Hound." He abandoned his career as a physician to devote himself to wood-

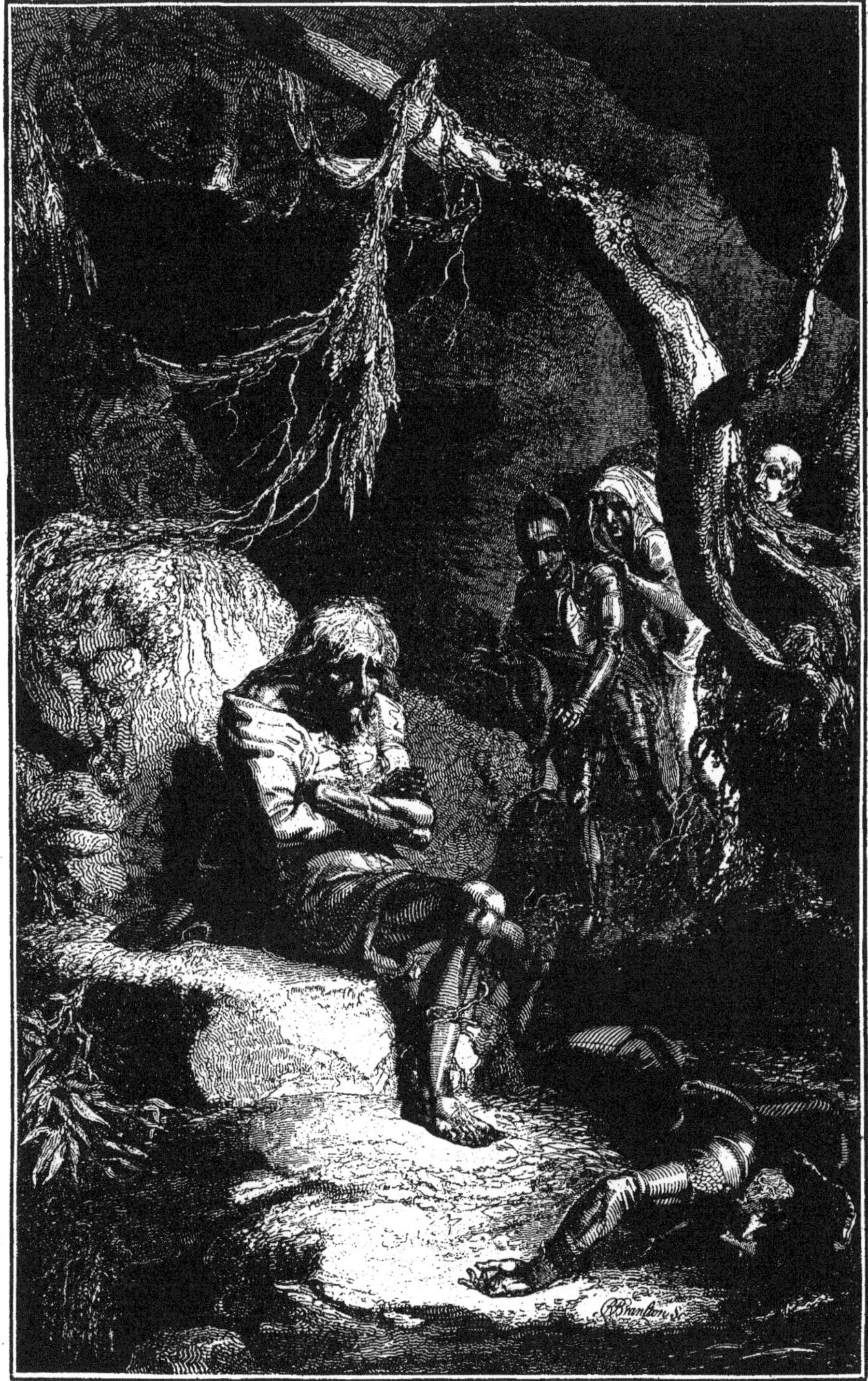
R Branston Sc

engraving, in which art he was an imitator of Bewick, although in every way greatly the inferior of that master. The earliest American wood-cuts of any considerable excellence were those of Joseph Alexander Adams, which appeared in Harper's Illuminated Bible, published in 1843. For a long time, however, following the example already set in England, delicacy and fineness of line were the engraver's chief aims, and his work was generally regarded as successful according as it imitated the effects of engravings upon copper or steel.

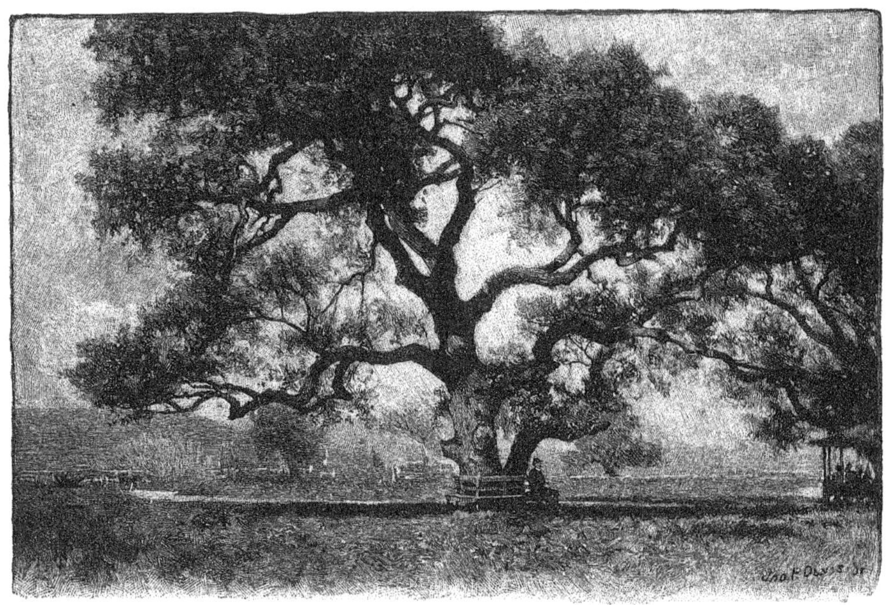

LIVE-OAK NEAR LOS ANGELES, CALIFORNIA
Engraved by John P Davis

In 1850 Harper's Magazine was established, followed by *Scribner's*, the *Century*, and various other illustrated periodicals, creating a steady demand for wood-cut illustrations which soon led to the formation of a school of wood-engravers. To the influence of these publications the present condition of the art in our own country is in great part attributable. As typical engravers of this middle period may be named A. V. S. Anthony and Henry Marsh. The exquisite skill of the latter is shown in his cut of the 'Water-Lily,' here given, and in his marvellous cuts of butterflies and other insects engraved for Harris's *Insects Injurious to Vegetation.*

In our own time the acme of perfection in printing wood-cuts has been reached by the "overlaying" process, by which the pressure is nicely adjusted to the character and resistance of the work, giving little to light parts, and much to heavy lines and solid blacks. The finest quality of Turkey boxwood responds to almost any texture and degree of refinement, and the electrotype process renders possible an unlimited edition of the most delicate work. We judge an etching or line engraving from the earliest and most carefully printed proofs; a wood-cut is entitled to the same consideration, and some of the fine proofs of modern work are in their way almost as perfect in quality.

The so-called "new school" of wood-engraving is an outgrowth of the altered conditions of the art. After passing through successive stages of development, it remained for our own engravers to still further extend its limits, and to develop its possibilities as an imitative art. The black-line process, now so generally employed, is by no means the fac-simile process known to the early engravers. Much more is required of the wood-engraver of the present day than was required from his predecessor. He must render the most subtile qualities of his original, its tones, textures, and effects. He imitates the effects of other graphic arts, even to the brush-marks of the painter. As an original artist he works from nature, giving to his work the freshness of fields and woods.

It is impossible to mention the names of the many skilful engravers who have assisted in bringing about this radical change in the practice of their art. Among the leaders in the "new departure," however, may be named Juengling, Hoskin, Davis, Smithwick, French, Muller, Whitney, Morse, Wolf, King,

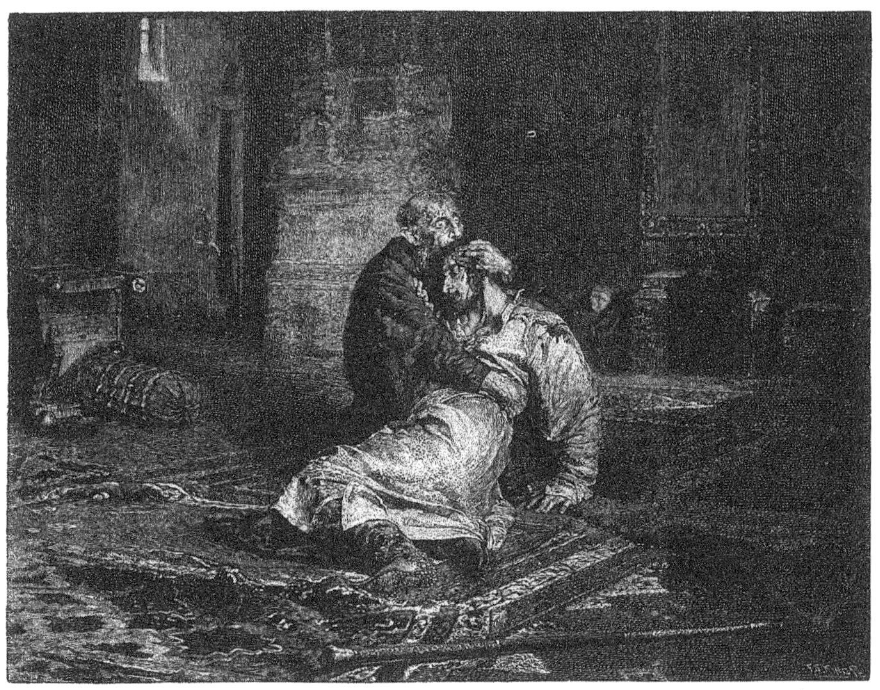

IVAN THE TERRIBLE AND HIS SON

Engraved by F. S. King from the painting by Répine

Closson, Kruell, Johnson, Kingsley, and Cole. In manual skill, in variety and delicacy of handling, and in knowledge of all the resources of their art the American engravers have no equals; their works show the culmination of modern wood-engraving.

CHAPTER VIII

VARIOUS MODERN ENGRAVERS

The Modern Engravers of Italy — Raphael Morghen — Giuseppe Longhi — The Milanese School — Anderloni, Garavaglia, Gandolfi, and Rosaspina — Paolo Toschi — Calamatta and Mercurj — Modern German Engravers — J. G. von Müller — J. F. W. Müller — Steinla, Amsler, and Felsing — Mandel — Modern Etchers — Méryon — Jacquemart — Lalanne — Rajon — Various Modern Etchers — Engraving in the United States — Collections of Prints — Conclusion

IN the preceding chapters we have followed the progress of engraving in the works of its great masters, each school having its own traditions and national predilections. The present chapter will be devoted to individual engravers of different countries, with little regard for historical arrangement.

The modern engravers of Italy first claim our attention. To them we are indebted for many beautiful engravings from Italian paintings of the fifteenth and sixteenth centuries. Adapted by size and character for framing, their prints have long been favorites for home adornment. They engraved, in many instances for the first time, many beautiful paintings and frescos by Raphael, Leonardo, Correggio, Parmigiano, and other eminent painters, preserving to posterity a rich inheritance which will long survive the fading glories of the originals.

The most famous of these engravers was Raphael Morghen, whose abilities, like those of his contemporary, Bartolozzi, have been the subject of much difference of opinion. While England and France possessed a number of eminent engravers,

Morghen stood alone in Italy during the greater portion of his career, and his accidental superiority was proclaimed genius. His great celebrity in his own time was undoubtedly due in great part to his happy selection of subjects. Although his technic was soft and pleasing, and his mechanical facility great, yet as an engraver he was inferior to Bervic and Longhi, and much of his work is deficient in taste and variety, and fails to realize the spirit of his originals. But after making due allowance both for the blind enthusiasm of his worshippers and the jealousy of his detractors, there are a few of his engravings which must always rank high in art, although he no longer stands at the head of all modern engravers in the popular estimation.

Raphael Sanzio Morghen was born at Portici, near Naples, June 14, 1761. At first a pupil of his father and uncle, he displayed such abilities as draughtsman and engraver in a series of Masks from the Carnival held at Naples in 1778 that he was sent to Rome for better instruction under Volpato, who with Bartolozzi had been a pupil of Wagner at Venice, and is now best known by his series of large engravings, beautifully colored, from Raphael's Stanze in the Vatican. Here Morghen made rapid progress, and in 1781 engraved from Raphael's lunettes in the Vatican the allegorical figures representing Poetry and Theology, to which he afterwards added those of Justice, Philosophy, and Jurisprudence. He also worked for a time in conjunction with Volpato, whose daughter Dominica he married, and soon surpassed his master, although this certainly required no very exalted abilities.

Morghen's reputation was soon afterwards established upon the appearance of his well-known plate of the Aurora, from Guido's fresco at the Rospigliosi Palace; Aurora, as the harbinger of day, accompanied by the dancing Hours, scatters flowers before the Chariot of Phœbus. Although not a great work, yet the beauty of the subject, and the soft, pleasing manner in which it was engraved rendered it extremely popular, and it commanded an enormous sale. Of a number of recent copies of this print, that by Burger, of Munich, is perhaps the most interesting.

A few years later, at Florence, whither Morghen had removed with his wife, appeared his famous plate of 'The Last Supper,' from the masterpiece of Leonardo. The original, twenty-eight feet long, was painted in oil upon the wall of the refectory of the Dominican Monastery of Santa Maria delle Grazie, at Milan; it was commenced in 1488, and, with Leonardo's usual dilatoriness, completed about ten years later. No great work of art has ever been more wilfully or more shamefully abused. Armenini stated that it was already half decayed when he saw it fifty years afterwards; according to Scanelli, the expressions of the faces had almost disappeared by 1642, and Belotti, who "restored" it in 1726, practically repainted it. Morghen's engraving, upon which he worked for nearly three years, and which appeared in the year 1800, was made from a drawing by Matteini, after the restorations, and from old copies which he is said to have consulted; that his engraving should give an adequate idea of the sentiment and spirit of the original was manifestly impossible. The original painting suffered still further injuries from the French who occupied Milan under Napoleon, and afterwards, as a climax of vandalism, a doorway was cut through the wall, destroying a portion of the lower part of the picture, so that in our own time Leonardo's masterpiece presents little more than a spectre of its former grandeur. Morghen's engraving is highly interesting as well as valuable for having assisted in preserving the fading glories

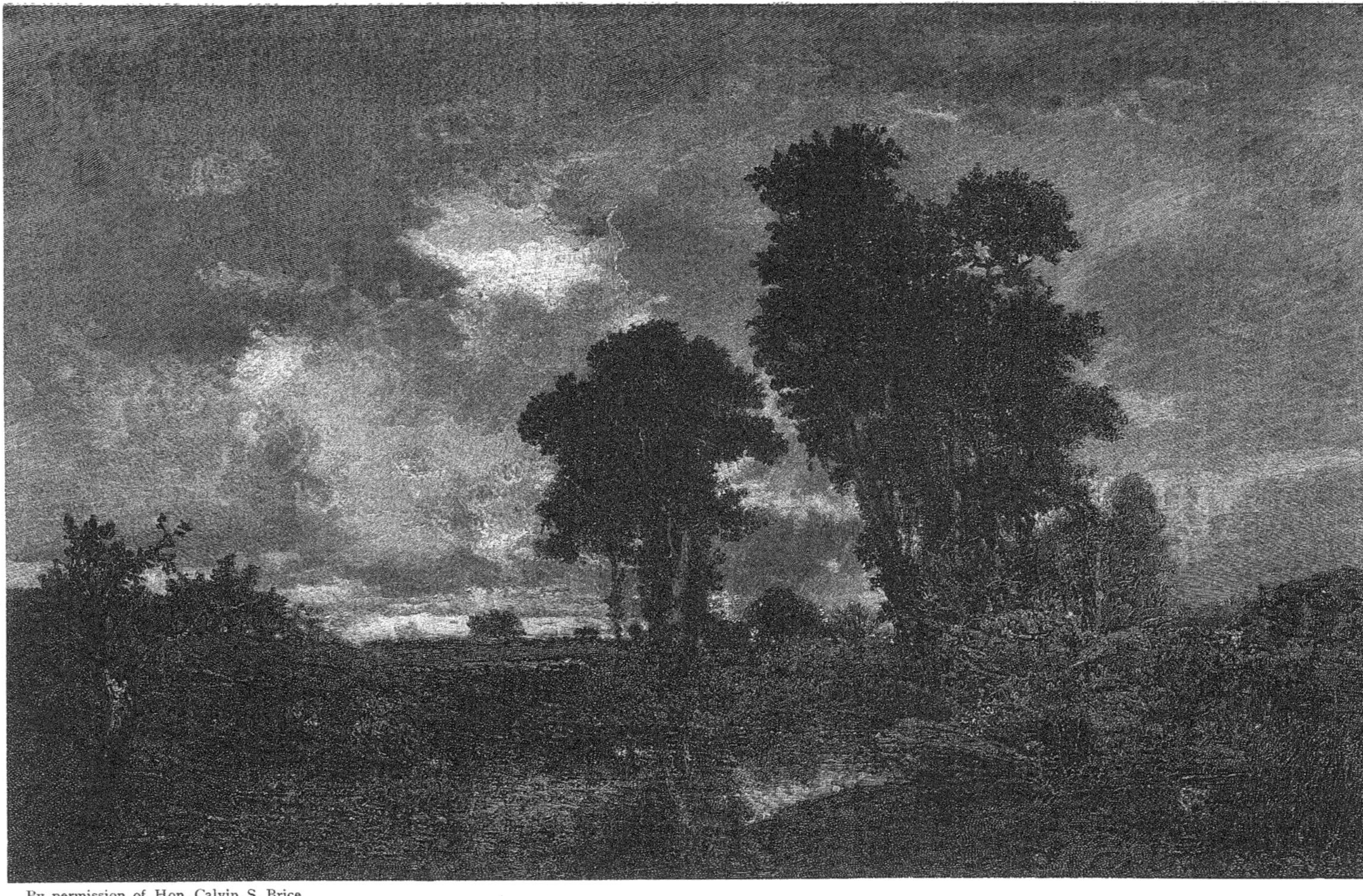

By permission of Hon. Calvin S. Brice

of the original, although this has been more perfectly accomplished by a number of old copies. No other similar work ever achieved such immense popularity, or has been so highly extolled. The demand for impressions was so great that the plate, which, like many of Morghen's, was delicately cut, soon showed signs of "fatigue," and had to be frequently retouched; Morghen's engraving should therefore be judged from early impressions before the delicate lines and dry-point work had become worn. Among the many copies of this print is the fine plate engraved by Charles Burt, of Brooklyn, which bears the signature, however, of A. L. Dick, who was only its publisher.

Among other popular subjects engraved by Morghen were the 'Madonna della Sedia' and 'Transfiguration,' after Raphael, and the 'Madonna del Sacco,' after Andrea del Sarto. But Morghen's best work is to be found in his engraved portraits. To the engraver of the large equestrian portrait of the Spanish soldier and ambassador Francesco di Moncada only praise can be given. This portrait, from Van Dyck's painting, now in the Louvre, is a masterpiece of the art, remarkable alike for its artistic excellence and great technical skill, and for its complete realization of the original. This portrait, sometimes called "Raphael Morghen's Horse," was engraved at Rome in 1793, in which year the engraver was appointed professor in the Academy at Florence. There is also a fine portrait of Leonardo da Vinci, engraved in 1817 from the great painter's own portrait of himself in the gallery at Florence, showing the marvellous intelligence of this many-sided genius, who placed painting last among the things he could do "as well as any man;" and scarcely less interesting are the portraits of the five great Italian authors, Dante, Petrarch, Tasso, Ariosto, and Boccaccio. There are two portraits erroneously inscribed as those of Raphael, and the mysterious beauty known as 'La Fornarina,' and there is a portrait of Napoleon, engraved for a magnificent folio edition of the *Code Napoléon.*

Morghen is said to have given an impression of nearly every state of each plate to his pupil Nicolò Palmerini, who compiled a catalogue, the last edition of which, published at Florence in 1824, contains little more than a chronological list of the plates which appeared before that time; its author might have given us much interesting and valuable information concerning the engraver, of whose life we know so little, considering his great reputation, and that it is but little more than half a century since his career closed. The collection of Raphael Morghen's engravings in the British Museum is by far the finest in existence. There is an excellent descriptive catalogue by Mr. Frederick R. Halsey, who enumerates 182 prints by the master.

Morghen's fame continued unabated up to the time of his death. He was honored not only in his own country, but throughout Europe. He was an associate of the Institute of France, and a member of various academies, and was invited by Napoleon to take up his residence in Paris. His death, which occurred in 1833, is said to have been given the importance of a national event. Sonnets were written extolling his talents and lamenting his death, and a monument was raised to his memory in the Church of Santa Croce at Florence.

Notwithstanding the fame of Raphael Morghen, he exercised much less influence upon his art than a number of his contemporaries. His chief imitators were Giovanni Folo and Pietro Bettelini. The former engraved a number of fine subjects after various Italian masters, of which 'Christ raising the Widow's Son,' after Annibale Caracci, and the 'Mater Dolorosa,' after Sassoferrato, are the best examples. He also took advantage of the popularity of Morghen's plate of 'The Last Supper,' and engraved the same subject. Bettelini had been a pupil of Gandolfi and Bartolozzi, but afterwards took Morghen as his model. His masterpiece, 'The Entombment,' after Andrea del Sarto, is a work of great merit.

Contemporary with Morghen was an engraver to whose influence and example we owe many beautiful engravings after the Italian masters, and in whom we recognize great ability united with correct ideas of art. Giuseppe Longhi, painter, engraver, teacher, and author, was born at Monza, October 13, 1766. Abandoning the Church for engraving, he became a pupil of the Florentine engraver Vincenzio Vangelisti, a pupil of Wille, who had gone to Milan upon the invitation of Leopold II. to assume direction of the school of engraving which that prince had founded at the Brera. Going afterwards to Rome, Longhi formed the acquaintance of Raphael Morghen, then at the zenith of his fame, and soon acquired considerable reputation by his engravings and miniature paintings. Upon his return to Milan he was commissioned to engrave Gros's portrait of Napoleon at Arcole, which appeared in 1798, in which year he also succeeded to the professorship at the Brera, made vacant by the death of Vangelisti, who in a moment of insanity had defaced his plates and committed suicide. Longhi's eminence as an engraver was equalled by his success as an instructor, and the school at Milan soon became famous.

Upon matters pertaining to his art Longhi is considered a high authority. Although a descendant of the school of Wille, he was an earnest student, and in close sympathy with Edelinck and Nanteuil. His famous work, *La Calcografia*, published at Milan in 1830, contains many sound views upon the theory of his art, and accurate estimates of the abilities of different engravers. The first volume concludes with a biographical notice of its author by Francesco Longhena, and has been translated into German by Carl Barth. The unpublished manuscript of the second and concluding volume is still preserved at Milan.

Longhi engraved with great success both subjects and portraits. Of the former are the large plate, 'Lo Sposalizio,' after Raphael, representing the marriage of the Virgin according to the apocryphal books of the New Testament; 'The Holy Family' and 'Vision of Ezekiel,' also after Raphael; the exquisite engraving of the 'Reclining Magdalen,' from the picture in the Dresden gallery, long attributed to Correggio, but now regarded as probably one of a number of copies of a lost original; the 'Madonna del Lago,' after Leonardo da Vinci; the 'Entombment,' after Crespi; 'Galatea,' after Albani; six plates of the 'Fasti di Napoleone il Grande,' engraved in the "semilibero" manner from Appiani's designs, and published at the Emperor's expense; and besides these are many fine subjects after Raphael, Rembrandt, Carlo Dolci, Correggio, and other masters, mostly Italian. In some of his prints he received assistance from his pupils in the backgrounds and accessories.

Of the many fine portraits engraved by Longhi, there is none more interesting than that of Eugène Beauharnais, Napoleon's step-son and Viceroy of Italy, a magnificent full-length portrait with flowing plume, engraved in 1812–14 from the painting by Gérard. There are also two portraits of Napoleon as King of Italy, one with the Crown of Laurel, and the other with the Iron Crown of the Lombards; the former was engraved for Napoleon's *Code Civile*, and the latter for that rare series published at Milan, the *Vite e Ritratti di Illustri Italiani*, for which the portraits of Enrico Dandolo, Doge of

Venice, and Michael Angelo were also engraved. There is also a rare portrait of Washington, engraved in 1817 for Bettoni's series, resembling, although somewhat remotely, the Stuart head. The hair in this portrait was engraved in imitation of that in Masson's portrait of Brisacier, known as the "Gray-haired man." Longhi died in 1831 at Milan, leaving unfinished plates of Michael Angelo's 'Last Judgment' and Raphael's 'Madonna del Velo,' the latter of which was completed after his death by Toschi. His own portrait was engraved by his pupil Samuele Jesi.

While Morghen received more than his full share of praise, to Longhi was accorded the still more flattering homage of imitation. The school at Milan became the most important of its time, and sent forth many distinguished engravers, learned in the theory and principles of their art as well as in its technical processes. Of the many Italian engravers who profited directly or indirectly by his teachings were Pietro Anderloni, Garavaglia, Gandolfi, and Rosaspina, all engravers of great ability.

Pietro Anderloni (1784–1849), the chief of these engravers, was Longhi's favorite pupil, and assisted him in engraving many important plates, among them the second plate of the 'Vision of Ezekiel,' upon which his name appears with that of Longhi as engraver. His beautiful engraving of the 'Virgin and child adored by Angels,' after Titian, is always greatly admired. Other fine examples are 'The Judgment of Solomon,' 'The Holy Family,' and a number of Madonnas after Raphael, besides the 'Defeat of Attila,' and 'Heliodorus driven from the Temple,' from Raphael's frescos in the Vatican; 'Moses at the Well defending the daughters of Jethro,' after Poussin, and 'St. John,' after Luini. He also re-engraved the background of

Longhi's plate of the 'Reclining Magdalen,' the work of the first engraver having proved unsatisfactory.

Anderloni's pupil Garavaglia engraved a number of fine plates, among them 'Jacob and Rachel,' after Appiani; the 'Madonna della Sedia,' after Raphael; 'The Ascension' and 'Beatrice Cenci,' after Guido; the 'Magdalen,' after Carlo Dolci; 'Hagar and Ishmael,' after Baroccio; and the 'Virgin and Child,' after Gimignano.

Mauro Gandolfi supplemented his Italian training by studying in England the styles of Sharp and Bartolozzi. His 'Cupid

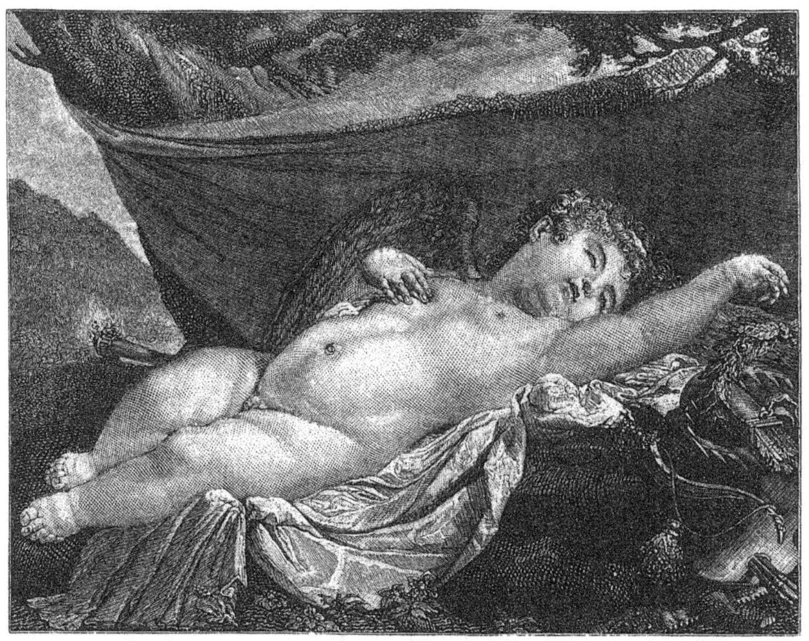

CUPID SLEEPING
From the engraving by Gandolfi

Sleeping,' from his own design, and 'St. Cecilia,' after Raphael, are good examples of his work.

Rosaspina was also a pupil of Bartolozzi, and worked at first in the dotted manner, but afterwards in line. His engraving of 'Christ lowered from the Cross and wept over by St. John and the Holy Women,' from the painting by Correggio, at Parma, and the beautiful 'Dance of Cupids,' after Albani, are his best works.

Another famous engraver belonging to this period, Paolo Toschi, was born at Parma, the home of Correggio and Parmigiano, in 1778, and died there in 1854. A pupil of Bervic, at Paris, he first distinguished himself by a fine engraving from the painting by Gérard, representing the entry of Henry IV. into Paris in 1594. Returning to Parma, he became professor at the Academy, and commenced his well-known series of engravings from the injured frescos of Correggio and Parmigiano. Of these the famous 'Madonna della Scala' and the 'Incoronata,' after Correggio, are beautiful examples. The 'Madonna della Scodella,' after Correggio, and 'Lo Spasimo di Sicilia,' after Raphael, also show Toschi at his best.

But two other Italian engravers will be named, Luigi Calamatta (1802–69), and Paolo Mercùrj (1808–86), both of whom, by art education, belong rather to France than to Italy. At Paris Calamatta became a disciple of Ingres, after whom he engraved one of his finest plates, 'The Vow of Louis XIII.' Returning to Italy, he resided for a time at Florence, but soon went to Brussels, and afterwards settled at Milan, where he died. Of his engravings after Italian masters the 'Madonna della Sedia' is a beautiful example. Mercurj possessed great technical skill, and received many marks of distinction at the Salon. His masterpiece is the 'Reapers in the Pontine Marshes,' from Léopold Robert's painting in the Louvre.

The Hessian gunsmith, who in the early part of the eighteenth century wandered about in Germany until chance led him to Paris, and to fame, was destined to have many eminent disciples in his own country as well as in France and Italy. Among the greatest of these was Johann Gotthard von Müller, who was born at Bernhausen, near Stuttgart, in 1747. At the age of twenty-three he went to Paris, and under the instruction of Wille became one of the foremost engravers of the time. Returning to Stuttgart, he founded there, under the patronage of Duke Karl Eugen of Wurtemberg, the Academy of Design, of which he was successively professor and director, in the meantime becoming a member of almost every important academy on the Continent, and engraving many fine plates. He died at Stuttgart in 1830, but after the death of his son in 1816 he devoted but little attention to his art. His large portrait of Louis XVI., published during the Revolution, and his beautiful engraving of Raphael's 'Madonna della Sedia,' engraved for the Musée Français in 1804, have already been mentioned. His other works include 'The Battle of Bunker's Hill,' after Trumbull, published at London in 1798, portraits of his master Wille and Madame Le Brun, and a fine half-length portrait of Napoleon's brother, King Jerome of Westphalia, in his robes, engraved in 1813, in conjunction with his son and pupil Johann Friedrich Wilhelm Müller, the latter engraving the face and lace kerchief.

The younger Müller was born at Stuttgart in 1782. At an early age he went to Paris, where he studied the works of Bervic, Tardieu, Desnoyers, and other eminent engravers; thence he went to Italy to complete his studies. He made many drawings after the Italian masters, principally Raphael, and upon his return to Germany was appointed court engraver to the King of Wurtemberg and professor at the Dresden Academy. Soon afterwards he entered upon the great undertaking which has forever associated his name with that of Raphael.

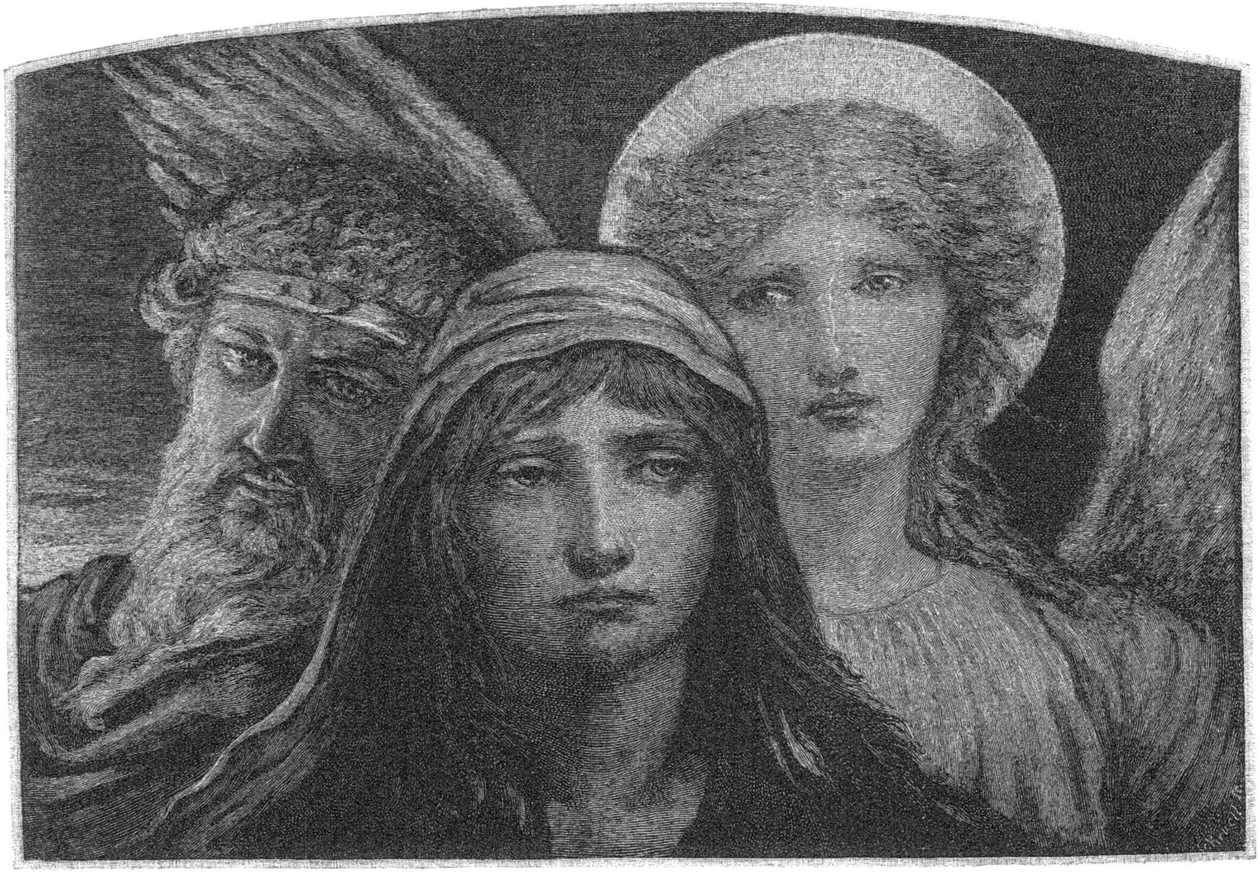

BETWEEN DOUBT AND FAITH — Engraved by G. Kruell

Of a melancholy disposition and feeble in health, Müller devoted his last energies to the completion of the great work which so pathetically ended his career: his engraving of Raphael's 'Madonna di San Sisto.' After years of incessant labor his task was completed, but his mind and health were destroyed. At length the plate was sent to Paris to be printed, and, relieved from the excitement which had sustained him, he broke down utterly, and in a moment of exasperation stabbed himself with a graver, from the effects of which he died May 3, 1816, in his thirty-fourth year. After his death the proof of his plate arrived from Paris, and was suspended over his bier.

Müller's plate of the Sistine Madonna is one of the masterpieces of modern engraving, far superior to any of the numerous other engravings from the famous picture at Dresden. In 1827, when the painting was cleaned by Palmeroli, a portion of the canvas which had been turned over the frame was unrolled, and the top of the curtains with the rod and rings exposed. These parts were still concealed when Müller made his engraving, but are shown in the later engravings of Steinla and Mandel. The popularity of Müller's engraving was so great that the plate soon showed signs of wear, and was retouched slightly by Bervic, and afterwards extensively by Desnoyers, since which time it has been almost wholly re-engraved, so numerous have been the retouches. Other important engravings by the younger Müller are 'Adam and Eve,' after Raphael, and 'St. John the Evangelist,' after Domenichino. Most of the remainder of his eighteen plates are portraits.

Chief among the German engravers who followed the Müllers were Steinla of Dresden, Amsler of Munich, Felsing of Darmstadt, and Mandel of Berlin. The engraver who called himself Steinla, from his birthplace in Hanover, but whose real name was Moritz Müller (1791–1858), was at first a pupil at the Dresden Academy, but was afterwards sent to Italy by the King of Saxony to complete his studies under Morghen and Longhi. Upon his return he engraved some of the finest subjects in the Dresden Gallery, among them the famous 'Meyer Madonna' of Holbein, for which he received a gold medal at Paris, and his well-known plate of the 'Madonna di San Sisto,' engraved in 1847. He also went to Madrid, where he engraved Raphael's 'Madonna del Pesce.' In the latter part of his career he became professor of engraving at the Dresden Academy.

The works of Samuel Amsler (1771–1849) show his preference for the classical models of Dürer and Marc Antonio. An artist of great ability, he was also instructor in the Royal Academy at Munich, where he numbered among his pupils Merz, Gonzenbach, and others, by whom we have admirable engravings after Kaulbach, Cornelius, Overbeck, and other German painters.

The Darmstadt engraver George Jacob Felsing (1802–83) was a pupil of Longhi at Milan, studied the style of Raphael Morghen at Florence, and that of Desnoyers at Paris; returning to Darmstadt he was appointed professor and court engraver. Felsing displayed exceptional abilities in a number of fine engravings, among them 'Christ on the Mount of Olives,' after Carlo Dolci; the 'Madonna Enthroned,' after Andrea del Sarto; 'The Violin Player,' after Raphael; 'The Marriage of St. Catherine,' after Correggio; and 'St. Cecilia,' after Hoffman.

Our list of line engravers closes with Johann August Eduard Mandel, an engraver of great ability, who was born at Berlin in 1810, and died in 1882. In the earlier part of his career, Bervic and Desnoyers divided the honors in France, Raphael Morghen and Longhi were famous in Italy, and Sharp

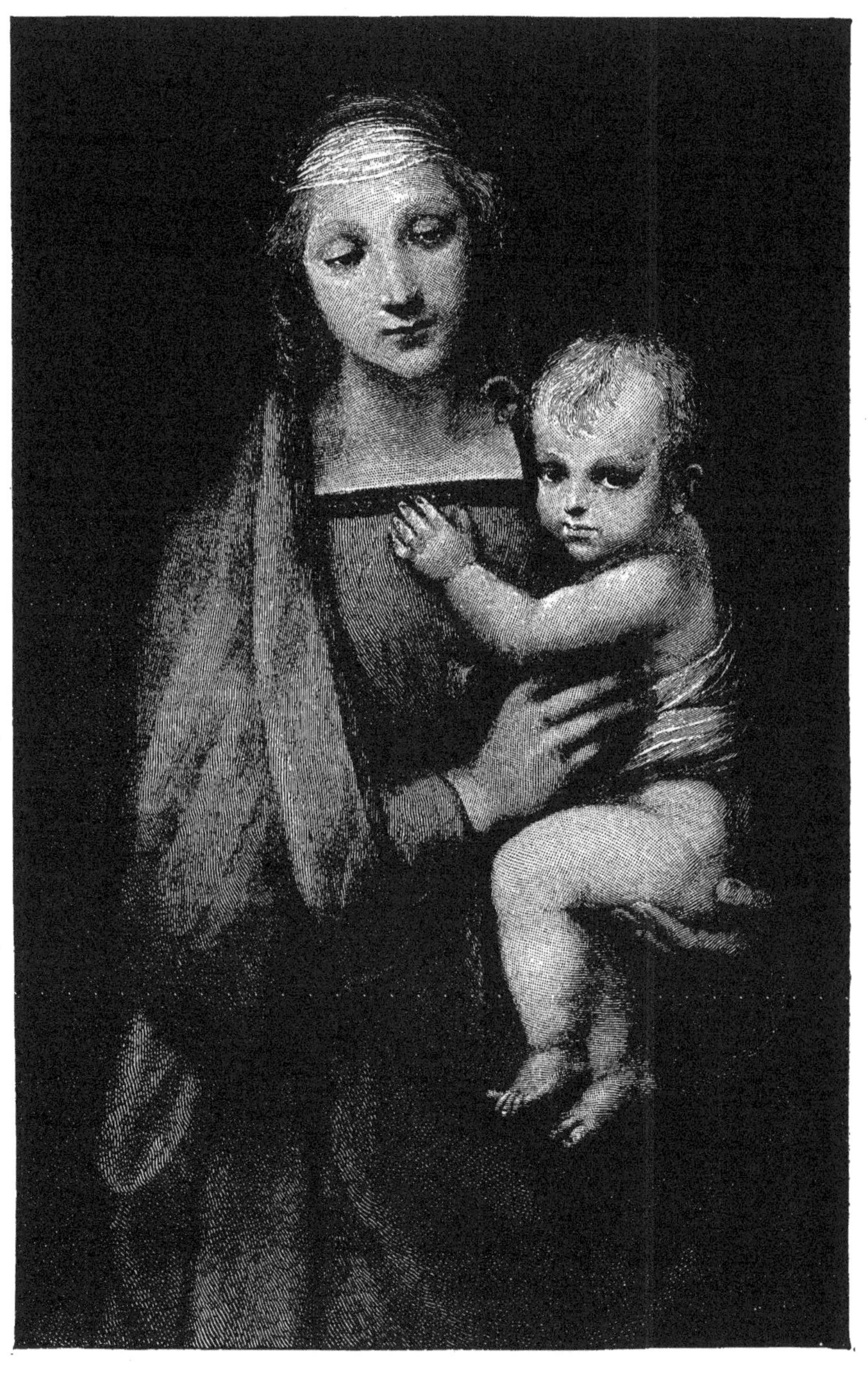

THE MADONNA DEL GRANDUCA

From Raphael's painting in the Pitti Gallery, Florence — Engraved by W B. Closson

still practised his art in England; all of these Mandel survived, to become one of the last worthy representatives of a once glorious art. Mandel engraved fine plates of Raphael's 'Madonna della Sedia' and 'Madonna di San Sisto,' the latter second only to Müller's beautiful engraving of the same subject, and, like it, published posthumously. There are also fine portraits of Charles I. after Van Dyck, and Titian, after that master's portrait of himself at Berlin, the latter contrasting strangely in technic with the famous portrait by Agostino Caracci.

To Adam Bartsch, of Vienna, we owe the famous work, *Le Peintre-Graveur*, the standard authority with collectors, indispensable until the recent *Manuel de l'Amateur d'Estampes*, by M. E. Dutuit, which embodies the results of previous research, and includes the interpreters of painting.

There are still a few line engravers of ability, but the great masters have departed and the schools are deserted. In our own day the art has assumed a commercial character, and has been abandoned for quicker and cheaper processes, in which excellence is less evident than haste. But if engraving with the burin has lost its former prestige, never were skilful etchers so numerous as now or their art so widely appreciated. Etching, unlike engraving with the burin, is an art which appeals directly to the painter. Rembrandt, Claude, and Van Dyck were typical painter-etchers of the early schools, while in our own time such masters as Millet, Fortuny, Daubigny, Meissonier, and Jacque have produced many characteristic works with the needle; besides this class is the great body of artists who devote themselves chiefly to this process. So much, however, has already been written about the modern revival of etching that only a few masters will be named, without attempting a comprehensive account of modern work.

Charles Méryon, "sailor, engraver, and etcher," was a type of that unfortunate class who have "lived poor and miserable and died so," and of whose fame others have reaped the reward. Méryon was born in Paris, November 3, 1821, the illegitimate son of an English physician and a French opera dancer. Abandoned by his father, he is said to have been tenderly cared for by his mother, to whose influence his biographer, M. Burty, attributes much of his peculiar sensibility. At the age of sixteen he entered the naval school at Brest, and afterwards sailed around the world, visiting many foreign lands. But his constitution was unequal to the seafaring life, and he returned to Paris to devote himself to art, of which he had already become a passionate student. He entered the studio of Phelippes, but color-blindness soon put an end to his career as a painter. He then turned his attention to etching, and became for a time a pupil of M. Eugène Bléry, and copied works by the old masters, principally views of old Paris by the Dutch artist Renier Zeeman. His beautiful view of the Old Louvre from the painting by Zeeman shows how completely he had already mastered his art.

Méryon soon entered upon his great work, his views of old Paris. In our own time but little remains of the Paris of Zeeman, Della-Bella, and Callot. The work of reconstruction, inaugurated under the First Empire and completed by Baron Haussmann, has left but few traces of the labyrinth of dark, narrow, winding streets, and the curious architecture of the picturesque city of mediæval days. Méryon witnessed a great portion of these changes, and with a sombre and philosophical spirit set to work to obtain memorials of the picturesque buildings which were being demolished. His work was at first scarcely noticed, and it was with great difficulty that he could dispose of the prints, now so precious, to obtain the means of living. Of a melancholy disposition, difficult to approach, he soon grew morbidly sensitive and irritable, and repulsed every attempt to patronize and encourage him, and was soon tormented with delusions which ended in hopeless insanity.

Mr. Haden relates that he once visited Méryon, whom he found in a little room high up on Montmartre, and who received him with every courtesy, and upon his return allowed him to take away a few proofs of his work, for which, knowing Méryon's circumstances, he was scrupulous to leave, surreptitiously, a sufficient compensation. After he had walked a considerable distance on his return, he was overtaken by Méryon, who, greatly agitated, demanded the return of his proofs, determined from what he knew of Mr. Haden's work that he should not take them to England. Méryon afterwards warned M. Burty that Mr. Haden was an impostor who had discovered or bought a quantity of plates which he was signing and adopting as his own, but which were far too good to be the work of any etcher of our degenerate century, an extremely flattering if unintentional compliment. In 1858, after his return from Belgium, whither he had gone to make some drawings, Méryon was placed in the asylum at Charenton, the certificate stating that he was "suffering from melancholy madness aggravated by delusions." After a few months his health so improved that he left the asylum, and for seven years this eccentric creature led the same isolated life, in constant difficulties with the few who remaïned his friends, practising his strange art in his own peculiar way. In 1866 his malady so increased that he was again confined at Charenton, and here, two years later, February 14, 1868, he died, and was buried in the cemetery of the asylum. He lies beneath a large slab of copper, upon which his epitaph was engraved by his friend Bracquemond, who has also etched his portrait. There is another portrait, by Léopold Flameng, taken shortly before Méryon was removed to Charenton.

Méryon's etchings, about one hundred in number, comprise studies, views of architecture, phantasies, souvenirs, rebuses, inscriptions in verse, and portraits. Both in sentiment and execution they are absolutely personal in character, unlike the works of any other artist. The well-known series "*Eaux-fortes sur Paris*" contains the most characteristic examples of his art. The famous 'Abside de Nôtre Dame' is his most important plate, although less characteristic than some others. 'Le Stryge,' 'La Pompe Nôtre-Dame,' 'Le Pont Neuf,' 'La Morgue,' 'L'Arche du Pont Nôtre-Dame,' 'Tourelle rue de la Tixéranderie,' and 'Saint Etienne-du-Mont,' are all notable examples. An extended account of Méryon's life and work will be found in the memoir and descriptive catalogue by M. Philippe Burty, of which there is an English translation.

In striking contrast to the originality of Méryon is the copyism of Jules Jacquemart (1837–80), the marvellous etcher of vases, gems, ornaments, and other similar objects of still-life. For beauty, delicacy, and truth, as well as for exquisite taste, his works of this character are unrivalled. The work for which he is famous is to be found in the plates illustrating the *Histoire de la Porcelaine*, by his father, Albert Jacquemart; the *Gemmes et Joyaux de la Couronne*, of Barbet de Jouy, and in other pieces of a similar character, notably his exquisite masterpiece, the "Trépied ciselé par Gouthière," a work inimitable in execution. Jacquemart also etched many plates, some of great excellence, from paintings, besides views, flower-pieces, portraits, etc. His works number nearly four hundred, of which there is a descriptive catalogue by Louis Gonse. During the

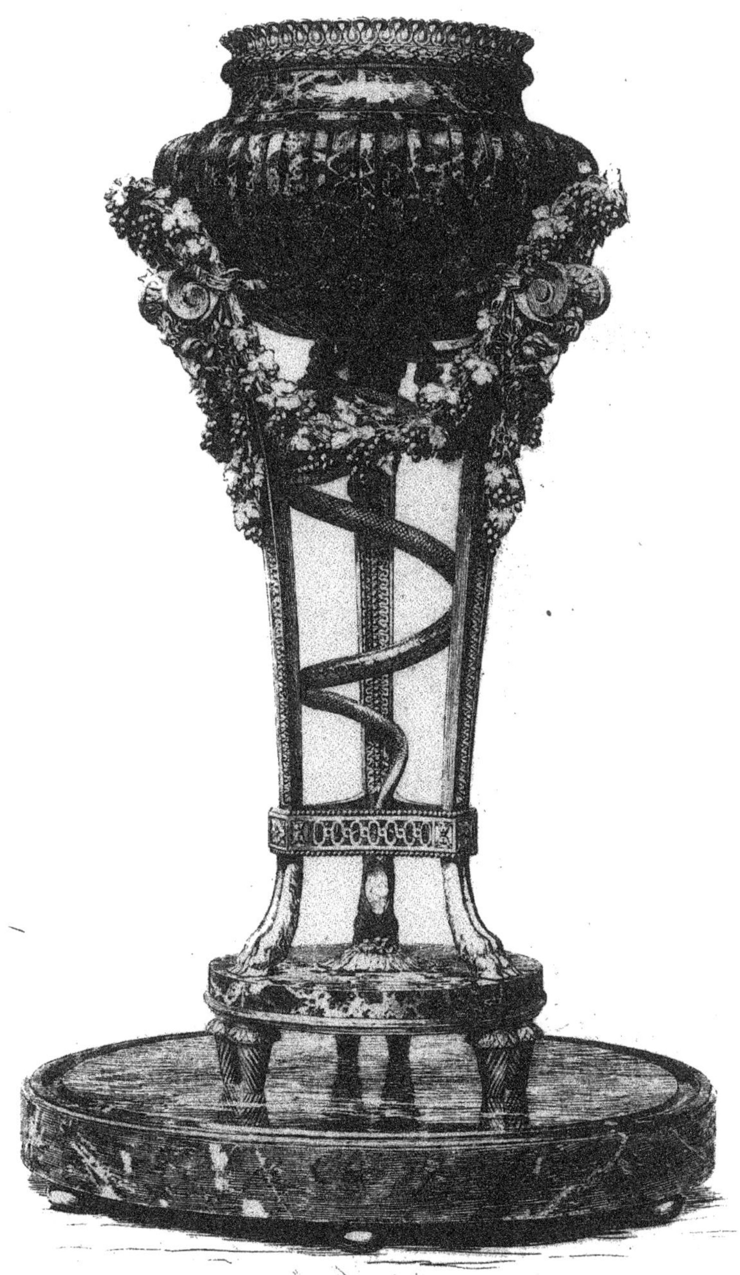
Jules Jacquemart.

latter part of his life, owing to failing health, he abandoned etching for water-color painting, and became one of the leading spirits in the Société des Aquarellistes.

No less characteristic are the works of Maxime Lalanne (1827–86), painter, etcher, and author, the most graceful etcher of architecture and landscape who ever lived. His works present rare refinement of character and great delicacy in execution, and are picturesque and beautiful. As representative examples may be named 'Démolitions, rue des Écoles,' 'Rue des Marmousets,' 'Aux Environs de Paris,' 'The Quay at Bordeaux,' 'The Canal at Montigny,' 'View from Pont Saint-Michel,' 'View from the Trocadero,' 'View from the Pont de la Concorde,' the last two of large size, and the set of little prints 'Chez Victor Hugo.' In 1866 Lalanne published his *Traité de la Gravure à l'eauforte*, illustrated with etchings, a practical and standard treatise on his art, of which there is an English translation by Mr. S. R. Koehler. Among many medals and marks of distinction received by Lalanne were the Order of Christ, conferred upon him by the King of Portugal, himself an amateur in the art, a medal from the Philadelphia Centennial Exposition, and the decoration of the Legion of Honor. An exhibition of his works was held in New York in 1890, the proofs shown being those selected by the artist for a projected exhibition in London, prevented by his death.

But one other master will be named, Paul Rajon, one of the greatest of the modern etchers from pictures by other artists. Born at Dijon in 1843, Rajon went to Paris and became the pupil of Léopold Flameng and Léon Gaucherel, masters eminent in the revival of their art. He also made frequent visits to England, and in 1886 and 1887 visited the United States. During the latter part of his life he lived at his country-house at Auvers, on the Oise, near Paris, and of this place many delightful reminiscences are related by his friends. He died here in 1888.

Rajon is well known through his many fine subjects after Meissonier, Alma-Tadema, Bréton, Turner, and other artists, ancient and modern, but it is in portraiture that he stands preeminent. His masterly portraits of Charles Darwin, John Stuart Mill, and Susanna Rose are among the representative examples of the art; nothing finer of the kind has ever been accomplished. Rajon was also an excellent draughtsman, painter, and artist in pastel and crayon.

An account of the works of living artists cannot be attempted here. It would require a volume to do justice to the achievements of such accomplished masters as Charles Jacque, Seymour Haden, James McNeill Whistler, Félix Bracquemond, Alphonse Legros, Samuel Palmer, Félix Buhot, Storm van s'Gravesande, Léopold Flameng, Charles Waltner, William Unger, Charles Courtry, Henri Lefort, Laguillermie, Brunet-Debaines, Delauney, Chauvel, Haig, Tissot, Zilcken, and the multitude of other skilful etchers, original artists, and interpreters of pictures.

Nor has the art of engraving been without its representative masters in the United States. In mezzotint, Charles Willson Peale, A. H. Ritchie, and John Sartain are well-known names; in line, A. B. Durand, Joseph Andrews, the Smillies, Charles Burt, William E. Marshall, and others, have engraved works of great excellence and historical value; and the American bank-note engravers have long been the acknowledged masters in that branch of the art. In etching we may claim Whistler, but only by birth, Stephen Parrish, Charles A. Platt, Joseph Pennell, Thomas and Peter Moran, Mrs. Moran, Frank Duveneck,

F. S. Church, Otto H. Bacher, R. Swain Gifford, Reginald Cleveland Coxe, and other original artists whose works are widely known and justly appreciated. An account of contemporary work will be found in M. Beraldi's *Graveurs du XIX*^{e} *Siècle* and Mr. Hamerton's *Etching and Etchers.*

In conclusion, the importance of forming public collections of prints in the different cities of our country cannot be too strongly urged, both in advancement of art education and as a means of intellectual enjoyment. While it is no longer possible to form great collections like those at Paris, London, or Berlin, smaller collections of representative works will in most instances accomplish the same purpose. As the masterpieces of the art have come down to us as a heritage from the past, so let us regard ourselves as their custodians for future generations.

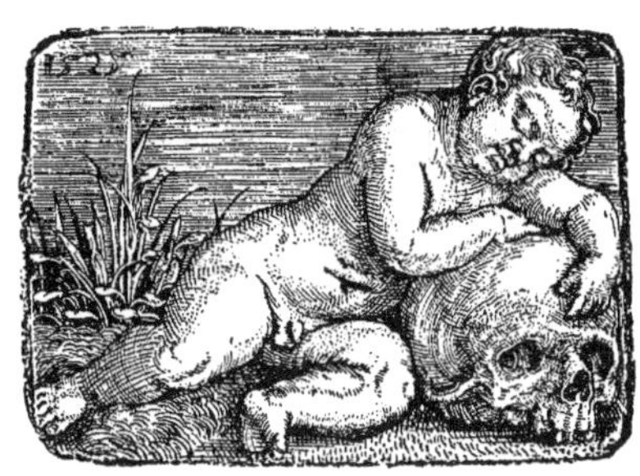

INDEX

THE END

CPSIA information can be obtained
at www.ICGtesting.com
Printed in the USA
BVHW041132290119
538945BV00010B/224/P

9 780266 750192